D0602717

FINDING
ANYTHING
ABOUT
EVERYTHING
IN TEXAS

100 Credible Books
and 100 Reliable Web Sites

Edward M. Walters

A REPUBLIC OF TEXAS PRESS BOOK

TAYLOR TRADE PUBLISHING

Lanham • New York • Dallas • Toronto • Oxford

A REPUBLIC OF TEXAS PRESS BOOK

Published by Taylor Trade Publishing
An imprint of The Rowman & Littlefield Publishing Group, Inc.
4501 Forbes Boulevard, Suite 200
Lanham, Maryland 20706

Distributed by NATIONAL BOOK NETWORK

Library of Congress Cataloging-in-Publication Data

Walters, Edward M. 1944-
 Finding anything about everything in Texas : 100 credible books and 100 reliable
web sites /
Edward M. Walters.
  p. cm.
 Includes bibliographical references and index.
 ISBN 1-5879-199-1 (Paper : alk. paper)
1. Texas—Miscellanea. 2. Texas—Bibliography. 3. Texas—Computer network
resources. I.
Title.
 F386.W34 2005
 976.4'002—dc22

                              2004018358

∞™ The paper used in this publication meets the minimum requirements of
American National Standard for Information Sciences—Permanence of Paper
for Printed Library Materials, ANSI/NISO Z39.48-1992.

Manufactured in the United States of America.

To Tracey L. Mumford and Meridith B. Walters,
who, with resilience and buoyancy, somehow
survived their father's wandering
around in academic circles.

CONTENTS

PREFACE

Have you ever wanted to know how to find out who was the real "Yellow Rose of Texas?" Do you know where to find the names of the three American soldiers who captured Santa Anna's favorite wooden leg during the Mexican War? Do you know how President Lyndon B. Johnson acquired the nickname "Landslide" Lyndon, a name he detested all his life? *Finding Anything about Everything in Texas* shows you where to find answers to questions like these.

Consider this book an explorer's field guide to finding information about Texas in printed and electronic form. With descriptions of one hundred credible books and one hundred reliable web sites, it leads you to the sources of "just about" everything in Texas. The structure of this book is simple. Each chapter poses ten questions about a general topic of importance in understanding Texas. The book provides short answers to the questions assembled from the books and web sites. So, *Finding Anything about Everything in Texas* describes one credible book source and one reliable web site that answer a question and supply additional information on a Texas subject.

Newcomers to the Lone Star State typically experience a cultural shock upon crossing the border, whether arriving from another U.S. state or another continent like Europe, China, or India. Trying to figure out Texas resembles the process of deciphering a secret code. Migrating to a new culture constitutes a challenge for the sturdiest individual, but coming to Texas produces an experience so profound that authors do not write typical travel books. They write survival guides. *Finding Anything about Everything in Texas* offers a crash course on Texas information survival for anyone trying to get up to speed on a Texas subject in a hurry.

The Texas economy exceeds the economies of many nations, the state's oil production ranks in the top ten among world nations, and the state itself acts and boasts like a sovereign nation. The range of information about this multiethnic, multifaceted Texas culture spans wide, deep, seemingly endless, and frequently overwhelming terrain. Coping with the corpus of information requires a plan and a guide. This book provides both.

You will detect in these pages information about three "states" of Texas information. A Texas of myths, legends, movies, cowboys, tycoons, and cattle barons fills volumes of books, autobiographies, family histories, and stories of the Lone Star State. A real and authentic Texas of many landscapes, peoples, cultures and customs, rich and diverse, full and complex, lies almost submerged underneath this giant, mythical veneer. The internet, the worldwide web, and electronic publishing create another Texas: a virtual Texas where a blending of the supernatural and the real takes place in a wired world of images, media, story, and song. Separating these three states requires an understanding of the sources, an information strategy, and sound tactics. *Finding Anything about Everything in Texas* is your explorer's guide to Texas information.

In the Lone Star State, traditions, legends, myths, characters, heroes, and villains require little cultivation and watering. They grow naturally abundant and durable like mesquite trees and prickly pear cacti, and they expand without end. Searchers face a daunting task of locating reliable Texas facts and information among vast quantities of printed and electronic records. Books right now in print contain more than 200 million words about Texas and Texans, and this number excludes the millions of pages of documents about Texas on the worldwide web.

Organized around a simple design, *Finding Anything about Everything in Texas* divides information about Texas into broad subjects. An introductory chapter provides a sample of the type of questions, answers, subjects, books, and web sites in the book and introduces the presentation format. The next eight chapters highlight the history, people, geography, folklore, music and art, law, commerce, and science of Texas. The final chapter guides readers to unique electronic information services provided to citizens of Texas. It elaborates special sources of information for readers seeking special materials like photographs, manuscripts, and government publications. Because searching for information about Texas stimulates the imagination and provokes infectious humor, *Finding Anything about Everything in Texas* approaches Texas without traditional academic encumbrances.

So if you are curious about why the artificial leg of General López de Santa Anna resides in a military museum of the Illinois National Guard who won't give it back, then *Finding Anything about Everything in Texas* guides you to the information. The museum maintains Santa Anna's leg in excellent condition except for the names of the three conquering Illinois volunteers carved into the shin.

ACKNOWLEDGMENTS

Many individuals provided generous assistance to me in writing this book, and I wish to express my appreciation to them. Principally, I am indebted to many professional librarians in public and university libraries, archives and special collections, state agencies, and museums. Their knowledge of Texas information resources informed this book from conception to completion. Librarians of the Fondren Library and the Underwood Law Library at Southern Methodist University assisted with many general and legal research problems. The staff of the Dallas Public Library, particularly the Texas/Dallas History Collection, provided easy access to a wide variety of Texas materials. Carol Roark, Rachel Howell, Michael Smith, and Amie Treuer suggested many valuable materials. Joe Milazzo, government information and map resources librarian at Central University Libraries, Southern Methodist University, retrieved and cataloged government publications from remote storage for my use. The reference departments of four fine state libraries never failed to return my phone calls: the Texas State Legislative Reference Library, the Texas State Library and Archives Commission, the Eugene C. Barker Texas History Center at the University of Texas at Austin, and the Texas Medical Center Library. Marilyn P. Duncan, director of communications for the Lyndon Baines Johnson School of Public Affairs; Brian Schwegmann, wildlife web coordinator of the Wildlife Division of the Texas Parks and Wildlife Department; and Cynthia R. Banks of the Geographical Information Systems Laboratory of the Parks and Wildlife Department helped solve special problems and provided information on state agency services. Don Carrick, archaeologist at Big Bend National Park, provided useful background on national park history. Kirk Cole, public information officer of the Texas Commission on Alcohol and Drug Abuse, supplied information on the newly reorganized Department of State Health Services. Vivi Sooy, Neva Lindell, Paul Scott, Happy Nelson, and Linda Magee Nelson made material available to me from their private collections which proved highly useful. Bill Evans, president of the Evans Group, made helpful suggestions on the manuscript, as did Wayne Ruhter, senior economist at Ruhter and Reynolds, and Barry Johnson of Needham and Johnson. Finally, I thank Karl Griffith, Mary Hansen, Kara Larson, John Hanicak, Bruce Romig, Barry Pullman, Tracey Mumford, Chris Mumford, Meridith Walters, Lee Nodwell, Larry Dennis, and Mitzie Stewart for their individual contributions.

1

FINDING ANYTHING ABOUT EVERYTHING IN TEXAS

- What notorious Texas villain dug up his amputated leg, paraded it through the streets, and gave it a full military burial to manage a political comeback?
- What Texas Indian tribe believes the Creator made the Big Bend National Park out of rocks, boulders, and building materials left over from creating the world?
- Who won the race between the carnivorous *Theropod* dinosaur and the vegetarian *Sauropod* dinosaur on the Glen Rose Trackway 107 million years ago?
- How did an emaciated herd of unbranded cattle on the frontier open range of South Texas originate a new word, movie, and television character called a *maverick*?
- Is it true that a prostitute once brought suit against the Missouri-Kansas-Texas Railroad for receiving an electrical shock in a signal tower while making love to a railroad employee?
- What famous Texas song about a cowboy dying on the prairie was actually an imported tune about a sailor being buried at sea?
- What Texas steer-wrestling rodeo performer developed a method of bulldogging a steer by the lip?
- How many official state agencies are there in Texas government? (a) less than 100? (b) more than 400? (c) somewhere between 120 and 247? or (d) none of the above?

- What Texas town incorporated *and* disbanded in a single day to enable 40,000 spectators to watch two locomotives, traveling seventy miles per hour pulling twelve cars, crash head-on?
- How many pounds of night-flying insects do Texas's 500 million cave-dwelling bats eat in a typical night?

SANTA ANNA'S LEG: FATHER OF THE MODERN POLITICAL CAMPAIGN

General Antonio López de Santa Anna, the Mexican dictator who used his amputated leg to revive his tainted political career, may be the best known villain in Texas history. In spite of attempts by some observers to revise his reputation, Santa Anna remains the supreme villain of Texas history. He ordered the take no prisoners Degüello at the Alamo and fathered the ultimate treachery at Goliad. For these dark deeds, Texans remember. But when it comes down to using a war wound to promote a political career, Santa Anna's activities with his leg make a good case for giving him the title "Father of the Modern Political Campaign."

Many generals would have trouble resurrecting a career after a humiliating defeat and capture like Santa Anna's debacle at the Battle of San Jacinto. But not Santa Anna! He found a new war, the Pastry War of 1838, fought bravely, and lost his leg when his horse was shot out from under him. He gave the leg a tasteful burial on his estate and appeared to retire.

As political tensions rose in Mexico, General Santa Anna plotted and waited for an appropriate time to make a comeback. Capitalizing on his war wound with a grandiose promotional scheme, he dug up his leg in 1842, paraded it through the streets, and buried it with full military honors in Mexico City. After the leg's second funeral, he built a monument to it in Santa Paula Cemetery. Two years later, the fortunes of politics turned, and a Mexican mob dug up his leg and dragged it through the streets. Santa Anna barely escaped with his cork leg.

Returning to power again in 1846, he lost the Battle of Cerro Gordo to General Winfield Scott in the Mexican War. In this defeat, his leg problems continued. Elements of the 4th Illinois Regiment Volunteers captured his favorite cork leg and took it back to Illinois. For a while, they displayed it and even permitted veterans and the public to hold it for a nominal fee. Eventually they moved it to a museum.

Today Santa Anna's leg resides in the Illinois State Military Museum in Springfield. Mexico wants the leg back, but Illinois refuses to relinquish it. So, the leg sits in a museum case on the second floor of a site where the Illinois National Guard comes for military training. Inscribed on the shin of the leg are the names of the three men who captured this ultimate trophy of war: "Private A. Waldron, First Sergeant Sam Rhodes, Second Sergeant John M. Gill, April 18, 1847."

Finding Anything

So Far from God: A History of the Mexican War, 1846–1848 by John S. D. Eisenhower gives an account of the travels of Santa Anna and all his legs leading up to, and through, the Mexican War. Eisenhower vividly describes Santa Anna's life from the Pastry War of 1838 through surrender to General Winfield Scott. For a work of fiction drawing heavily on history, consult James Michener's *The Eagle and the Raven* (1990). He paints a vivid romantic portrait of Santa Anna and devotes much space to Santa Anna's grandiose, flamboyant use of his wounded leg.

To see a photograph of Santa Anna's leg on exhibit, check out the Static Exhibit menu of the Military Museum homepage of the Illinois National Guard. It resides at Camp Lincoln at Springfield, Illinois. The web site is www.il.ngb.army.mil/. Santa Anna paid $1,300 to Charles Bartlett, a New York cabinetmaker, to carve this leg out of cork, and it occupies a proud position in the museum. A well-researched newspaper article on the leg by Paul Wood provides the Illinois side of the story. See the web site www.news-gazette.com/story.cfm?number=2464 entitled "Santa Anna's Leg Took a Long Walk," which appeared in the *The Champaign, Illinois News-Gazette*.

CREATING THE BIG BEND FROM LEFTOVERS

A popular explanation of the creation of the Big Bend country, attributed to Indians, holds that after the Creator finished putting up the earth, sky, and stars and stocking the sea with fish, and the air with birds, he had a lot of leftover stones, boulders, and rubble. So he threw them down in Southwest Texas, creating the Big Bend. Texans and Texas authors have often repeated this story without attributing it to any specific Indian source.

The legend appears in the early writings of geologist Ross Maxwell, the first superintendent of the Big Bend National Park. He opened his 1968 guidebook to the Big Bend with the story which he recites as "according to Indian legend." By 1985, in Maxwell's history of the Big Bend National Park, the story had become an "Apache legend." A historical expert on the Big Bend recently dropped Apache from the Indian legend without naming any specific Indian source.

Some archaeologists suggest a logical scenario that may account for confusion over the legend. When the Big Bend National Park first opened in 1944, it had to compete with the grandeur of the Yellowstone National Park to attract visitors to its remote location. A cowboy once described Big Bend as "not close to nowhere, so people ain't had a chance to ruin it." The Park Service initiated a massive publicity campaign to promote the new park. They paid historian Walter Prescott Webb $20 a day for two months to write two articles promoting the park and to take a four-day rafting trip in Santa Elena Canyon.

Some archaeologists suspect that the Big Bend Indian leftover legend may be one of those appealing Indian legends created by white people to sound like an ancient Indian myth. Perhaps the Big Bend National Park needed a good Indian legend to attract the public out to a remote corner of Southwest Texas. What better way to do it than with a good Anglo-Indian myth?

Whether the Big Bend legend is Anglo or Indian in origin, no doubt ancient Indians occupied the lower Pecos and Trans Pecos areas of Texas 10,000 years ago. They left projectile points and other evidence of their culture all over the area. Far more revealing than spear points and arrowheads, Indians in this area left a special form of art. From the Early Archaic period 5,000 years ago, they painted rocks and boulders and the walls of caves and rock shelters with impressive pictographs.

These remains are dramatic evidence of their culture, and Indians left similar rock paintings in other Texas locales well into the period of European colonization. In these caves and rock shelters, they painted a living record of their lifestyles in bright colors on stone. They painted panthers, bison, catfish, figures throwing spears, shamans practicing their craft, masks, designs on pebbles, and horses. These pieces provide a time-span of unique evidence of the culture of ancient Indians along the Rio Grande and other locations in Texas.

In 1938, before this art could be defaced, artist Forest Kirkland visited the sites, took notes, and rendered 160 faithful water colors of many Texas Indian rock paintings. He arrived just in time. In one location in

Central Texas, he noted that hunters already had begun to use Indian paintings of a buffalo and a turkey for target practice. "They are gradually being destroyed by bullets from the guns of hunters who choose them as targets," Kirkland noted. One of the most prominent of the rock art sites of the Trans-Pecos area of Texas is now being preserved in Hueco Tanks State Park near El Paso.

Finding Anything

The Indians of Texas: From Prehistoric to Modern Times (1961) by W. W. Newcomb, Jr. provides a thorough description of all Indian cultures who occupied Texas from prehistory to their "extermination and oblivion." Newcomb's work is a classic survey of Texas Indian cultures. Beginning with the earliest prehistoric cultures, the author devotes chapters to the Coahuiltecans, Karankawas, Lipan Apaches, Tonkawas, Comanches, Kiowa, Kiowa Apaches, Jumanos, Wichitas, and Caddoes. Texas acquired its name from the tribes of the Caddo Confederation who referred to themselves as "taychas" or "tayshas," meaning allies or friends,.

To get a sharp visual perspective of the rock art styles of early Indian cultures in the Trans-Pecos region, consult the web site of The Texas Rock Art Foundation at www.rockart.org/. The foundation gallery provides color photographs of four major styles of rock art found in the Trans Pecos Region. Multicolored rock paintings of many shamans in a trance-like pose appear in the Pecos River Style. The small red stick figures in action scenes dominate the Red Linear Style. Indian artists of the Red Monochrome Style painted bows and arrows in red tones that date to 1000 A.D., and in the Historical Style beginning after 1600 A.D., Indians painted subjects like horses, churches, guns, Europeans, and vaqueros herding cows, reflecting the beginnings of European contact.

RUNNING ON "THREE VICIOUSLY CLAWED TOES"

Ancient Indians left dramatic rock paintings as evidence of a complex culture. Dinosaurs left equally dramatic evidence of their presence in Texas through their bones, skeletons, and tracks. Archaeologists, students, school children, and their parents still discover dinosaur bones and tracks in Texas right down to their bird-like, clawed toe-nails.

Thousands of dinosaur tracks and fossils survive across Texas on private and public land. In the Triassic and Cretaceous geological periods, much of the Texas environment of the dinosaurs was a muddy coastal plain surrounding an interior seaway. The seacoast moved back and forth as the sea level fluctuated.

Dinosaurs roamed these tidal flats, shorelines, swampy marshes, and lagoons. A dinosaur would plant his big, heavy foot on firm, limy sand making a "footprint" or track. Afterward, mud and silt from the shifting seas filled up the tracks. With the movements of the seawater, laden with microorganisms, layer after layer of sedimentary rock like limestone and shale built up. These layers of rock formed a protective covering that preserved the tracks for millions of years. But, millions of years of erosion from rivers like the Paluxy in Glen Rose would wear down the sediments and expose the tracks.

Dinosaur tracks and fossils blanket the central part of Texas in the rock formations of the Triassic and Late Cretaceous period from about 220 million to 66 million years ago. At the end of this period, they abruptly and mysteriously disappeared. A number of these track sites are among the most popular tourist attractions in Texas. Dinosaur Valley State Park at Glen Rose is the state's premier location for viewing dinosaur tracks. So popular were these dinosaur tracks that early ranchers in the area made a business of manufacturing and selling fake tracks. One of the counterfeits led to the discovery of the real set of tracks at Glen Rose by archaeologist Roland T. Bird in 1938.

After the *Jurassic Park* blockbuster movies created a dinosaur rage, even Texas politicians moved in to capitalize on the popularity of dinosaurs. The Texas Legislature, never widely known for its scientific opinions, named the *Brachiosaur Sauropod, Pleurcoelus* as the official Lone Star State Dinosaur in 1997, acclaiming this species as *"indigenous"* to the state of Texas.

Glen Rose preserves tracks from the two-legged, three-toed carnivorous *Theropod* and "four-legged" vegetarian *Sauropod*. Erosion in the riverbed of the Paluxy River exposed the most famous dinosaur race in the world, a perfectly preserved "chase scene" between the carnivorous *Theropod* and herbivorous *Sauropod*. Two sets of tracks lead more than a hundred yards down the Paluxy riverbed in Somervell County. Almost all tracks are preserved in two museums: the American Museum of Natural History and the Texas Memorial Museum. Who won this contest more than 100 million years ago remains a cretaceous mystery, but the heavy money is on the lighter carnivorous *Theropod* who could run on his tiptoes.

Finding Anything

Roadside Geology of Texas (1991) by Darwin Spearing renders a lucid explanation of the geology of Texas for nonprofessionals. The author describes the dinosaur tracks at Dinosaur Valley State Park at Glen Rose, and he explains the origin of Texas dinosaur tracks. Think of this book as geology a second time around, or Texas geology clarified for dummies. Texas is divided into seven major geological regions according to their characteristic features. After describing Texas geology, the author furnishes readers with 7,500 miles of driving tours through all seven regions. These driving tours reveal Texas geology in roadcuts, formations, and riverbeds with easy-to-follow instructions. The book contains hundreds of maps, photographs, and illustrations.

For a photograph of the perfectly preserved chase scene of the *Sauropod* and *Theropod* dinosaurs, go to the web site of the American Museum of Natural History at www.amnh.org/exhibitions/expeditions/treasure_fossil/ Treasures/Glen_Rose_ Trackway/glenrose.html?dinos. The museum houses an excavated section of the trackway discovered by Roland T. Bird. The largest footprint of the *Sauropod* is three feet long and two feet wide. The Texas Memorial Museum at the University of Texas at Austin preserves another large section of the trackway. Archaeologists estimate the date of the great race at 107 million years ago.

MAVERICK AND "MAVERICKING"

Part of the Texas character was formed out of the fight for independence against Santa Anna, taming the frontier, and battling a harsh climate. Other traits grew out of a different form of idiosyncratic behavior. The "maverick" and "mavericking" fall into the latter category of the Texas experience. As the word is presently used in American English, a "maverick" is an independent person who does not go along with a group, refuses to conform, and takes unorthodox positions on issues. Fair enough. Extreme mavericks are considered obstinately defiant of authority or restraint of any kind. Not surprisingly, the origin of the word "maverick" is a product of the frontier South Texas open range cattle culture.

Several accounts of the origin of the terms "maverick" and "mavericking" survive, and all the accounts involve a man by the name of Samuel Maverick and his herd of cattle. This one appears credible. A man named Samuel Augustus Maverick came from South Carolina to South Texas in

1833. He joined the Texas volunteers and signed the Texas Declaration of Independence from Mexico. After the war, he acquired some land in Matagordo County and began some ranching operations. The story goes that Maverick reluctantly accepted 400 head of cattle in payment of a debt and put the cattle under the care of a family who were supposed to brand and care for the stock. The family neglected the cattle and residents in the coastal region soon began to refer to these unbranded cattle as "one of Maverick's."

When Samuel Maverick finally got around to selling his herd, the new owner, rancher A. Toutant Beauregard, had to go searching all over the open South Texas range for these unbranded "mavericks." Unfortunately, Beauregard's cowboys were overzealous, and whenever they found any unbranded cattle, they branded them and claimed them as "mavericks." By 1857, people in a wide area south of San Antonio referred to all unbranded cattle as "mavericks."

Mavericking became the practice of going out on the open range, finding, and branding unbranded cattle. Range laws effectively ended this practice in the 1880s. Samuel Augustus Maverick became famous enough as a Texas patriot of the revolution and a rancher to get the new county named after him in 1857. The county lies at the extreme point of South Texas bordering the Rio Grande, and Eagle Pass serves as the County Seat.

Finding Anything

The Longhorns (1941) by J. Frank Dobie contains history, stories, theories, and folklore of the origin of Texas cattle like the longhorn. Stories about "mavericks" and "mavericking" in South Texas appear in Dobie's classic work. Dobie describes four accounts of the origin of "mavericking," and three involve Samuel A. Maverick.

Go to the *New Handbook of Texas*, a six-volume authoritative encyclopedia of Texas history, culture, geography, and county history. It contains both a history of "maverick" and "mavericking," the history of Maverick County, and the biography of Augustus Maverick. Sponsored by the Texas State Historical Association, the handbook provides a history of all of the 254 counties in Texas. Fortunately, all of the information in the handbook plus additional updates can be found in *The Handbook of Texas Online*. The information on the web is more recent with many more articles than the printed version as well as many new articles. Check out the online version at www.tsha.utexas.edu/handbook/online/.

THE "SHOCKING" TRUTH ABOUT THE KATY RAILROAD

As a state, Texas got a late start in railroad building, but it can claim one major achievement in the American railroad industry: there are more miles of railroad line in Texas than in any other state. Texas constructed almost 19,000 miles of railroad lines and still had more than 12,000 miles in 1980.

Workers completed the first 20 miles of Texas railroad track in 1853 from Harrisburg to Stafford's Point. One of the first locomotives to operate regularly in Texas was called the "General Sherman." In 1870, the first railroad to come into Texas from outside the state was the Missouri-Kansas-Texas Railroad, popularly known as the Katy. The Katy participated in the great period of Texas railroad expansion of the 1880s when more than 8,000 miles of track were laid. Soon afterward, Katy was serving Houston, San Antonio, and Austin.

The Missouri-Kansas-Texas Railroad is colored with railroad history and legend from ownership by Jay Gould in the 1880s, train robberies, runs through Indian country, and crashing two locomotives head-on in a promotional scheme. Little wonder a railroad of many adventures and some misadventures would undergo its share of litigation damage claims.

One hobo sued the railroad for losing his leg while trying to jump on board, and another one sued for getting his head cracked when a box car door slammed while he was sleeping. A farmer asked for damages because the fireman on a passenger train blew the whistle too long and scared the horse that was pulling a bailer. The scared horse tripped, broke his leg, and had to be shot. In one case, when a Katy train hit four cows on the tracks, the engineer testified about what he did when he realized he was going to hit the cows. "I ducked" was his reply.

One of the most notorious damage claims against the Katy occurred in the Signal Tower Case brought by a plaintiff for an incident on Friday, the 13th day of September 1934. The facts brought out in the trial revealed that the plaintiff had "propositioned" an employee of the Katy Railroad who worked in the signal tower. Against company policy, the employee, for the sum of $1 "in advance," had invited the plaintiff into the signal tower "to indulge with him."

The Katy Railroad testified that it "had not equipped its said signal tower for any such passionate purposes" and had in fact instructed its employee to admit no visitors to the signal tower. While "reclined upon a cushioned chair," the plaintiff's "bare knee did touch an open electric

"Good Bye."
WE'RE GOING TO KANSAS AND TEXAS.

Scene in one of the Through Cars running to Kansas and Texas from Hannibal, St. Louis, Moberly, Kansas City and Sedalia, over the Great Emigrant Route, the Missouri, Kansas & Texas Railway.

"Good Bye." We're going to Kansas and Texas. Advertisements appeared frequently in magazines in the 1890s to attract riders for "the Great Emigrant Route" of the Missouri, Kansas and Texas Railway. From the collections of The Dallas/Texas History and Archives Division, Dallas Public Library.

switch upon the wall of said tower." This action created "an electrical contact quite different from the contact for which she was prepared." And, it
interrupted the session. The Katy Railroad argued that this session was
"completely outside the scope of the employment" of the signal operator
and that he "manifestly was on a frolic of his own." The Katy Railroad did
ask for the court's help in getting its employee's $1 back because the ses-
sion was never completed.

Finding Anything

Humor Along the Katy Lines (1970) by Lloyd W. Jones discloses a
unique picture of a railroad's history from the point of view of its legal
counsel. The author wrote the book on the occasion of the centennial celebration of the Missouri-Kansas-Texas Railroad Company. He provides a
view of the railroad taken from primary sources, court filings, and contemporary news accounts.

To obtain a photographic history of the Katy Railroad, visit the web site
of the Katy Railroad Historical Society at http://katyrailroad.org/.
Through an extensive photographic gallery, the society documents the
Katy Railroad's history from the earliest wood-burning engines through
steam engines and diesels. The site highlights the restored station at
Denison, now the Red River Railroad Museum.

"BURY ME NOT ON THE LONE PRAIRIE"

Like many immigrants to the Texas prairies, many popular cowboy songs
had histories of their own before they arrived in the Lone Star State. Com-
paring the life of a nineteenth-century cowboy to the life of a sailor at sea
is the way "Bury Me Not on the Lone Prairie" originated. The last request
of a dying cowboy on the prairie, and the philosophical supplication of a dying sailor aboard ship are ignored by colleagues. Neither the sailor nor the
cowboy wanted to be buried far away from home, but he didn't get a choice
in the decision because his workmates "gave no heed" to his dying prayer.

Before it got to Texas, the somber tune to "Bury Me Not on the Lone
Prairie" had been affixed to a poem called "The Ocean Burial," published
in 1839 by the Reverend Edwin Chapin in *Southern Literary Messenger*.
George N. Allen set the poem to music in 1850, and it became a popular
ballad. This sailor clearly does not want to be buried at sea. He wishes to
be buried in the "old churchyard, on the green hillside by the bones of his
father." The cowboy wants to be buried in the "little churchyard on the

Bill "Hopalong Cassidy" Boyd, the "Galahad of Range," starred in sixty-six movies that forged an indelible image of the media cowboy. He posed for a Holsum Bread promotion at the Cotton Bowl in Dallas in 1952. From the collections of The Dallas/Texas History and Archives Division, Dallas Public Library.

green hillside" by his father's grave. Cowboys and sailors lived rough and lonely lives. So, they lowered the sailor "o'er the vessel's side," and they buried the cowboy in a "narrow grave, just six by three" on the lone prairie.

Finding Anything

Singin' Texas (1994) by Francis Edward Abernethy traces the origin and background of "Bury Me Not on the Lone Prairie" and ninety-one other Texas folk songs. Spending many years in collecting these songs, the author crossed paths with folklorist John Lomax and others in the Texas Folklore Society and the Texas Folklife Festival. This collection includes cowboy songs, outlaw ballads, religious folk hymns, children's songs, and dance music. The selection is wide enough to include historical songs commemorating events like the "Galveston Storm" in 1906.

For articles that deal with the history of Texas music, consult the web site at the Center for Texas Music History at Texas State University in San Marcos. The web site is found at www.txstate.edu/ctmh/. The center makes available online *The Journal of Texas Music History,* which publishes articles on musicians as diverse as Willie Nelson and Selena to Bob Wills and Tish Hinojosa. The Southwestern Writers Collection at Texas State University now adds songwriter's collections to their archives and contains material from songwriters like Waylon Jennings and Ray Wylie Hubbard. They have an "early" handwritten songbook of Willie Nelson written when he was eleven years old.

BULLDOGGING A STEER BY THE LIP

The 75th Texas Legislature, the same group of legislators who designated *Brachiosaur Sauropod, Pleurcoelus* as the official Lone Star State Dinosaur in 1997, went on a state-symbol designating spree. Before they were through, they had created ten new official state symbols, more than any legislature in Texas history. The *Texas Observer* suggested that the "Official State Legislative Pastime" ought to be filing "Official State Resolutions." They created so many new symbols, in fact, that subsequent legislatures had to place restrictions on designating state symbols.

Here's more of what the 75th Legislature accomplished. They designated the guitar as the official state musical instrument, the sweet onion as the official state vegetable, and cotton as the official state fiber and fabric. Still overflowing with Lone Star pride, they proclaimed the rodeo as the official state sport, no doubt without consulting any football coaches' association. In the House resolution making it official, the Legislature pointed out that "the world's first" recorded rodeo was held in Pecos in 1883, and the first indoor rodeo was held in Fort Worth in 1917. Bill Pickett of Rockdale made a distinctive contribution to steer wrestling by developing "a method of bulldogging a steer by the lip."

The story of Bill Pickett's legendary feat of biting down on the lower lip of an angry longhorn who was not behaving goes back to Rockdale, Texas, in 1903. Pickett subdued a longhorn by jumping on its back from his horse and wrestling the steer down by its horns. In the struggle, he bit down on the lower lip of the animal and jerked the animal flat. Steer wrestling, according to some Texans, originated with Bill Pickett. Soon people paid to see Pickett "bulldog" steers. There is a sculpture of Bill Pickett, who died in 1932, biting the lower lip of a steer in Fort Worth at the Cowtown Coliseum.

Finding Anything

The *Texas Almanac, 2004–2005,* published biennially by the *Dallas Morning News,* contains basic information about Texas official state symbols. Consult the latest edition of the almanac for the name of each symbol, the number of the legislative session, and the year it passed. A computer searchable version of the *Texas Almanac* furnishes the same information on the Web free for most Texans through a program called TexShare at www .texshare.edu/. Obtain a password from a local Texas public library.

The Texas Legislature creates official state symbols by passing bills and resolutions. The full text of all bills and resolutions of the Texas Senate or House are found in the *General and Special Laws of the State of Texas* published by the Office of the Secretary of State every two years as session laws. All the laws and resolutions of each legislature are printed in this periodical. All laws and bills of the Texas Legislature passed since 1995 are posted on the Legislature's web site at www.capitol.state.tx.us/.

WHO RUNS THE SECOND BIGGEST STATE?

There's a short answer and a long answer to the question of how many state agencies make up Texas government. Even some of the state's best political scientists are not precisely certain, and the best they can do is provide a range between 120 and 247 agencies. They say it depends on how you define an "agency."

Here is the problem. Texas, like other states, has departments, agencies, commissions, boards, bureaus, and other organizational units in state government. This is confusing enough for most people. But in state government agencies, Texas has many different types of top policy makers: elected executives, appointed executives, elected commissions, elected boards, ex officio boards and commissions, and appointed boards and commissions. Sometimes one board is responsible for the policies of several agencies, and sometimes many separate agencies deal with related functional areas. More than 30 policy-making boards deal with education alone, and more than 100 boards and commissions set policy for their agencies. So, determining the number of Texas state agencies is not as easy as one might think.

The *Texas State Directory,* a commercial directory which takes a broad approach to defining a state agency, includes approximately 220 agencies that support the executive, legislative, and judicial branches of state government. The *Guide to Texas State Agencies,* an academic directory issued by the Lyndon Baines Johnson School of Public Affairs at the University of Texas at Austin, uses a conservative definition of an agency and comes up with approximately 130 agencies. TRAIL, the Texas Records and Information Locator, is a web site maintained by the Texas Library and Archives Commission that lists 173 agencies in state government that have web site home pages and provides an easy link to these home pages.

None of these sources includes all the state universities and community colleges. The official position of *Finding Anything About Everything in Texas* is that Texas has plus or minus 180 agencies, excluding universities and colleges, within a confidence interval of 5 percent.

Finding Anything

The *Texas Fact Book* (2004), a biennial publication of the Texas Legislative Budget Board, provides substantial, authoritative information on Texas state government. The fact book gives phone numbers and internet addresses of all major state agencies and maintains a contact page of toll-free telephone numbers for many important agencies.

Access to the homepages of state agencies has been simplified. For a convenient alphabetical list of 173 of the most important state agencies, the Texas State Library and Archives Commission maintains a list of web sites of agencies and a direct link to all their home pages. TRAIL is an acronym for Texas Records and Information Locator, and its web site is located at www2.tsl.state.tx.us/trail/. It also links to a large supply of current electronic publications and archived Texas documents.

THE CRASH AT CRUSH, TEXAS

The Texas business climate can create a promoter faster than Texas weather can whip up a funnel cloud in tornado season. The railroad industry holds the distinction of the most sensational promotional event in Texas History: the "Crash at Crush." A historical marker now memorializes the site of Crush, Texas, the town that grew into Texas's third largest city in a single day and then disbanded—all so 40,000 people could witness the head-on collision of two locomotives.

In 1896, the M. K. & T. Railroad, the "Katy," hired George Crush, a young ticket agent, to increase passenger traffic. He created a town fifteen miles north of Waco, laid four miles of rails, offered free viewing to the public if they paid to ride chartered trains to the site, and staged a crash of two locomotives. When the boilers on the trains exploded unexpectedly, three people were killed and several injured, including the official photographer who lost an eye. The stunned crowd reacted with shock and horror, recovered quickly, and began scouting the area for souvenirs.

The Katy Railroad fired Crush on the spot but rehired him the next day when newspaper coverage of the crash brought international notoriety to the railroad. Crush, Texas, disappeared. The railroad settled with the injured parties, including the photographer, Jervis Deane, who received $10,000 and a lifetime pass on the Katy Railroad. He soon recovered and advertised in the Waco paper: "Having gotten all the loose screws and other hardware out of my head, am now ready for all photographic business." Except for an occasional chunk of metal plowed up by a farmer, a historical marker near West, and Scott Joplin's "Crush Collision March," little remains of the event but colorful railroad history. An event of minor significance to history, Crush stands as an early example of the effectiveness of negative publicity.

President Dwight D. Eisenhower's father, David, worked at the Katy Railroad Roundhouse in Sherman, Texas, when the future president was born on October 14, 1890. From the collections of The Dallas/Texas History and Archives Division, Dallas Public Library.

Finding Anything

Texas Trains (2002) by Richard K. Troxell gives an account of the Crash at Crush and describes all the major railroads that operated in all seven regions of Texas. The book richly illustrates railroad history with photographs from museums and archives depicting old locomotives, depots, bridges, tunnels, conductors, and cabooses. The author organizes the book like a railroad history tour of Texas through the surviving relics.

To view photographs of the collision and hear Scott Joplin's *Crush Collision March*, log on to the Lone Star Junction web site at www.lsjunction.com/. Several photographs of Engines 999 and 1001, the two locomotives given the honor of crashing, appear at this web site along with an accurate narration of the event. Explore this site for many other primary documents of Texas heritage.

TEXAS CAVE-DWELLING BATS

The Texas urban bat colony in Austin, located at the Congress Avenue Bridge, has achieved the status of an icon in the media. In the summer months, 1.5 million bats attract crowds as they make their three-foot drop from their roosts and take off into the night for an evening's feast on hundreds of pounds of mosquitoes, moths, and miscellaneous crop pests. They have grown into the largest urban colony of bats in North America. World fame follows them. A public sculpture, *Night Wings* by artist Chuck McCann, honors their place of residence. A Bat Hot Line reports information on their flight times. These bats hog all the publicity and get most of the media attention.

All the media attention given to urban bats overshadows the role of the huge cave-dwelling bat population of Texas and underreports the role of Texas as home to more species of bats than any other state. The state's extensive network of caves harbors a bat population at times estimated to be 500 million bats. These bats are mostly of the Brazilian free-tailed and cave myotis species. Since bats prey heavily upon all kinds of night-flying insects, these cave-dwelling bats are estimated to consume six million pounds of insects per night. Some biologists estimate the nightly intake of these bats may be as high as fifty percent of their body weight.

The world's largest bat colony is Bracken Cave near New Braunfels. In the summer, this colony may exceed 20 million bats. Other regions of the state have sizable bat populations, too. The Big Bend region has more than twenty species of bats including the rarest Texas bats. Unfortunately, one-third of the more than thirty species of Texas bats fall into some category of the threatened list. Bat Conservation International (BCI), headquartered in Austin, works to increase the public level of awareness of the bat's useful role in ecology and the importance of its conservation.

Finding Anything

The Bats of Texas (1991) by David Schmidly describes thirty species of bats known to inhabit Texas. The author illustrates the text with color plates, drawings, and tables, making the information clear to beginning and advanced readers. Each entry provides a description, distribution map, and life history of each species.

Check out the web site of Bat Conservation International at www.batcon.org/ to keep track of activities dealing with all Texas bats and with efforts to promote awareness of bats everywhere. The organization works with many groups in a nonconfrontational manner to educate the public on the usefulness of bats and the preservation of bat habitats.

BOOKS AND WEB SITES

Santa Anna's Leg: The Father of the Modern Political Campaign

Eisenhower, John S.D. *So far From God: the U.S. War with Mexico 1846–1848.* Norman, OK: University of Oklahoma Press, 2000, 1989.

Illinois National Guard. Military Museum. Static Exhibits. Santa Anna's Leg. www.il.ngb.army.mil/.

Creating the Big Bend from Leftovers

Newcomb, Jr., W.W. *The Indians of Texas.* Austin: University of Texas Press, 1961.

The Rock Art Foundation. www.rockart.org/.

Running on "Three Viciously Clawed Toes"

American Museum of Natural History. Search "Glen Rose Trackway." www.amnh.org/.

Spearing, Darwin R. *Roadside Geology of Texas.* Missoula, Montana: Mountain Press Publishing, 1991.

Maverick and "Mavericking"

Dary, David. "Mavericks and Mavericking." *Handbook of Texas Online*. Texas State Historical Association. www.tsha.utexas.edu/handbook/online/ (accessed June 13, 2004).

Dobie, J. Frank. *The Longhorns*. Boston: Little, Brown & Co., 1941.

The "Shocking" Truth About the Katy Railroad

Jones, Lloyd W. *Humor Along the Katy Lines*. Dallas, Texas: Southwest Railroad Historical Society, 1970.

Katy Railroad Historical Society. www.katyrailroad.org/.

"Bury Me Not On the Lone Prairie"

Abernethy, Francis Edward. *Singin' Texas*. 2nd Edition. Denton: University of North Texas Press, 1994.

Center for Texas Music History. Texas State University. www.txstate.edu/ctmh/.

Bulldogging a Steer by the Lip

General and Special Laws of the State of Texas. Austin: The Office of the Secretary of State. www.capitol.state.tx.us/.

Texas Almanac, 2004–2005. Dallas, Texas: *Dallas Morning News*, 2004.

Who Runs the Second Biggest State?

Legislative Budget Board. *Texas Fact Book*. Austin, Texas: Legislative Budget Board, 2004.

TRAIL. Texas Resource and Information Locator. www2.tsl.state.tx.us/trail/.

The Crash at Crush, Texas

Lone Star Junction. www.lsjunction.com/.

Troxell, Richard K. *Texas Trains*. Plano, Texas: Republic of Texas Press, 2002.

Texas Cave-Dwelling Bats

Bat Conservation International. www.batcon.org/.

Schmidly, David J. *The Bats of Texas*, College Station: Texas A&M University Press, 1991.

2

HEROES, HEROINES, HOAXES, AND HISTORY

- How did the legend of "The Lady in Blue" inspire the establishment of the first Spanish missions in Texas?
- How did French explorer and hero La Salle, who planted the second flag over Texas, die before his dream of a colony could be realized?
- What prominent New England woman did Stephen F. Austin actively recruit to his colony with a land grant to add a civilized tone to Texas society?
- What well-known Texas ranch, whose red barn made frequent appearances in Marlboro commercials, allegedly was acquired in a high stakes card game?
- What Texas ghost town achieved fame as the port of entry for 188 camels and their Arab trainers as part of the U.S. Army's experiment with camels?
- How did the pecan tree gain its high position as the officially designated State Tree of Texas?
- What Texas historic fort today has adopted the Oozlefinch, "a rare featherless bird that flies backward," as its mascot?
- How many million head of cattle and horses made the northward trail drives to Kansas and other cattle markets from the end of the Civil War to the turn of the century?
- Which one of the legends of gallantry and bravery surrounding Colonel William Travis and the Alamo defenders probably never happened?

- Did Emily Morgan, the Yellow Rose of Texas, turn the tide at the Battle of San Jacinto by her battlefield "afternoon delight" with General Santa Anna?

LADY IN BLUE

Records of the first European penetration of Texas reveal a motivation to find precious metals, the quest for a route to the Orient, and the drive to store up spiritual treasure in heaven. Following close on the heels of conquistadors and treasure hunters, the Franciscans, using New Spain as a base of operations, took spiritual aim on the souls of Indian inhabitants of Texas.

María de Agreda, a Franciscan nun and spiritual advisor to King Philip IV of Spain, reputedly possessed a special spiritual gift called "bilocation." Bilocation enabled her to be physically present in two locations at the same time without ever having to leave her native Spain. Sometime after 1620, Sister Agreda vividly recounted her transportation experiences as a missionary to New Mexico. In one of her trances, she ministered to an Indian group called the "Titlas" or "Ticlas." Missionaries thereafter periodically reported contact with Indians who had received spiritual blessings from a mysterious "Lady in Blue."

The bilocations of María de Agreda, the "The Lady in Blue," achieved enough fame to be depicted in a seventeenth-century woodcut showing her spreading the doctrine to a small circle of Indians. In 1628, María reported her revelations about Indians in the "Kingdom of the Ticlas" to a new Archbishop preparing to depart for Mexico. On his orders, missionaries began work among the Jumano and Tejas. Revelations of María de Agreda inspired other explorations into eastern Texas and influenced the founding of the first mission in East Texas, San Francisco de los Tejas, in 1690.

The first extensive exploration of the Texas interior occurred by accident of a shipwreck. In 1519, Spaniards first scouted and mapped the Texas coast through the work of Alonzo Alvarez de Piñeda, who had strict orders to keep Hernando Cortés from acquiring it. The scheme failed, and Alonzo died a prisoner in Mexico. On the promise of Florida as a spoil, Pánfilo de Narváez tried again to block Cortés, but his enterprise ended in a disastrous shipwreck.

Of those who survived the Age of Exploration of Texas, Alvar Núñez Cabeza de Vaca lived a life so full of adventure that in today's terms it would merit a lucrative publishing contract and Hollywood credits. Cabeza de Vaca escaped Narváez's second shipwreck on Galveston Island, overcame shipmates' eating the expedition's horses, cannibalism of his shipmates, and capture by Indians. Indians enslaved him, and he learned medicine from a comrade to survive.

Cabeza became the first European to cross Central Texas on foot, trading his skills as a healer for safety. One historian credits him with performing "the first surgical operation recorded in the history of medicine within the present limits of the United States." Some Indians near the Chisos Mountains brought a man to him who had been pierced with an arrow. He removed the arrow and sewed the incision with hair from animal skin and bone from a deer. In 1536, he finally made his way to New Spain where citizens took him to Mexico City. He published an account of these adventures in 1542 producing a big success in Europe.

Spanish Texans' impact on the Lone Star State looms large. For three centuries they ruled Texas; they imported new laws, new technologies, a new government, and a new social organization; they established a powerful and influential religion; they mapped the land, set its first boundaries, and chose Tejas as its name. More than two million Texans today bear Spanish names and carry Spanish blood. Millions more speak, read, and write the Spanish language.

The Spanish Texans never found the gold and precious metals they were seeking, but they left an economic impact in another important industry as permanent as metals. Texas ranching owes much to the Spanish. Cattle, sheep, horses, goats, oxen, and mules constituted a main ingredient in the economy of South Texas early in Texas history. Rancher Don Juan Joseph Flores registered the first Texas-owned brand at Bexar in 1762. The Spanish "vaquero" initiated practices of roundup and branding that became permanent parts of the western tradition.

Finding Anything

Our Catholic Heritage in Texas, 1519–1936 by Carlos E. Castaneda is a multivolume analysis of the influence of Spanish penetration of Texas. Published in 1936, the first volume, *The Mission Era: The Finding of Texas, 1519–1693*, describes the first Spanish explorations up to the establishment of missions. The book contains a reproduction of a woodcut of the Lady in Blue during her ministry to the Jumano and Tejas Indians from 1620 to 1631.

The web site of the Institute of Texan Cultures of the University of Texas at San Antonio offers extensive information on twenty-six cultural and ethnic groups who have come to Texas and contributed to development of the state. Check the web site at www.texancultures.utsa.edu/ publications/texansoneandall/texansnav.htm. The web site highlights Spanish, Mexican, and Tejanos groups with photographs, art, and primary documents. This web site contains an abbreviated version of a book called *Texans One and All* by John Barnes containing information from the institute's established monographic series, The Texians and Texans.

FLEUR-DE-LIS ON THE TEXAS FRONTIER

The Age of Exploration in the 16th and 17th centuries unleashed the European passion to sail, explore, claim land, colonize, and name rivers, forts, missions, and mountains after European monarchs, Catholic saints, and characters of the Bible. The way Europeans went about the process of claiming land is curious indeed. Sometimes they followed the Portuguese practice of erecting a stone cross called a "padrao." The cross was sometimes two meters high and carried an inscription setting forth the name of the "most serene, most excellent" prince who had ordered the land in question "to be discovered." At other times, the explorers just came ashore and read a proclamation to the first natives they ran into, claiming the land for the monarch they had contracted with for the expedition. They also made very imprecise maps to establish these claims.

Under this open-ended, haphazard system, millions of acres of conflicting land claims in the New World came to be held by the various European countries. These claims led to continuous, internecine warfare. Professional historians must study for a lifetime to keep straight the causes of these wars, the names of these wars, and the flags of the countries these explorers represented.

Spain planted the first flag over Texas when Cabeza de Vaca and his four colleagues survived a long eight-year trek through much of central Texas. France, concentrating its efforts on the Mississippi Valley, gave permission to Réne Robert Cavelier, Sieur de la Salle, to found a colony in the New World after he successfully returned from navigating the Mississippi River to its mouth in 1683.

Leaving Rochelle, France, in July 1684 with four ships of colonists, laborers, mechanics, and single women looking for husbands, La Salle lost one ship to the Spanish, another ran aground, and a third returned to France over a dispute. With his final ship, he put into Lacava Bay and erected Fort St. Louis. The failure of La Salle's colony followed a familiar pattern. After erecting buildings, planting crops, and raising some livestock, the colony deteriorated from Indian conflicts, illness, and drought. The Karankawas who occupied the coastal plain practiced cannibalism.

With supplies running low and his men nearing mutiny, La Salle made a desperate decision to lead a party to the Mississippi River in hopes of making it to the French outposts in the Illinois country. With colonists ill and supplies exhausted, he left Fort St. Louis in command of a subordinate and embarked on his final journey in January 1687. He reached Cole on the Brazos where his troops mutinied, killed him, and left his corpse in the woods to be devoured by animals. France's greatest explorer died at only forty-three years old near the Trinity River on March 19, 1687.

Only eight members of La Salle's party made it to the forts of the Illinois country. They sent out a rescue party to Fort St. Louis but could not find anything. The Karankawas and smallpox, or both, left no trace of the colonists. Only in recent years have archaeologists pinpointed the exact location of Fort Louis by discovery of a steel spearhead stamped with a fleur-de-lis. La Salle's influence endured, for it established a United States claim to the greatest single territorial acquisition in its history, the Louisiana Purchase.

Finding Anything

Lone Star: A History of Texas and the Texans (2000) by T.R. Fehrenbach gives a comprehensive interpretation of Texas history from the initial European explorations to the twentieth century. The author describes this book as, not a book of facts and figures, but a "panorama of perceptions" largely drawn from contemporary sources. *Lone Star* is more readable and engaging than a typical textbook.

For a realistic look at the ill-fated colonial venture of La Salle, examine the articles and photographs of the La Salle web site of the Texas Historical Commission. This site contains the descriptions of the archaeological discovery and excavation of one of La Salle's ships, the *Belle*, which became stranded on a sandbar. More than one million artifacts have been preserved from this excavation, providing a rich picture of what provisions were required to establish a colony. See the commission web site at www.thc.state.tx.us/lasalle/lasdefault.html.

Réne-Robert Cavelier, Sieur de La Salle, 1643–1687, established the U.S. claim to the Louisiana Territory. This statue in Navasota, Texas, memorializes the site where some think he was killed. From the collections of The Dallas/Texas History and Archives Division, Dallas Public Library.

STOPPING THE BIRDS FROM FLYING OVER TEXAS

Mary Austin Holley, cousin of the impresario Stephen F. Austin, was not the typical Texas settler of the "Old Three Hundred" who settled Austin's Brazos Valley colony. Born in New Haven, Connecticut, wife of a well-known Unitarian minister and college president, and a gifted writer, Mary perhaps would have lived out her life as a minister's wife but for her husband's untimely death of yellow fever on board the ship *Louisiana* in 1827.

Faced with the prospect of surviving the loss of a spouse, Holley found herself in the circumstances of many immigrants who looked westward. "Emigration," she would write, "is often undertaken with expectations so vague and preposterous" that disappointment is almost inevitable. In Mary Austin Holley's case, however, the emigration experience had a favorable beginning.

Her cousin, Stephen F. Austin, was so anxious to have her in his colony that he offered her a league of choice land, 4,428 acres, near his own plantation, on the condition that she come to Texas to claim it. Arriving in Texas in 1831, she caught the spirit of westward expansion almost immediately by putting her literary skills to work for the new, struggling colony. If population would grow, land prices would rise and the colony, and she, would prosper. By 1833, Mary published her first book under the laborious title, *Texas. Observations, Historical, Geographical, and Descriptive, in a Series of Letters, Written During a Visit to Austin's Colony, with a view to a permanent settlement in that country, in the Autumn of 1831.* The book brought her attention in the east where she had connections, and she determined to try another literary project.

The on-again, off-again relations between the Mexican government and the colonization project of Moses Austin would have a dramatic impact on the most important book of Mary Austin Holley's literary career, her second book called simply *Texas.* After Mexico achieved independence from Spain in 1821, Texas autonomy was subsumed under the flag of Mexico and frequently dependent upon the shifting loyalties of López de Santa Anna. Colonization was alternately encouraged and rebuffed. Mary quoted an old Spanish provincial General saying that, if it were in his power, he would "stop the birds from flying over the boundary" between Texas and Mexico.

Mary began her second book on Texas with the purpose of writing a guide for immigrants. It would have chapters on geography, climate, trade, cities, customs, and people. She set to work on this guide and turned out a highly readable and entertaining travel guide designed to lure settlers with passages suggesting that the agriculture was so rich that "Yankees could luxuriate in a paradise of pumpkins." Texas sugar cane was said to "sweeten a foot and a half higher up than Louisiana cane."

Before Mary could complete her "strictly matter of fact" guide book, historical forces transformed her book into a primary source of Texas history. With events in Texas having moved into full-scale revolt, Stephen F. Austin visited Mary at her Kentucky home bringing written accounts of the Alamo, Goliad, the Texas Declaration of Independence, and his appeal for aid to Texas. Hastily, Mary added these primary documents to her book, making it one of the earliest histories of the Texas Revolution. Mary died in 1846, a decade after her more famous cousin, but with a lasting literary reputation.

Finding Anything

Texas (1836) by Mary Austin Holley can claim to be the first history of Texas. The Texas Historical Association has reprinted a new edition of the book with an introduction by Marilyn McAdams. Holley described the geography, customs, society, and history of Texas, and she included a chapter on "The History of General Austin and His Colony." She forecast the legacy of her cousin Stephen F. Austin with a piece of prophecy: when Texas eventually takes her place among the powerful empires of the American continent, "children will be taught to hold his name in reverence."

For a short account of the life of Mary Austin Holley, check the web site of the Unitarian Universalist Historical Society at www.uua .org/uuhs/duub/articles/maryaustinholley.html. This site provides a biography of her life and the life of her husband, a Unitarian minister. Her interaction with influential political leaders and academics in New England contributed to her success as a literary figure and advocate for Texas.

PUNCHING COWS TO RANCHING EMPIRES

In Texas, there are very few things that have not been won, or lost, in a card game. Houses, horses, saddles, oil wells, land, brides, and guns are all alleged to have changed hands across a poker table. Such has been alleged about the founding of the Four Sixes Ranch (6666) headquartered in Guthrie. As the story goes, Rancher Burk Burnett, a player remaining in the high stakes game, won the hand that secured him a large ranch in West Texas with four sixes.

The only problem with the story is that the principal in the story, Burk Burnett, a major figure in the Texas stock-raising industry, said it never happened. The source of the name of his major ranch was probably a herd of cattle he bought in Denton that already carried the four sixes brand. Whatever the case, the Four Sixes Ranch has been a mainstay in Texas ranching for more than 100 years.

Richard M. Kleberg, Chairman of the Board of the King Ranch Corp., talks with Winthrop Rockefeller at a Santa Gertrud cattle sale on November 15, 1953. From the collections of The Dallas/Texas History and Archives Division, Dallas Public Library.

Burk Burnett came from Bates County, Missouri, and began as a cowboy on the Chisholm Trail just as trail drives began to accelerate in 1868, after the Civil War. He switched to ranching with his father and first ranched near Wichita Falls. Burnett negotiated with major figures of his day in building his ranching empire, including Theodore Roosevelt and Quanah Parker. In an event which turned tragic in Fort Worth in 1885, Burk and W.T. Waggoner invited Parker, the Comanche Chief, and his father-in-law, Yellow Bear, to Fort Worth for the Fat Stock Show.

Unfamiliar with the operations of a gaslight, Yellow Bear extinguished the flame of the light without turning off the gas supply. Yellow Bear died from asphyxiation, and Quanah Parker was saved fortuitously by rescuers who smelled gas. Burnett interceded with tribal members who suspected foul play and used an experiment to show the dangers of the gas. Through Parker's assistance, Burnett leased 300,000 acres of grazing land for about six cents per acre.

Burnett died in 1922, but his descendants continued to build the ranching holdings until they reached a half million acres. Good management, the discovery of oil, and Marlboro commercials have managed to keep the Four Sixes Ranch (6666) active and prosperous in the twenty-first century. The ranch main headquarters is at Guthrie on Highway 83. A small Texas town named Burkburnett in Wichita County is testimony to the contributions of a big Texas rancher.

Finding Anything

Historic Ranches of Texas (1980) examines twelve of the largest ranching operations in the state. The book provides survey histories, scope of the land holdings, ranching operations, photographs, and artist renderings of the primary structures of the properties. It includes ranches from all parts of Texas, such as the King Ranch in South Texas and others in Central and East Texas.

For the family history of the Four Sixes Ranch (6666), check the web site at www.6666ranch.com. The site provides details of the ranch holdings, photographs of Burk Burnett, Teddy Roosevelt, Quanah Parker, and ranch operations. With 480,000 acres spread over the north central plains from Guthrie, Panhandle, Paducah, and Granbury, the Four Sixes Burnett Ranches are among the largest individually owned ranching properties in Texas. Today, they are owned and operated by the great-granddaughter of the founder, Ann Burnett Windfohr Marion.

INDIANOLA: A FORGOTTEN PORT

Of the many ghost towns that sprang up and disappeared in Texas history, Indianola witnessed some of Texas's most dramatic events and the climate's most ferocious forces. A list of the many names considered for the town reveals its storied history. At different times, the location was known by the names of Karlsshafen, Indian Point, Powderhorn Lake, Old Town, New Town, La Salle, and Miller's Point. Reflecting the optimism of the founders, the citizens chose to combine the exotic appeal of *Indian* with the Spanish word *ola*, meaning wave. They envisioned a wave of people and supplies spreading westward from Matagorda Bay, making Indianola the Gateway to the West.

The town prospered initially just as the founders hoped. Prince Karl zu Solms-Braunfels used Indianola as a port of entry for thousands of German immigrants who fought off typhoid, cholera, and yellow fever to establish successful German settlements. The town developed rapidly into a warehousing and shipping point. A big government contract from the U.S. Army Quartermaster Department constructed a Government Wharf, a big boost to the local economy. Wells Fargo prominently shipped silver bullion from mines in northern Mexico in heavily guarded, mammoth wagons pulled by sixteen mules hitched in four rows of teams, adding romantic pride to the citizenry.

The city continued to develop and even had to concern itself with some of the pressing moral issues of the day. It constructed a large Temperance Hall, and the city council made unlawful the keeping of a "house of ill-fame within the city." In 1856, Indianola achieved national fame as the port of entry for 188 camels. The U.S. War Department experimented with these camels as a possible alternative to mules for supply and support in the arid southwest desert. The first ship dispatched to Indianola could not unload the camels because of its draft, so the camels had to be transferred to a lighter ship which finally unloaded the cargo on May 14, 1856. Many reasons have been offered for the failure of the camel experiment: the Civil War, opposition of the mule handlers, lack of support from the War Department, and the camels' "sore feet."

Indianola suffered from the Federal blockade during the Civil War and the city was captured for two years. After the war, Indianola survived another yellow fever epidemic and appeared on its way to a prosperous recovery. The Indianola Railroad increased the city's reputation as a shipping and receiving center. In 1875, nature foreshadowed the event that would ultimately bring down the city. On September 15th, the effects of a hurricane flooded Indianola with five feet of water in an 18-hour period killing 250 people.

After the flood, a plan to move the city to higher ground north of Powderhorn Lake failed to receive backing, and some merchants abandoned the city. The remaining citizens faced an uphill battle to rebuild. The grim end of the city finally came through another peril of Mother Nature. On August 20, 1886, the second hurricane in eleven years struck Indianola with even more force than the first. A newspaper reported that buildings that had withstood the cyclone of 1875 "went down as if made of pasteboard." Most of the buildings that escaped destruction perished in a fire the following spring. The ruin was complete, and the post office closed on October 4, 1887.

Finding Anything

Texas Forgotten Ports (1988) by Keith Guthrie gives an account of the rise and demise of Indianola. The book also describes other coastal ports on the Mid-Gulf Coast from Corpus Christi to Matagorda Bay and includes Indianola. Volume two covers inland river ports served by paddle-wheel steam boats.

For an illustrated view of Indianola's rich history, go to the web site of the Texas Settlement Region at www.texas-settlement.org/indianola. This not-for-profit organization preserves the local history of the coastal region through activities, publications, and coordination of seven museums along the Indianola Trail. The web site displays a picture by artist Helmuth Holtz of Indianola in September 1863 from the deck of the ship *Texana,* anchored in the bay. It has photographs of most of Indianola's noteworthy historical events, including the camel disembarkation, scenes before and after the hurricanes, and the major cemeteries.

FROM A BULLET IN THE BACK TO THE GOVERNOR'S MANSION

The pecan tree acquired its symbolic position in Texas political life from its association with Governor James S. Hogg. The respected governor achieved his first measure of fame as the first native governor. Born in Cherokee County, he worked at small newspapers in East Texas until he passed the bar. While helping the sheriff at Quitman, Hogg was ambushed by outlaws who lured him across the county line and shot him in the back.

He became attorney general in 1886 and advocated regulating railroads and corporations. He worked hard to eliminate abuses in the railroad industry common at the time: rate discrimination and monopolies. His crowning legislative achievement in April 1891 proved to be the creation of the state's most powerful regulatory agency: the Texas Railroad Commission.

Often regarded among the most effective Texas governors, Hogg walked a middle position between support of working classes on the one hand and trying not to impede private enterprise and economic growth and development on the other. In addition to his political programs, he and his wife, Sarah Ann Stinson, raised four children, and he earned the reputation of a devoted family man. The Hoggs' only daughter, whom they named Ima after the heroine of the novel *The Fate of Marvin,* authored by James Hogg's brother Tom, became permanently enshrined in Texas folklore. Her name gave impetus to the myth that the Hoggs had a second daughter named Ura. Generations of Texans held to the untruth even after Ima Hogg and her foundation gave millions to Texas for educational and humanitarian projects.

James Stephen Hogg desired no stone monument erected in his memory. The night before he died, he gave simple instructions to his children to plant a pecan tree at the head of his grave and a walnut tree at the foot. He wished that walnuts and pecans be "given out to the plain" and that they would "make Texas a land of trees."

The Governor died on March 5, 1906, and his family carried out his wishes, burying him in the Oakwood Cemetery in Austin. The well-loved governor could not prevent the erection of a later statue.

In 1919, the 35th Legislature passed Senate Bill 42 designating the pecan tree as the official Texas State Tree, the second official state symbol after the Bluebonnet State Flower. To further honor the pecan tree and Hogg, they also established a new policy for planting trees on state property. Henceforth, planting trees on state property must be for "ornamentation" and "use." Fruit and nut bearing trees would be planted at "eleemosynary asylums, the State Capitol, and public schools."

Finding Anything

The Chief Executives of Texas from Stephen F. Austin to John B. Connally, Jr. (1995) by Kenneth E. Henderson recounts short biographical sketches of all Texas governors from Texas Independence to 1970. Authored by a historian, the book weaves a continuous thread of Texas history through the biographies of its chief executives. It supplies references to additional sources of information for each governor.

For additional biographical sketches of Texas governors, see the web site of the Texas State Library at www.tsl.state.tx.us/ref/abouttx/governors.html. In addition to providing portraits, photographs, and other memorabilia, this site links the reader to the biographical sketches in the *Handbook of Texas Online* by the Texas State Historical Association.

THE BIRD THAT FLEW BACKWARD

Few of the twenty-seven historic frontier military forts of Texas remain active military concerns today. Most of the forts have become the focus of tourists, museums, heritage organizations, or archaeologists. Some became state parks. But a few, like Fort Bliss, survived the vicissitudes of history, politics, base closures, and changes in military technology to remain healthy, functioning concerns.

A clue to the longevity of Fort Bliss may be found in the mascot that adorns the flag that hangs over the fort: the Oozlefinch. Instead of a mascot that reflects the historical origins of the post like an elegant stallion, rugged mule, soaring eagle, or a cunning and fierce animal, the mascot of Fort Bliss is a mythical bird of the twentieth century, a featherless bird that flies backward and carries a Nike missile in the crook of its left leg. It flies backward to keep the dust out of its piercing red eyes so that it can never be surprised. The Oozlefinch knows where it has been, and it doesn't miss a thing.

Fort Bliss owes its creation to the post-Mexican War period when six companies of the Third Regiment were ordered to *El Paso del Norte* in 1848. In June, 275 wagons, 2,500 head of livestock, some passengers, and the six companies began the 673-mile journey from San Antonio under the command of Major Jefferson Van Horne. The Army abandoned the post for a time, only to reopen it in 1854, naming it after William Wallace Smith Bliss whose career ended prematurely at the age of thirty-eight.

Life in such a remote Army post as Fort Bliss was not entirely monotonous. With its proximity to Mexico across the river, there were times of excitement. One lieutenant commented that the boredom disappeared during fiestas. Life changed from a routine as "monotonous as the desert" into "gay and noisy scenes" with bullfights and billiards, bailes and monte, and intrigues and crime.

Fort Bliss's record of service to Texas and the nation proved durable and distinguished, participating in many of the important engagements of the times. The Army Camel Train went on maneuvers through Fort Bliss. The post functioned ably in containment of the Apache forays and participated in the hunt for Apache Chief Victorio. By the end of the nineteenth century, it appeared that the days of Fort Bliss were numbered. It shrank to a population of one lieutenant, one chaplain, one doctor, and five cavalry.

Fort Bliss's strategic proximity to Mexico played a role in preserving the base and more than once in history brought it into Mexican-American affairs. The most prominent case occurred with the flamboyant leader of the anti-Huerta Mexican revolutionary faction, Pancho Villa. When the legendary leader invaded Juarez in 1913, five thousand Mexicans crossed the Rio Grande and took sanctuary in Fort Bliss. With Pancho Villa contributing to further unrest south of the border, Fort Bliss became a permanent fixture on the American military landscape under the command of its first general officer, John J. Pershing.

Continuing into the twentieth century, Fort Bliss adapted again by de-emphasizing the cavalry function that had been its history and by moving into the modern weapons technology of anti-aircraft artillery and guided missile systems. Today, it is a thriving base of 3,500 buildings situated on more than 1 million acres. Consistent with the antiaircraft and missile technology it teaches, the base adheres to the motto of the legendary Oozlefinch: "If it flies, it dies."

Finding Anything

Frontier Forts of Texas (1966) is a collection of historical essays on famous Texas forts, including Fort Bliss. The book covers the history of eight of Texas's most prominent frontier forts: Belknap, Bliss, Brown, Clark, Concho, Davis, Mason, and Sam Houston. A prominent historian or military historian contributes a separate article on each fort, and historian Joe B. Frantz authored the article on Fort Bliss.

For an illustrated history of Fort Bliss, check the Historic Fort Bliss web site at http://147.71.210.21/adamag/district/district.htm. Because Fort Bliss is on the national registry of historic sites, many of its buildings are landmarks and excellent examples of the architectural styles of the era. The narrative and photographs provide a 100-year look at the changing nature of the base.

"HEAD 'EM UP, MOVE 'EM OUT"

Finding a more enduring image of Texas than the cowboy and the cattle drive may be impossible. Cattle forging a swollen river, the stampede, roping and branding, chuck wagons, horse thieves and rustlers, drudgery, dust and bandannas, hardship, and violence comprise one of Texas's lasting contributions to the reality and the myth of the frontier experience.

The reality is that, between 1865 and 1900, approximately 30,000 men and a few women drove an estimated 10,000,000 head of cattle and 1,000,000 horses north to markets in Kansas and beyond. Even the names of the routes they took, the Western Trail, the Chisholm Trail, the Shawnee Trail, the Goodnight Loving Trail, are permanently etched in history, folklore, and song. For many who hired on for these drives, the experience was "the most unforgettable experience of their lives."

To preserve interest and save for posterity as many of their trail driving experiences as possible, George W. Saunders founded the Old Time Trail

Drivers Association in 1915. In 1917, he got the idea to publish a book to record the recollections of the members' experiences on trail drives. By this time, the membership in the association had risen to 1,000. Saunders obtained the interest of Marvin Hunter, a San Antonio newspaperman, to edit the work. In 1924, Hunter and Saunders published the book under the title *Trail Drivers of Texas*.

Even though recollections of cattlemen and trail drivers thirty years after the events may contain enhancements of the facts, reading trail drivers' stories provides a stark glimpse into real trail life. Charles Goodnight's and W. J. Wilson's firsthand accounts of the killing of Oliver Loving, perhaps Texas's first trail driver, reads like a movie script. Loving died while trying to make his way through Indian country to bid on contracts in New Mexico and Colorado for the herd Charles Goodnight was driving. Goodnight wanted him to travel only at night. A brave man, according to Goodnight, "devoid of caution ignoring the warning to travel at night," Comanches caught and killed him. W.J. Wilson, his companion, escaped to tell the story.

Other stories of trail drivers paint a picture of trail driving with self-effacing simplicity. Sam H. Nunneley, who came to Texas in 1869, met Frank James in McKinney, Texas, and traveled with him for part of a year while James was using an assumed name. Nunneley went on one drive of 14,000 cattle from Uvalde to Wichita, Kansas, purchased a saddle for $40 and a horse for $16, and rode with his young friends 900 miles to Silver City, New Mexico. When that didn't work out, he hooked up with a buffalo hunter who he said killed more than 5,000 buffalo for the "hides and tongues." They sold the hides to Fort Worth people for "six bits to a dollar each." He said he was also in the "run" in Oklahoma, and he helped make the Oklahoma Territory a state.

Finding Anything

The Trail Drivers of Texas: Interesting Sketches of Early Cowboys and Their Experiences on the Range and on the Trail during the Days That Tried Men's Souls—True Narratives Related by Real Cowpunchers and Men Who Fathered the Cattle Industry in Texas (1925) provides eyewitness accounts of the experiences of Texas trail drivers. The book contains more than three hundred recollections of life on the trail collected by George W. Saunders between 1915 and 1923. The sketches are richly illustrated with photographs of the trail drivers and trail scenes.

For another viewpoint of the trail drive, check the history section of the county web site of Wilbarger County. Under "Cattle Drives and Trail Drives," there are photographs of cattle drives that came through Wilbarger County on their way to Doan's Crossing on the Red River. One historical marker records sixty-one brands of cattle from the herds that crossed the Red River on the Western Cattle Trail on the way to Kansas. The web site is www.co.wilbarger.tx.us/cattle.htm.

DRAWING A LINE IN THE DIRT

In slogan, song, film, novels, and history, the Alamo permeates the spirit of Texas character in much the same way that the cowboy and trail drives have colored the landscape. If anyone in America has not read about, heard of, or seen films about the Alamo, "The Shrine of Texas Liberty," they are recent arrivals or they haven't been paying attention. The little mission in San Antonio provided the fortified stage for a cast of giant characters to make their heroic defensive stands in the fight for Texas independence. Subsequent history and the mythmaking impulse did the rest.

Every word written by the 187 combatants killed at the mission fortress, stacked in three piles, and burned between oil-soaked wood has been repeatedly dissected for clues to the battle and siege. Reports of the thirty or so survivors have been equally scrutinized for details of the engagement. Even with all the study of the event, one historian noted that only a rash man would claim to have the final answer to "everything that happened at the Alamo." Debate over the exact number who died at the Alamo continues.

For certain, William Barrett Travis received orders to go to "the defense of San Antonio" in January 1836. He wrote to Henry Smith on January 28th that desertions and difficulty in obtaining provisions delayed his departure and he was departing with only thirty men. With the news of Santa Anna on the march with an army of thousands, Travis wrote Smith again on February 11th from San Antonio: "For God's sake, and the sake of our country, send us reinforcements." Travis followed his request on February 23rd with a short note saying, "The enemy in large force is in sight."

Thirty-seven years after the Alamo battle, a story surfaced that Travis took his sword, drew a line in the dirt, and asked all defenders who would stay and die with him to cross the line. The others could slip away. The story was attributed to a noncombatant survivor, but few historians believe it. They believe that William Barrett Travis more likely would have demanded his men remain at their posts no matter what the cost. He and they did, and that is the valor of the Alamo.

Travis answered the demand to surrender with a cannon shot. Santa Anna hoisted a "blood-red" flag indicating his take-no-prisoners policy in this engagement. On March 6, 1836, after a siege of ten days, Santa Anna assaulted the Alamo. After the bugle sounded the *deguello,* an ancient Spanish no-quarter call to attack, the Mexican Army attacked. The defenders held on for three hours through the first assault. The Mexican army returned to pierce the fortress, and savage fighting took place.

When the fighting ended and the Alamo defenders' corpses smoldered, the process of counting the bodies produced another lingering myth: how many Mexicans did the Alamo defenders kill? Santa Anna claimed 600 American dead in his official report to the Mexican government, and he reported his own losses at 70 dead. Some Mexican historians claimed 1,500 defenders had been in the Alamo fortress. Some say the Mexican Army lost 670 dead in its assault force and over 25 percent in its other units for a total of 1,600 killed. The Mexican officer Ruiz in charge of burning the bodies of the Alamo defenders reported cremation of exactly 182 bodies. Whatever the case, each side possessed fuel for it version of how many died at "The Cradle of Texas Liberty."

Finding Anything

Alamo Defenders: A Genealogy: The People and Their Words (1990) by Bill Groneman contains biographies of 200 people who died in, or escaped from, the Alamo. In a section called "The People," the author sketches the lives and genealogies of the combatants and noncombatants at the Alamo. The second section, entitled "Their Words," provides excerpts from their letters and stories from November 11, 1835, to March 3, 1836, three days before the Alamo assault.

For keeping track of general information about the Alamo, consult the web site of the Alamo Society at www.thealamosociety.com. Founded in 1986 during the Texas Sesquicentennial celebration, this society of both amateur and professional historians tracks Alamo history and popular culture through annual conventions, newsletters, and support of preservation projects. Coverage of the depiction of the Alamo in popular film is one of the society's special interests.

THE YELLOW ROSE OF TEXAS

When the presence of mystery surrounds the clash of great historical figures in a history-shaping event, conditions are ripe for the making of great myth. Sam Houston, the steed Saracen, General Santa Anna, the cannons called the Twin Sisters, and the Battle of San Jacinto comprise the ideal conditions to create one of the most romantic and enduring myths of the Texas Revolution: the legend of the Yellow Rose of Texas. Embellishment of the life of Emily Morgan, the Yellow Rose of Texas, provides a good glimpse into the process of Texas mythmaking on a grand scale.

As narrated in a journalist's account of the battle, *The Day of San Jacinto*, and an English professor's book, *The Yellow Rose of Texas: Her Saga and Her Song*, the actions of a captured slave woman by the name of Emily Morgan turned the tide of the battle. Presumably, Emily accomplished this feat by being privy to some of Houston's plans, getting advance word to Houston of Santa Anna's advance near San Jacinto, and by seducing the Mexican general at noon on the day of the attack. For these brave acts, legend anointed Emily D. West as a heroine of the Texas Revolution: the Yellow Rose of Texas.

Unfortunately, as appealing as this legend is to the modern Texas psyche, the facts of the Battle of San Jacinto hardly support much of this account. In the first place, Emily Morgan was not a slave; she was born Emily D. West, a free black in New Haven, Connecticut. She signed a contract with agent James Morgan in October 1835 to work one year as a hotel housekeeper in Morgan's Point, Texas. She had barely arrived in Texas before the Alamo defeat and the Goliad massacres threatened Texas with extinction.

On April 16, 1836, advance forces of Santa Anna captured her and others and forced her to accompany his army. Little contemporary evidence exists proving any amorous play on her part delayed Santa Anna's readiness for battle. His own incompetence appears to have sealed the fate of the Mexican army. The general's soldiers returning to Mexico after the defeat did not mention the presence of a woman or that Santa Anna was in a state of undress. At siesta time, they were not anticipating an attack, and they posted no sentries. Emily West could not have known of any of Houston's plans.

The erroneous story of her exploits surfaced first in 1842 in conversation between an Englishman, William Bollaert, and a veteran on a ship bound for New York. Bollaert recorded the veteran's suggestion that the battle was "probably" lost because of the influence of a mulatto girl named Emily who was "closeted in the tent" with Santa Anna. A university press published his diary in 1956, which footnoted the conversation but never named the veteran of the war.

When a journalist and university publicist got hold of the unnamed source, the myth of the Yellow Rose of Texas took on Texas-sized proportions. Though no contemporary description of her exists, the Emily of myth became a "long-haired mulatto girl" of about twenty. A Texas A&M publicist expanded the myth by declaring that the most exciting event in New Washington was Emily's "deliberately provocative amble down the street." He concluded a speech in Austin by suggesting that a monument should be erected to her at San Jacinto. It should be inscribed: "In Honor of Emily Who Gave Her All For Texas Piece By Piece." He said that she was a fitting candidate for the girl in Mitch Miller's version of the "Yellow Rose of Texas."

By the time of the Texas Sesquicentennial in 1986, the myth had too much momentum to stop. A college professor had accumulated the fact and the fiction into a full blown monograph called *The Yellow Rose of Texas: Her Saga and Her Song.* And the myth goes on!

Finding Anything

Legendary Ladies of Texas (1994) edited by Francis Edward Abernethy recounts the legend of Emily D. West, alias Emily Morgan, and the Yellow Rose of Texas. This collection of legends includes the stories of eighteen Texas women. It ranges widely from the bandit Belle Starr and singer Janis Joplin, to artist and sculptress Elizabeth Ney and golfer Babe Zaharias.

To separate the legend from the facts about Emily West, see the article by Margaret Swett Henson at the web site of the *Handbook of Texas Online* at www.tsha.utexas.edu/handbook/online/. Tracing the origin of the legend, the author reveals many original sources that fueled the myth.

BOOKS AND WEB SITES

Lady in Blue

Castaneda, Carlos E. *Our Catholic Heritage in Texas, 1519–1936.* Austin: Von Boeckmann-Jones Company, 1936; reprint Arno Press, 1976.

Institute of Texan Cultures. *Texans One and All.* Spanish, Mexican, and Tejanos. www.texancultures.utsa.edu/publications/texansoneandall/texansnav.htm.

Fleur-de-Lis on the Texas Frontier

Fehrenbach, T.R. *Lone Star: A History of Texas and the Texans*. Updated Edition. Da Capo Press, 2000.

Texas Historical Commission. La Salle Project. Fort St. Louis Project. www.thc.state.tx.us/lasalle/lasdefault.html.

Stopping the Birds From Flying Over Texas

Holley, Mary Austin. *Texas*. Lexington, KY: J. Clarke & Co., 1836; Austin: Texas State Historical Society, 1990.

Trask, Kathi. "Horace and Mary Austin Holley." *Dictionary of Unitarian and Universalist Biography*. Unitarian Universalist Historical Society. www.uua .org/uuhs/duub/articles/maryaustinholley.html (accessed June 13, 2004).

Punching Cows to Ranching Empires

Clayton, Lawrence and Salvant, J.U. *Historic Ranches of Texas*. Austin: University of Texas Press, 1993.

Four Sixes Ranch (6666). www.6666ranch.com.

Indianola: A Forgotten Port

Guthrie, Keith. *Texas Forgotten Ports: Mid-Gulf Ports from Corpus Christi to Matagorda Bay*. Austin: Eakin Press, 1988.

Texas Settlement Region. Indianola Trail Guide. www.texassettlement.org/ indianola/.

From a Bullet in the Back to the Governor's Mansion

Hendrickson, Kenneth E., Jr. *The Chief Executives of Texas from Stephen F. Austin to John B. Connally, Jr.* College Station: Texas A&M University Press, 1995.

Texas State Library and Archives Commission. Governors of Texas, 1846–present. www.tsl.state.tx.us/ref/abouttx/governors.html.

The Bird That Flew Backward

Historic Fort Bliss. http://147.71.210.21/adamag/district/district.htm.

Neighbours, Kenneth, F., Frantz, Joe B., Proctor, Ben, et al. *Frontier Forts of Texas*. Waco, Texas: Texian Press, 1966.

"Head 'Em Up, Move 'Em Out"

Hunter, J. Marvin, ed. *The Trail Drivers of Texas: Interesting Sketches of Early Cowboys and Their Experiences on the Range and on the Trail during the Days That Tried Men's Souls—True Narratives Related by Real Cowpunchers and Men Who Fathered the Cattle Industry in Texas*. 2nd Revised Edition. Cokesbury Press, 1925. Reprinted Austin: University of Texas Press, 1985.
Wilbarger County Texas. www.co.wilbarger.tx.us/cattle.htm.

Drawing a Line in the Dirt

Groneman, Bill. *Alamo Defenders: A Genealogy: The People and Their Words*. Austin, Texas: Eakin Press, 1990.
The Alamo Society. www.thealamosociety.com.

The Yellow Rose of Texas

Abernethy, Francis Edward. *Legendary Ladies of Texas*. Denton: University of North Texas Press, 1994.
Henson, Margaret Swett. "Emily D. West." *The Handbook of Texas Online*.
Texas State Historical Association. www.tsha.utexas.edu/handbook/online (accessed June 13, 2004).

3

WHO CAME, WHO STAYED, WHO WAS RUN OFF?

- What is the significance of the giant bones discovered by Texas ex-slave George McJunkin at White Horse Arroyo in 1908?
- What tool has been called the "Swiss Army Knife" of Texas Palaeo-Indian culture?
- How did the first African American in Texas survive as a faith healer and a "medicine man?"
- Whose book of travels across Texas earned him the reputation of the "first Texas braggart in the English tongue?"
- What did Apache relatives of deceased tribal members do to prevent the ghosts of the dead from doing great injury to the living?
- Who was the Irish Conquistador Indians called Captain Colorado because of his red hair?
- What Houston family of German descent allegedly acquired an in-law through a victorious duel in a poker game?
- How did Texas acquire the distinction of being home to the oldest Polish community in America?
- How did circus memorabilia of P.T. Barnum, Tom Thumb, the Flying Wallendas, and Buffalo Bill Cody end up in a San Antonio library?
- What Texas preacher, physician, cattleman, and circuit rider did not "allow the Commandment in Exodus to rest too heavily upon his conscience?"

GEORGE McJUNKIN AND THE GREAT BONE PIT

Homo sapiens wandered in, and out of, the 268,580 square miles of the unique landscape we call Texas for a long, long time—11,000 years or more. Archaeologists push back the date of the first arrivals with each new discovery. At some time during the retreat of the great glaciers, the first humans trekked here for the same reasons some German immigrants did in the 1830s: the land was free, the game was abundant, and there were no fees for hunting and fishing licenses.

Arriving first in the Panhandle-Plains area looking for woolly mammoths, bison, and ground sloths, the first arrivals to Texas left unique spear-points like fluted Clovis points, Folsom spear points, and other campsite debris in many places. An ex-slave born before the Civil War near Midland, Texas, named George McJunkin accidentally discovered one of their early "kill sites." He found giant bones in a gully just across the present northwestern border of Texas on the Crowfoot Ranch near Folsom, New Mexico.

After a fierce flood nearly wiped out the town of Folsom, on August 29, 1908, George rode out to inspect fences. An amateur fossil collector, he noticed a giant bone protruding from a washed out gully in a place called White Horse Arroyo. George never lived to see it, but his discovery of the Great Bone Pit led to the excavation of a perfectly preserved spear-point embedded in the rib-cage of a bison. His discovery set off a chain of events that changed the course of American history and archaeology. Analysis of his discovery proved conclusively that *homo sapiens* arrived in North America several thousand years earlier than previously believed. George became more famous in the history of archaeology than in western American history as a black cowboy.

The life of George McJunkin eradicates a number of western myths and constitutes an ironic legacy. An African-American ex-slave from Texas with his master's Anglo surname tired of blacksmithing and became a cowboy. He worked his way up to ranch foreman. As a hobby, he collected fossils, and one day, by accident, he found some old bones in a gully. His bones proved conclusively that "Native Americans" had occupied a continent for 11,000 years Europeans had named the "New World."

Finding Anything

The Life and Legend of George McJunkin (1973) by Franklin Folsom tells the life story of George McJunkin and the discovery leading to the excavation of the bone pit. Based on primary documents and interviews of people who knew McJunkin, the book spans his life from pre-Civil War days as a slave in Texas to his life as foreman of the Crowfoot Ranch in New Mexico where he made the discovery.

To see photographs and artifacts of McJunkin's discovery, check the web site of the Folsom Museum at www.folsommuseum.netfirms.com. The site contains several photographs of George, relics, and projectile points. A Folsom Point Historical Mile Marker now marks the spot on Highway 72, twelve miles northwest of Folsom, New Mexico, where George McJunkin discovered the bone pit. Archaeologists recovered twenty-three bison skeletons and nineteen Folsom projectile points from excavations begun in 1926.

THE FIRST TEXANS

The oldest extensive collection of artifacts of Paleo-Indian culture recovered in Texas dates 12,000 years ago at the Gault site on Buttermilk Creek forty miles north of Austin. Even after a century of active looting by amateur collectors, the Gault site excavations preserved more than a million artifacts. Clovis culture peoples, once believed to be the oldest arrivals in North America, occupied the Gault site for several thousand years. They left unique fluted projectile points along with animal bones of bison, mammoths, and paleo-horses. The Gault site functioned as a base camp for a wide range of hunting and food-gathering activities.

The first people to arrive in Texas were called Palaeo-Indians. They employed a long, thin flaked stone tool made of chert or flint as their own version of the "Swiss Army Knife." They used it for everything. They sharpened it into a lethal weapon that could stab and penetrate the hide of a mammoth or bison. They employed it as a cutting tool to process food from kills, and in time they fashioned points, knives, and scrapers to process the hides. They sometimes fixed the point to a wooden shaft to make a more potent weapon for the hunt. The oldest, most distinctive of these "projectile points" are the Clovis and the Folsom points. They are found at mammoth and bison kill sites and at campsites along streams in Texas.

Crafting of these flint and chert implements is Texas's oldest manufacturing industry. In the Panhandle Plains about 11,000 years ago, a prehistoric mining operation sprang up to support this industry. It continued uninterrupted for 10,000 years. Several hundred pit quarries survive along the red bluffs of the Canadian River in Moore and Potter counties. Think of these quarries as the Pittsburgh steel mills of Texas for ten millennia. In

1965, because of their antiquity and historical significance, the Alibates Flint Quarries became Texas's only national monument.

Bison kill sites furnish much of the information that exists about the culture of Paleo-Indians. Lake Theo in Caprock Canyons State Park yielded remains of one of several bison kill sites of the Folsom culture dating 10,000 years ago. Paleo-Indian peoples had no horses and hunted exclusively on foot. Like other kill sites in Texas, such as Bonfire Shelter in Langtry, the Folsom people at Lake Theo drove bison over a cliff to their death and then skinned and butchered them at the site. They used specialized scrapers, points, grinding stones, knives, gravers, and abraders to kill hundreds of *Bison antiquus*. At this site, they removed the hides and scraped the fat and flesh from the carcasses and possibly observed some kind of religious ceremony in the process. The active collection, documentation, and reinterpretation of Texas prehistory continues at an active pace with frequent discoveries and changing theories.

Finding Anything

Digging up Texas: A Guide to the Archaeology of the State (2003) by Robert Marcom is a survey of 14,000 years of Texas prehistory and history in archaeological excavation. The author features many archaeological sites, interviews specialists, describes the major Indian cultures of Texas, and explains some of the major methods of archaeological research. He describes and interprets several of the state's best-known excavation sites such as the Alibates Flint Quarries and the Gault site. In a single chapter, the author provides a useful overview of the culture of the major Indian tribes who occupied Texas from prehistory to Indian removal.

To take an excellent virtual tour of thirty archaeological sites in Texas, check the web site of the Texas Archeological Research Laboratory, TARL, at the University of Texas at Austin. TARL contains the largest collection of artifacts in Texas. The site contains photographs of artifacts, illustrations of excavations, maps, newsletters on current activities, and updates on legislation and grants. The TARL web site is www.utexas.edu/research/tarl/.

AFRO-AMERICAN MEDICINE MAN TO THE INDIANS

The experience of the first Afro-American in Texas foreshadowed later black experiences in America. He did not come to the state willingly. Enduring harsh conditions at sea, he survived a shipwreck. He learned Christian faith healing from the ship's commander, who was the son of a Spanish physician, and he used his wits to survive five years enslavement among Indians.

Being one of four of 242 sailors to survive eight years on the American mainland, he finally arrived in Mexico City only to be sold to a new master. In his mission into New Mexico, searching for the mythical city of gold, Zuni Indians killed him. They killed him because the owl feathers on the gourd rattle he used in faith healing and sprinkling ceremonies were an evil omen to the Zuni.

Estevanico, also known as Estevan, Esteban, Estebanico, Black Stephen, and Stephen the Moor, became the first Afro-American to traverse the territory of Texas. He did it as the personal slave of Andrés Dorantes de Carranza of Spain. Estevanico sailed on the ill-fated voyage of 1528 with Cabeza de Vaca that wrecked near Tampa Bay. The original party of 242 sailors steadily shrank as it encountered frequent adversity.

One group of five struck out on their own to find refuge, but fell to eating their dead when they ran out of food. They were discovered with only one member "unconsumed." With make-shift barges, the remaining sailors reached Galveston Island only to wreck again. With about fifteen survivors, they headed south and then west along the Rio Grande.

By 1533, the group dwindled to four survivors, including Estevanico. He and his mentor introduced their methods of faith healing among the coastal and interior Indians, a tactic which probably enabled their party to survive. Estevanico and his mentor practiced a ritual of prayers and gently blowing their breath on the afflicted natives. After several years among hostile Indians, the party escaped and made their way eventually to Mexico City. Dorantes had no thoughts of giving Estevanico his freedom. He sold him to the Viceroy Antonio de Mendoza, who sent him on his final and fatal expedition.

Still hoping to find the legendary Seven Cities of Cibola, the Viceroy assigned Estevanico to a Franciscan, Fray Marcos de Niza, and sent them on an expedition to find Cibola. Estevanico traveled as the advanced scout for the lead party, and sent back wooden crosses of various sizes to indicate how favorable conditions looked.

In 1539, he reached Cibola, thought to be the pueblo village of Hawikuh. He told the villagers he had been sent by white men who would soon arrive. They intended to make peace, heal the sick, and instruct the people in divine matters. When he demanded turquoise and women to take back to the expedition, the village elders killed him as he entered the village. Estevanico survived slavery on three continents by three peoples and died a slave in pursuit of another's fortune.

Finding Anything

Black Texans: A History of African-Americans in Texas, 1528–1995 (1996) by Alwyn Barr reviews four centuries of the black experience in Texas. The book chronicles the black experience from European exploration, slavery, the Civil War, Reconstruction, and the civil rights movement in Texas.

A shorter account of the Afro-American experience in Texas can be found at the web site of the Institute of Texan Cultures. The site provides a narrative history, analysis, and photographs of the contributions of prominent black Texans in Texas development. A major mission of the institute, the web site contains the histories of major ethnic communities who have contributed to Texas life and culture. The institute's education section contains excerpts from a book called *Texans One and All* on ethnic groups. See www.texancultures.utsa.edu/publications/texansoneandall/texansnav.htm and select African American from the list of twenty-six major ethnic groups who made contributions to Texas. The site contains a short, illustrated history of each group.

"FIRST TEXAS BRAGGART IN THE ENGLISH TONGUE"

The first explorations of Texas by Englishmen resemble the misfortunes of the aftermath of Cabeza de Vaca's shipwreck. By Spanish and Portuguese standards, the English were greenhorns at the slave trade, and Spain quickly demonstrated her superiority. After clashing with a Spanish fleet and losing four of his six ships in the Gulf of Mexico, English sea captain Sir John Hawkins gathered the survivors of his slave-trading venture and set sail from Veracruz in 1668 in the *Minion*. In a dreadfully overcrowded vessel, he and his crew of undersupplied sailors hoped to make England or a friendly port. When it became clear that all would either drown or eat one another, they put 114 mariners ashore thirty miles from Tampico in New Spain.

Only three of the 114 castaways survived and returned to England. David Ingram, Richard Twide, and Richard Browne chose to walk north from New Spain, east to the Atlantic, and then up the Atlantic coast for a 3,000-mile journey to Cape Breton off Nova Scotia. Upon finally making it back to England, Ingram wrote an account of his travels. Ingram's travel narrative provides the first description of Texas in the English language. Impressed by the size of Texas, its fertile soils, and its natural resources, Ingram mixed exaggeration and reality in a way that made disbelievers out of the audience he wanted to impress. He observed vegetation, soil, grasses, and shrubs accurately, but he claimed seeing an elephant twice the size of a horse.

Hoping to stimulate interest in more voyages, Ingram waxed fantastic in picturing gems and minerals. He saw great crystals and rubies, an abundance of pearls, and "sundry pieces of gold, some as big as a man's fist." These exaggerations earned Ingram the title of the "first Texas braggart in the English tongue." He could arouse no interest in Texas among Queen Elizabeth's ministers. Some even believed he made up the whole story.

It would be a long time before Englishmen would come to Texas, but they would play an influential role in Texas development. English natives joined Stephen F. Austin's Old Three Hundred colonists, and men like Edward Mandell House and Charles Shearn fought in the Texas Revolution. After the revolution, English writers contributed to the massive effort of publicizing Texas in England, and the effort drew immigrants as ranchers, cowboys, lawmen, and soldiers. The British press scrutiny produced its share of controversy over Texas. Some anti-Texas Englishmen viewed Texas as a haven for scoundrels and fugitives, asserting that the initials G.T.T., "Gone to Texas," were an "internationally used symbol for runaway criminals."

Finding Anything

The English Texans (1985) by Thomas Cutter gives an account of English contributions to Texas. The author highlights major English figures, both men and women, in many periods of Texas development. He explores the careers of Englishmen who became physicians, ranchers, lawyers, soldiers, cowboys, newspapermen, and architects. The author emphasizes English men and women who traveled in Texas in the mid-nineteenth century, stimulating great interest about Texas in England and other parts of Europe.

For an account of David Ingram's journey across Texas and the subsequent publication of his book, go to the web site of the Institute of Texan Cultures at www.texancultures.utsa.edu/publications/texansoneandall/english.htm. It highlights contributions of English Texans with text and historic photographs.

APACHE LAST RITES

Of all the Indian tribes who occupied Texas, the Apaches and Comanches constituted the greatest threat to the state's security. Mastering the use of the horse with skills unmatched by any other tribe, the Apaches and Comanches constituted a potent force on the frontier. In Apache culture, horses played a prominent role in war, hunting, and burial rituals.

Sending the dead off on a proper journey after death required scrupulous attention to certain funerary practices. These practices ensured both a successful life-after-death journey for the deceased and also provided for the safety and well-being of those left behind. The Apache feared the return of dead relatives to haunt persons who had harmed the deceased. Even after entering the underworld, a ghost, or spirit of the dead, might return and avenge a past injury. Observing ceremonial rituals and exercising protective measures provided safe passage for the dead and long-term security for those remaining behind.

After a short period of grieving, the family buried the deceased during the daylight hours. After washing and dressing him in his finest clothes, the family next mounted him on his favorite horse with as many of his personal belongings as possible. A small burial party then led the horse and corpse away from the camp into the hills. After finding a crevice or space between rocks, the burial party covered the corpse and the personal possessions with earth, stones, and brush. The burial party killed the horse, believing the deceased would need it in the afterlife. They returned to camp by a different route and refrained from looking back at the grave.

Upon their return to the camp, they discarded their clothes and thoroughly washed themselves. They kept the location of the grave site secret for fear of provoking the return of the ghosts. Others burned sage and other plants considered to be "ghost medicine" and bathed themselves in the smoke. "Using the names of the dead was taboo, so names died with their owners." They destroyed the remaining possessions of the deceased and relocated his campsite. Survivors left no opportunity for the ghost's return to chance.

Apaches believed that ghosts struck at night and sometimes approached their victims through animals like the owl and the coyote. The hooting of an owl and the presence of a coyote near a camp usually suggested some kind of ghost sickness which required some type of curative ceremony. The Mescalero Apache had their own special owl ceremony.

The extraordinary precautions of the Apaches concerning the death ritual arose from the belief that at death a dead kinsman appeared and led the deceased on a four-day journey north to an underworld. How peacefully this journey went depended on how well the funerary practices were performed. Even after entering the underworld, a ghost could return and avenge some wrong. Two exceptions in funeral arrangements applied to infants and very old persons. Infants, it was believed, could not have developed animosities, and old persons had lived their lives fully and outgrown their rancor.

Finding Anything

The *Handbook of North American Indians. Volume 10: Southwest* (1983) edited by Alfonso Ortiz analyzes and describes the customs, religion, art, and culture of the major Indian cultures and tribes who inhabited the Southwest. The Apaches and Comanches are well covered in volumes 9 and 10. Eastern Texas Indian tribes are not included. Outstanding photographs enhance this handbook.

For additional text and visual information on Texas Indians, go to the web site of the National Museum of the American Indian at the Smithsonian Institution. The web site is located at www.nmai.si.edu/. Rotating photographic and art exhibits at this site feature southwest and frontier Texas Indians. In addition, the SIRIS database, the Smithsonian Institution Research Information System at http://siris.si.edu/, now includes many scanned images of thousands of the Smithsonian Native American photographs. For a historic photographic collection of Apache leaders like Victorio and Cochise, see http://impurplehawk.com/apgallery.html.

THE LUCK OF THE IRISH

Unlike some immigrant groups who came to Texas, the first Irish colonists did not fare much better than they had fared in the mother country. To some it appears that all they did at first was exchange one form of misery for another. The "luck of the Irish" followed them all the way.

The first Irishman to come to Texas came as a Conquistador in the employ of Spain. Born in Dublin in 1734 as Hugh O'Conner, he fled English oppression to Spain. He entered the military and rose to the rank of an officer in the Volunteer Regiment of Aragon. He first served the Spanish Crown in Cuba, then with increasing responsibility, he moved on to New Spain. He became governor of the province of Texas under the name of

Hugo Oconer in 1767. The Indians gave him the name "Captain Colorado" because of his red hair and scarlet coat.

Oconer earned a fine reputation for attempts to prevent incursions of Apaches and other Indians into Spanish territory. As Comanches drove the Apaches from their traditional hunting grounds, the Apaches made raids deeper into Texas and Mexico. In a twenty-five-year period in the mid-eighteenth century, the Spanish estimated Apache raids killed more than 4,000 people and destroyed or stole 12 million pesos worth of property.

Oconer's efforts to defend the northern frontier highlighted his military career. In an effort to stop Apache raids into Northern Mexico, the Spanish viceroy promoted Oconer to *commandante inspector*. In this position, he reorganized the northern defenses with a defense line of twenty-two presidios that extended 1,500 miles from Goliad all the way to Sonora, California. During this effort, he strengthened the defenses of San Antonio. His campaigns against the Apaches and his defensive strategy brought only modest success. It also ruined his health, and he died at the age of forty-five in 1779.

The motive for Irish immigration to Spain, to America, or to any country outside of England remained a constant for several centuries. The denial of land, voting rights, education, and political representation, coupled with religious persecution from the English government, remained a constant among the Irish people. Under English law, an Irish Catholic was not "presumed to exist." In 1833, when James Power, a Mexican impresario, returned to his home of Ballygarrett in County Wexford to recruit settlers to Texas, he had no difficulty generating optimism for his venture.

With handbills and notices, he announced the purpose of his visit. His sister supported the effort. After holding village meetings describing grassy plains, rich farmland, and thousands of cheap acres, Power signed up 250 families to come to Texas. Most of the families would never make it to their promised land grants. Of the first group of 108 settlers to depart Ireland for Texas, only eight reached the new Texas colony.

In December 1833, the first wave of immigrants traveled to Liverpool where they boarded the ship *Prudence* for the four-week trip to New Orleans. Each settler paid Power $30 per adult for transportation. They brought enough food, provisions, and seed for one year. They waited in port for the second group of Power's colonists to arrive on the aptly named ship the *Heroine*. Bad weather drove the *Heroine* off course, making it two and a half months late.

While waiting for the second group of colonists to arrive, the first group contracted cholera which was sweeping the United States at the time. Many in the first group died in New Orleans. The healthy colonists boarded two schooners sailing to the colonial settlement at Copano. Bad luck continued. Near Aransas Pass, a furious gale blew the schooners into a mud bank where they lost many supplies and farm implements.

Before the passengers could disembark, cholera broke out again, and the Mexican authorities refused to allow the colonists to come ashore until the epidemic abated. Two hundred and fifty Irish colonists died. As a conclusion to this first Irish colonial experiment, the authorities buried the bodies in the bay without providing final religious rites of their Irish homeland. The Irish foray into the Refugio colony had a most unfavorable beginning.

Finding Anything

The Irish Texans (1995) by John Brendan Flannery recounts the wide variety of Irish experiences in Texas. The book records many avenues of Irish enterprises in Texas from military participation in the Spanish army to establishment of the first Irish colonies. The author notes Irish contributions to Texas Independence and various industrial ventures in oil and railroads as well as professional achievements in medicine and education.

To keep track of current activities of interest to the Irish Texan community, check the web site of the Southwest Celtic Music Association at www.scmatx.org/. Although the site specializes in Irish, Celtic, and Renaissance music, it follows all aspects of Irish heritage in Texas through its links page in the main menu. It is possible to move easily to the Irish heritage interest groups in all of the major Texas cities from this site.

FREE LAND AND NO FEES FOR HUNTING LICENSES

In the nineteenth century, Germans made up the largest ethnic group coming directly from Europe to Texas. Today, by ancestry, they rank as the third largest national origin group in Texas behind Hispanics. Friedrich Ernst, the Father of Texas German Immigration, set up the first permanent German settlement in 1831 with a grant of a league of land in Stephen F. Austin's colony.

Anglo-American citizens of the nearby town of San Felipe referred to Ernst as an "industrious" man because he could produce a particularly fine cigar. The first German settlement became known as Industry. Legend has it that Indians taught him how to cultivate tobacco. German patterns of immigration followed a classic model of coming to Texas. A dominant personality writes many letters home overstating the positive, the letters are circulated, and a "chain migration" results. Friedrich Ernst's letters to his friends and neighbors in Germany got passed around and printed. Revolutionary unrest in Germany, combined with Ernst's promotional activities, stimulated a flood of immigration to Texas. By 1900, the German population had reached one million.

The lifestyles of German immigrants proved to be compatible with the lifestyles of Texans. Both groups worked hard, sang songs, played music, danced, drank beer, and told stories. Like many Texas stories, the German stories cannot always be verified from constant retelling over draughts of Pearl and Shiner beer.

Caroline Louise Sacks von Roeder, one of the earliest Germans to immigrate, shares a story of one of her relative's unorthodox arrivals to Texas. Sigismund von Roeder, the "wild" member of the family, had killed the Prince of Prussia in a duel. The King deported him, and he ended up in Texas. He lived an adventurous life, and Sigismund's propensity to gamble landed him in a high stakes card game with a man named Benjamin Buckingham at a Brazos Plantation. With Buckingham's new bride in attendance, Sigismund started a winning streak. After losing all his cash, Buckingham lost his mules, workhorse, oxen, slaves, and plots on the plantation. He lost it all! Buckingham then put his marriage certificate on the table.

As long as the lady agreed, it was okay with Sigismund. She gave her assent and they played the last hand. Buckingham lost again. When Sigismund moved to take possession of the marriage certificate, Buckingham drew a pistol and fired, missing his German target. In response, Sigismund drew his sword and ran Buckingham through. A coroner ruled the death self-defense. In a letter to her sister in Germany urging that she come to Texas, Caroline Louise related the story of Sigismund describing Texas as a place of "freedom and romance."

Finding Anything

The German Texans (1996) by Glen E. Lich documents the successful German immigration experience in Texas with history, stories, letters, folk tales, and recipes. The book contains documents and reminiscences of the first German settlements, collections of quaint customs, illustrations of German ranch brands, Sons of Hermann societies, and paintings by German artists.

To track current activities in the Texas German community, see the web site of the German-Texas Heritage Society at www.gths.net. A not-for-profit society devoted to all aspects of preserving German-Texas heritage, the society reviews important books on Texas German history and culture, language, genealogy, music, art, and film. The society's newsletter tracks activities in all parts of the state where German-Texans remain active.

MASS UNDER A LIVE OAK TREE

Creating the first Polish settlement in Texas developed from the idealistic goals of a Polish Franciscan Friar named Leopold Moczygemba. In 1852, the Bishop of Galveston recruited the twenty-eight-year-old Leopold to serve German Texans in the sprawling territory of West Texas. He needed missionaries to minister to German parishes that were beginning to fill up with immigrants.

Four Franciscan Fathers and a lay brother came to Galveston in September 1852 to work in churches at Fredericksberg, New Braunsfels, Castroville, and D'Hanis and to service a network of missions across the territory. The young Friar, observing the success of the German immigrants, adopted the standard practice of writing solicitation letters to his homeland in Upper Silesia. By 1854, a group of peasants in Poland began selling their property to come to Texas. Leopold's father and brothers joined the first group of 150 Poles to sail from Bremen. The voyage on board the *Weser* took nine weeks, arriving in Galveston on November 3rd.

One eyewitness recalls seeing the pilgrimage of the Poles from Galveston to their land plots on the San Antonio River and Cibolo Creek. "Some had on wooden shoes, and almost without exception, all wore broad-brimmed, low-crowned black felt hats, nothing like the hats that were worn in Texas."

After enduring the long journey and a yellow fever outbreak, the first group reached their plots of land on Christmas Eve 1854. Leopold led a mass under a live oak tree. The live oak tree still stands in Panna Maria (Virgin Mary) community, and it symbolizes all that the community overcame in transplanting itself from Upper Silesia to Central Texas. The colonists camped out until they could build dugout houses of sod, mud, straw, or wood. Later they built in stone with steep thatched roofs, and they finally built a permanent church.

From its completion in 1877, Saint Mary's of the Immaculate Conception Church provided the spiritual and social focal point of the Panna Maria Polish community. The architect designed a two-story Gothic Revival stucco church with a large 100-foot entrance tower visible in the distance.

Galveston, Texas, earned the title of "The Ellis Island of the West" and the U.S. government built two large custom houses to process immigrants. When it opened in 1891, the custom house above was hailed as "one of the most beautiful buildings in the state." By 1935, public tastes had changed, and a newspaper called it a relic "of an age when architects went slightly insane." From the collections of The Dallas/Texas History and Archives Division, Dallas Public Library.

Large lancet stained-glass windows enhance a simple interior and highlight a pointed arch. In 1966, President Lyndon Johnson honored the Panna Maria community as the oldest Polish settlement in the United States by presenting community officials with a mosaic of Our Lady of Czestochowa.

Finding Anything

The Polish Texans (1982) by T. Lindsay Baker recounts the unique Polish experience in Texas. Beginning with the conditions of unrest in central Europe, the author traces the Polish experience through biographies of significant figures. He analyzes distribution by trades and commerce and examines anti-Polish sentiment fostered by the Ku Klux Klan. The book includes photographs of significant Polish leaders and communities.

The web site of the community of Panna Maria at www.pannmariatx. com/ contains information on the founding of the community which celebrates its sesquicentennial in 2005. The web site contains excellent photographs of Saint Mary's Parish Church, the live oak tree where Father Leopold celebrated the first mass, the gravestone of Father Leopold, and other historical pictures of Polish Texans.

JEWISH TEXANS: "ONE GENERATION PASSES AWAY AND ANOTHER GENERATION COMES"

The record of Jewish Texans spans the revolutionary Texas era into modern times. Unlike other ethnic groups who immigrated to Texas, Jews came from many different regions of the world at many different times and distinguished themselves in many different pursuits.

Because of prohibitions against practicing the Jewish religion in New Spain prior to 1821, the records of Jewish settlers in Mexican Texas are difficult to verify. The family of Samuel Isaacks came to Texas from Tennessee. They settled on the Brazos in December of 1821, and Stephen F. Austin awarded the family land near present-day Rosenberg in Polk County.

Formal Jewish community life dates from the 1850s when the need to establish consecrated burial grounds led to the creation of cemeteries in Galveston, Houston, San Antonio, and Jefferson. The nearest rabbis served in New Orleans. To overcome this problem, the community held religious services in private homes, stores, or rented rooms.

In December 1859, the Houston Jewish community founded Temple Beth Israel, the first chartered congregation in Texas. It served forty-two men, twenty-six women, and forty children. Meeting in a wooden building used as a synagogue in the front and a meeting room in the back, the community hired Zachariah Emmich as Texas's first formally ordained rabbi for $1,000 on a one-year contract.

A common stereotype of Jewish contributions to Texas often revolves around great achievements of merchants and merchandising successes, the establishment of the first chain store in Texas, Zale Jewelry Corporation, or the Christmas catalog of Neiman Marcus. Examination of Jewish heritage reveals that Texas Jews entered almost all the vocations and professions attempted by immigrant groups—even farming and sheep herding.

From 1821, when it became legal to practice the Jewish faith in Texas, Jews became peddlers, merchants, slave owners, bankers, inventors, soldiers, spies, doctors, lawyers, and mayors. Some won Nobel prizes and some went bankrupt. Some were athletes like wrestler Abe Coleman, the

Jewish Adonis, and some, like Sam Dreben, were soldiers of fortune. It was said of Sam, a Russian immigrant, that he followed wars wherever he found them, and if he couldn't find one, "He'd start one."

Many successful Jewish Texans pursued personal interests and became avid collectors of art, sculpture, books, artifacts, and memorabilia. San Antonio Jewish lawyer, Henry Hertzberg, born in 1883, served in the Texas Senate for several terms. As a child, he developed a love of the circus. He turned this passion into a lifetime of collecting posters, art, memorabilia, letters, and circus lore that document the heritage of the circus and its impact on Texas and American life.

At his death, thousands of the items in his collection were donated to the San Antonio Public Library and opened for public viewing. Artifacts such as Tom Thumb's 1843 carriage, Buffalo Bill Cody's Wild West Show memorabilia, and a complete hand-carved miniature circus proved popular items in the exhibits. The Hertzberg Collection, which includes thousands of handbills and posters, grew with more donations into one of the largest collections of circus memorabilia in America.

Finding Anything

Deep in the Heart: The Lives and Legends of Texas Jews, A Photographic History (1990) by Ruthe Winegarten and Cathy Schechter provides an extensive, readable summary of the wide range of experiences of Jewish Texans over several centuries. The authors succeed in bringing together information culled from many archival and manuscript collections, articles, and newspapers. There are more than 500 photographs and many short biographies of major figures.

For a web site that stays current with the activities of Jewish Texans, check The Texas Jewish Historical Society at www.txjhs.org/. This site monitors important ongoing work at the state, region, county, city, and synagogue level. It has a detailed list of sources in book, video, and archive form.

CATTLEMAN IN THE PULPIT: REVEREND
GEORGE WEBB SLAUGHTER

Like other elements of Texas culture, religion and self-defense sometimes got mixed up together on the frontier and provided a martial flavor to the spiritual quest. The life of the Reverend George Webb Slaughter provides a good example. After coming to Texas from Louisiana, he practiced the vocations of part-time preacher, circuit rider, cattleman, Indian fighter, and physician. After he deserted his first form of faith, Methodism, and was ordained a Baptist in 1844, he once preached in Palo Pinto County with a long-barreled rifle leaning against the pulpit and a brace of pistols in his belt when the Indian relations in the county area were unstable.

When George Slaughter came to Texas from Louisiana in 1830, the practice of his Methodist religion, according to Mexican law, constituted a crime. In the Austin colony, nevertheless, eleven Baptist and three Methodist families managed to practice their faiths unofficially. Others longed for the opportunity. The growing tensions with Mexico consumed Slaughter almost from the day he arrived in Texas. Through a freight business he owned, he shipped Sam Houston's law books to Texas and soon became a military courier transmitting messages between Houston and William Travis.

After the Texas revolution, Slaughter married Sarah Jane Mason and began a family that grew to eleven children. The prospect of making a living and taming a frontier dominated the minds of most Texans during the period immediately after independence. Not surprisingly, many Texans neglected their spiritual lives. The Reverend Oscar Addison, a Methodist circuit rider, found nothing to cheer about on his circuit. He found members who had "backslidden" and were "spiritually dead." Some had been "going to dancing school" and some had "joined the Baptists." George Webb Slaughter was guilty on two counts. He joined the Baptists in 1842, and they ordained him in 1844.

From the time the Reverend Daniel Parker moved the Two-Seed in the Spirit Pilgrim Church of Predestinarian Regular Baptists into Fayette County near La Grange, the Baptists had been spreading their influence in Texas. While Methodists had frequently used circuit riders to extend denominational influence and maintain contact with local congregations, Baptists encouraged local congregations to make necessary financial arrangements to obtain local pastors. The result of this approach not infrequently was a poorly educated clergy or a layman. George Slaughter, though a man of many experiences, had three weeks of formal education.

In 1857, George moved his large family to Palo Pinto County, where he would spend the remainder of his life as a successful cattleman, preacher, and physician. For a number of years, he was the only physician in Palo Pinto County. During his years of ministering to the physical and spiritual needs of the citizens of the northwestern Texas counties, he is said to have baptized over 3,000 persons. At one time, he had ordained more preachers and organized more churches than any other minister in the state. He died at home in Palo Pinto on March 19, 1895 with his children and his old friend, the Reverend Rufus C. Burleson of Waco, by his side.

Finding Anything

Historic Churches of Texas: The Land and the People (1980) by Frank A. Driskell and Noel Grisham renders an account of the major sectarian influences on Texas. The authors relate the founding and evolution of the seven most influential Texas religions: Baptist, Catholic, Disciples of Christ, Church of Christ, Episcopal, Methodist, and Presbyterian. It focuses on the part each group has played in the development of Texas.

For a concise look at the development of Texas Baptists, see the article by J. W. Storey, "Baptist Church," in the *Handbook of Texas Online* at the Texas State Historical Association web site www.tsha.utexas.edu/handbook/online/. The author also analyzes all major Texas denominations at the same site in another article entitled "Religion."

BOOKS AND WEB SITES

George McJunkin and The Great Bone Pit

Folsom, Franklin. *The Life and Legend of George McJunkin*. Nashville: Thomas Nelson, 1973.
The Folsom Museum. www.folsommuseum.netfirms.com/.

The First Texans

Marcom, Robert. *Digging up Texas; A Guide to the Archaeology of the State.* Plano, Texas: Republic of Texas Press, 2003.
The University of Texas at Austin. Texas Arch eological Research Laboratory. TARL. www.utexas.edu/research/tarl/.

Afro-American Medicine Man to the Indians

Barr, Alwyn. *Black Texans: A History of African Americans in Texas, 1528–1995.* Norman: University of Oklahoma Press, 1996.
Institute of Texan Cultures. The University of Texas at San Antonio. *Texans One and All*. African Americans. www.texancultures.utsa.edu/publications/texansone andall/texansnav.htm.

"First Texas Braggart in the English Tongue"

Cutter, Thomas. *The English Texans*. San Antonio: The University of Texas Institute of Texan Cultures, 1985.

Institute of Texan Cultures. The University of Texas at San Antonio. *Texans One and All*. English. www.texancultures.utsa.edu/publications/texansoneandall/ texansnav.htm.

Apache Last Rites

National Museum of the American Indian. Smithsonian Institution. www.nmai.si.edu/.
Sturtevant, William C. and Ortiz, Alfonso, ed. *Handbook of North American Indians. Volume 10. Southwest.* Washington DC: Smithsonian Institution, 1983.

The Luck of the Irish

Flannery, John Brendan. *The Irish Texans*. San Antonio: The University of Texas Institute of Texan Cultures, 1995.
Southwest Celtic Music Association. www.scmatx.org/.

Free Land and No Fees for Hunting Licenses

Lich, Glen E. *The German Texans*. San Antonio: The University of Texas, Institute of Texan Cultures, 1996.
The German-Texan Heritage Society. www.gths.net/.

Mass Under a Live Oak Tree

Baker, T. Lindsay. *The Polish Texans*. San Antonio: University of Texas, Institute of Texan Cultures, 1982.
Panna Maria, Texas. www.pannamariatx.com/.

Jewish Texans: "One Generation Passes Away and Another Generation Comes"

Texas Jewish Historical Society. www.txjhs.org/.
Winegarten, Ruthe and Schechter, Cathy. *Deep in the Heart: The Lives and Legends of Texas Jews, A Photographic History*. Austin, Texas: Eakin Press, 1990.

Cattleman in the Pulpit: Reverend George Webb Slaughter

Driskell, Frank A. and Grisham, Noel. *Historic Churches of Texas: The Land and the People*. Austin: State House Press, 1980.
Storey, J.W. "Baptist Church." *Handbook of Texas Online*. Texas State Historical Association. http://tsha.utexas.edu/handbook/online/ (accessed June 14, 2004).

4

THE PLACE AND THE SPACE

- How did nature divide the Lone Star State?
- Where is the current reigning champion live oak tree of Texas located?
- What do the movies *The Texas Chainsaw Massacre* (1973), *Honeysuckle Rose* (1979), and *The Best Little Whorehouse in Texas* (1981) have in common?
- How did the towns of Dime Box, Ding Dong, and Direct, Texas, get their names?
- What is the longest highway in Texas?
- Why do some divide Texas culturally east to west between "Baptist biscuit eaters" and "callous-rumped sons of the range" and others North to South by legal sales of alcoholic beverages?
- What is the windchill factor for a resident of the Texas Panhandle when the temperature is near zero and the wind is gusting forty miles per hour?
- What Texas town recorded the most rainfall in a single 24-hour period?
- What is the significance of the Devil's Sinkhole, Moon Milk Falls, and the Enchanted Rock?
- What Texas fossil is the largest flying creature ever discovered?

NATURE'S DIVISIONS OF TEXAS

The long list of geographical, geological, environmental, and promotional names used to describe Texas spaces can be confusing even to native Texans. Scholars divide Texas into geological, ecological, biotic, vegetative, climatic, physiographic, and cultural regions. In turn, regional promoters, local tourism offices, and chambers of commerce christen their region with names like Heart of Texas, Gateway to the Golden Triangle, Sun Country, Winter Garden, and Metroplex. In 1977, geographer Terry Jordan identified twenty-nine different popular regions which some Texans identified in some way as their regional homes.

There is a practical way to identify the natural regions of Texas. The Texas Department of Parks and Wildlife employs a useful scheme in its guide to state parks. The *Official Guide to Texas State Parks* divides Texas into seven regions. Each region exhibits distinctive geographical and environmental characteristics. Most of the regions have at least twenty parks and historical sites. Examining the photographs and general descriptions of the seven regions and scanning specific features of individual parks, a newcomer quickly acquires a picture of the characteristics of the geography and environment of Texas.

The Pineywoods comprises the far northeastern section of Texas from Texarkana to Orange on the Louisiana border. A rich belt of forested pines and hardwoods cover much of East Texas. Because of the lumber industry, historians called it the "sawdust empire" or the "Old South" region of the state. The Big Thicket ecological region occupies 300,000 acres in the southern part of the Pineywoods.

The crescent-shaped Gulf Coast region comprises a 300 mile-long strip of land stretching from Louisiana to Mexico. The width of the strip varies between 50 and 100 miles. Long, narrow barrier islands protect the coast and inlets from storms. Padre Island, stretching 113 miles from the tip of Texas to Corpus Christi, is the longest barrier island in the U.S.

The South Texas Plains stretch from San Antonio and Del Rio in the north to the Rio Grande in the south. Grassland and brush country mesquite dominate the flat plains. The subtropical climate of the lower Rio Grande Valley supports many rare species of plants and wildlife.

The Hill Country comprises much of the area between Austin, San Antonio, Del Rio, and Midland. It consists of the hilly, rocky central part of the state known as the Edwards Plateau, an area known for spring-fed rivers and fine fishing. The oldest geological features in the state lie in the Llano Basin, which contains surface rock that is one billion years old.

The Prairies and Lakes region make up most of North Central Texas from the Austin-San Antonio area to the Gainesville-Denison area near the Red River. As its name suggests, this area once contained millions of acres of Blackland Prairie and tall grasses. After agriculture and settlement took its toll, perhaps only 5,000 acres of blackland prairie remain. Bands of trees like cedar elms, post oaks, and hackberries called the Cross Timbers run in a north-south direction through the region.

The Panhandle Plains encompasses almost 80,000 square miles of the northwestern corner of Texas bordering New Mexico and Oklahoma. The high plains and rolling plains extend southward to Midland and the Hill Country. The Llano Estacado dominates the highest area of plains. Palo Duro Canyon and the Canadian River break up the routine flat character of this southern end of the American Great Plains.

The Trans-Pecos, or the Big Bend Country, region of Texas exhibits more diversity than any other region. The Rio Grande forms the southern boundary of the land between El Paso and Del Rio and an east-west line between Midland and El Paso forms the northern boundary. All the area west of the Pecos River comprises the remainder of the Big Bend Country. The southwestern desert country intersects the highest mountains in Texas, producing spectacular scenery and rare plant and animal life. A cowboy called this region a place where the "rainbows wait for rain."

Finding Anything

The *Official Guide to Texas State Parks* (1997) written and photographed by Laurence Parent describes seven natural geographical areas of Texas. The guide contains more than 100 color photographs, and the author supplements the text with history, geology, natural history, and archaeology. *Texas Parks and Wildlife* magazine also provides current information on outdoor lifestyles in Texas and some of the best wildlife photography found in the U.S.

To see a more extensive treatment of Texas geography, go to the web site of the Texas Parks and Wildlife Department. The agency maintains a Nature section on the web site, including an Index of Natural Regions and Subregions of Texas. This web site further refines Texas natural regions into eleven categories at www.tpwd.state.tx.us/nature/tx-eco95.htm.

BIGGEST LIVE OAK ON RECORD

With only 53 of Texas's 254 counties having populations of more than 50,000 inhabitants in the 2000 census, miles and miles of rural back roads crisscross the state. In 1980, artist Earl Thollander traveled the back roads of the major regions of Texas in a pickup truck. Stopping at points along selected routes in each of the state's major natural regions, he sketched scenes of Texas that appealed to him. From the Gulf Coast to the Panhandle Plains, Thollander sketched a portrait of Texas from the back roads. After the trip, he gathered up his drawings, drew his own personal highway map with arrows, and marked the places he sketched. Then he added very short descriptions of the routes he took and put them in a book called *Back Roads of Texas*.

The artist drew a nostalgic picture of Texas, capturing the flavor of part of each region. Thollander made no apology for preferring the slower pace of rural life. He liked roads that were "narrow and winding, even bumpy and slow-going" that permit appreciation of the land. He sketched inscriptions on tombstones, operating windmills, old hotels, log houses, churches, trees, courthouses, farm animals, missions, signs, post offices, farm machinery, and boats. Alongside simple scenes of everyday life, he sketched the house of Sam Houston's widow, Margaret Moffette Lea. He liked Texas live oaks trees, one of the state's sturdiest trees.

On the road trip to Padre Island, he discovered Goose Island State Park and Live Oak Peninsula. On Goose Island Road, he saw a sign directing him to the Texas "champion live oak tree." He sketched it. The Goose Island Oak stood 44 feet tall, had a trunk with a 35-foot circumference, and showed a crown spread of 89 feet. Park officials estimated its age at 1,000 years. The Goose Island Oak held the title of largest live oak in Texas from 1966 to 2003. In 2003, it lost the title to a massive live oak in a coastal swamp.

In 2003, the Legislature recognized a new state champion live oak tree from Brazoria County, the San Bernard live oak. Estimated to be 200 years old, it stands 67 feet high and 10 feet wide. Michael Lange, a federal wildlife biologist, discovered it in the San Bernard National Wildlife Refuge. The tree has been added to the Texas Big Tree Registry, a list of the state's 250 largest trees, maintained since 1940. Texas hosts sixty-nine national champion big trees, behind only two other states in total number.

Finding Anything

Back Roads of Texas (1980) by Earl Thollander renders a rural perspective of the seven regions of Texas. This simple, well-executed book provides maps, sketches, and brief commentary on selected parts of each region. Creating a distinctive travel and guidebook, the author focuses on drawing sketches of Texas and limits his commentary to succinct descriptions.

See the Big Tree Registry sponsored by the Texas Forest Service for a listing of more than 300 species of the largest native trees of Texas at www.txforestservice.tamu.edu. The registry lists the common name, the Latin name, and the county of origin. It gives the tree's measurements in circumference, height, crown spread, tree index, and date of last measurement. For the stories behind historic trees of Texas, see the web site www.texasescapes.com/TexasHistory/TexasHistoricTrees.htm.

TEXAS CHAIN SAW MASSACRE AND *HONEYSUCKLE ROSE*

Movies filmed in Texas provide another way to gain a visual perspective of the Texas landscape. Since 1910, more than 1,000 movies and television programs have been filmed on location in Texas. All geographical regions of the state have provided landscapes for these movies, and many have employed Texas themes. The movie classic *Hud* (1963), filmed in Claude in the Panhandle Plains with Paul Newman, Patricia Neal, and Melvyn Douglas, employed cliché Texas themes of greed, oil money, and ethics. Warren Beatty and Faye Dunaway starred in a modern version of *Bonnie and Clyde* (1967), filmed in North Central Texas in Dallas and Denton. Robert Duvall played the role of a country singer who makes a comeback in *Tender Mercies* (1981), shot in East Texas and Waxahachie.

Central Texas, the Austin area, and Round Rock furnished the location for *The Texas Chainsaw Massacre* (1973), *Honeysuckle Rose* (1979), *The Best Little Whorehouse in Texas* (1981), and *Nadine* (1981). *The Texas Chainsaw Massacre* became a cult horror classic and spawned a sequel with Dennis Hopper in 1986. Willie Nelson starred in his first movie role in *Honeysuckle Rose* and sang "On the Road Again." *The Best Little Whorehouse in Texas* starred Burt Reynolds and Dolly Parton in an adaptation of Larry L. King's story of the legendary Chicken Ranch brothel in La Grange.

The Trans-Pecos region hosted its share of movies, including the Texas epic *Giant* (1956), filmed around Valentine and Marfa. With a cast of movie giants and future giants, it included Rock Hudson, Elizabeth Taylor, James Dean, Dennis Hopper, Sal Mineo, and Mercedes McCambridge. Texas oil money and ranching wealth closely resembling some contemporary Texas characters served as models for this movie. The science fiction thriller *The Andromeda Strain* (1970), about the spread of a deadly virus, was filmed in Schafter.

The Brush Country and Rio Grande Valley of Texas provided scenery for some of the oldest movies filmed in Texas. Appropriately, one of the first films shot in Texas used the siege of the Alamo as its subject, a subject that will not die. William F. Haddock directed the silent movie *The Immortal Alamo* (1911). It was shot in San Antonio, with battle scenes filmed at Fort Sam Houston using students from Peacock Military Academy as extras. John Wayne starred in the best-known version of the Alamo movies filmed in Texas at Brackettville, called simply *The Alamo* (1956). He produced, and directed, and starred in the role of Davy Crockett.

Finding Anything

Texas Production Manual (1988) produced by the Texas Film/Music Office provides the locations of all movies filmed in Texas from 1923-1988. The manual carries an article entitled "Motion Pictures Made in Texas, 1923-1988." The film office now operates under the Texas Film Commission and offers an extensive web site of information.

For the locations of recent and current projects of movies and television programs filmed in Texas, check the web site of the Texas Film Commission at www.governor.state.tx.us/film. In addition to an extensive filmography, the film commission provides detailed information on the Texas film industry and supplies information on how to apply to be an extra in a Texas film. Scenery from the state's seven major geographical regions provides movie producers a collection of "location photos" in the Regional Info section of the web site. This collection forms a fine "virtual" tour of all the state's geographical regions.

DING DONG AND DIME BOX, TEXAS

Early Texas settlers used a number of methods to christen counties, towns, and geographical features. Often the names proved distinctive, colorful and memorable. Texas place names reveal imaginative use of language, pragmatism, and problem-solving skills typically found among Texans.

The sources of the names varied widely. They came from individuals, groups, companies, the Bible, literature, combinations of names, spelling words backward, and from methods that defy classification. Dime Box, Texas, in Lee County, Ding Dong, Texas, in Bell County, and Direct, Texas, in Lamar County furnish a few examples of some Texas methods of naming cities.

A gorge called The Pass of the Camels in Culberson County and First Creek, Second Creek, Third Creek, Fourth Creek, and Fifth Creek in Lipscomb County illustrate how physical features acquired names. Sometimes canyons and creeks acquired their names from unique historical events, and sometimes they originated from peculiarities of the populace.

Before Dime Box, Texas, acquired an official post office, receiving mail tried the patience of the community. To solve the problem, the citizens erected a community mail box to receive mail from passing teamsters and freighters. They put a dime in the box to receive mail from places like Houston and Bryan. For about five years after the town got a post office, the community was called Brown's Mill, but people confused the new name with other cities. In 1884, they took back the previous name of Dime Box.

Ding Dong, Texas, took its name from a sign painted by John Hoover for two cousins, I.V. Bell and Z.O. Bell, who owned a store in the community. With a bell on each end of a three- by four-foot sign over the initials I.V. and Z.O., Hoover painted "Ding Dong" in the middle. The town never had a real bell until the Santa Fe Railroad gave them one. Direct, Texas acquired its name from an evangelist who allegedly told the citizens that they were going "direct to hell." Supposedly, he was disturbed because Indians were coming across the river "direct for whiskey."

The United States Army officially named a canyon The Pass of the Camels in Culberson County. The name constitutes a legacy of the Army's failed experiment of introducing eighty-seven camels into Texas in 1857. To see how camels would perform as supply animals in the arid conditions of the Southwest, the Army shipped camels to Indianola in 1857. They marched the camels to San Antonio and eventually stationed them at Camp Verde. The camels performed well, but their screams scared the mules. The Civil War put an end to their usefulness because Jefferson Davis had been the camel's main advocate in Washington. On a march through the Big Bend in 1859, one camel died and the army named the canyon in honor of all the camels. After the Civil War, the Army sold most of the camels and turned the rest loose in the wild.

Lipscomb County consecutively numbered five streams that flow southward into Wolf Creek, First Creek, Second Creek, Third Creek, Fourth Creek, and Fifth Creek. Texans name churches this way, too. For some unknown reason, they gave more practical names to the last two tributaries: Skunk Creek and Dugout Creek.

Finding Anything

1001 Texas Place Names (1980) by Fred Tarpley is a collection of information on the origin of unusual Texas place names. The author selected at least two place names from each of Texas's 254 counties, and the remainder he chose for their unique origins or significance of place. The work reflects ethnic settlement, history, folklore, humor, and geography.

For information on the background and history of more than 200,000 Texas cities, counties, place names, courthouses, historic landmarks, historical markers, and museums, check the web site of the Texas Historical Commission. Go to the Atlas of Historic Sites and search by the feature or landmark. This site enables a person to search for a specific site such as Dime Box or search for all the historic markers or museums in an entire county. The commission web site is www.thc.state.tx.us/.

THE LONGEST HIGHWAY IN TEXAS

U.S. Highway 83 runs from the tip of the Panhandle north of Perryman at the Oklahoma-Texas border due south to Abilene. The highway continues in a straight north-south direction until it reaches the Mexican border at Laredo. From Laredo, it follows the winding path of the Rio Grande to McAllen and ends at Brownsville. At a distance of 899 miles, Highway 83 is the longest highway in Texas. The last 198 miles of Highway 83 from Laredo to Brownsville go by two names: The Great Texas Coastal Birding Trail or the Texas Tropical Trail. Both names indicate the uniqueness of this part of the Texas environment.

To navigate the back roads, highways, and geographical regions of Texas requires a good map, and the state fortunately has a special atlas, the *Roads of Texas* (1999). Drawn from county maps issued by the Texas Department of Transportation, this roadmap-atlas covers the entire road system of Texas in seventy-three maps. With the exception of city streets, the atlas includes 25,000 roads from interstate highways and U.S. highways to state highways and county roads. These maps show all the state parks and recreational areas, access points to rivers and lakes, and the elevations of mountain peaks. They show all military bases, airports, railroad lines, and all bridges more than twenty feet in length.

In rural areas, maps in *The Roads of Texas* show symbols for churches, cemeteries, historic sites, and various local landmarks. The Cottage Hill United Methodist Church, for example, located near the intersection of State Highway 2478 and County Road 170 in Collin County provides a good example of the level of detail in this atlas. The tiny population of the community of Cottage Hill, lying between Weston and Celina, fails to merit space in standard Texas atlases.

The Roads of Texas shows county and state roads, the community of Cottage Hill, a church, a cemetery, and a historical marker. The historical marker indicates why Cottage Hill is on the map. The Cottage Hill United Methodist Church may be one of the oldest Methodist congregations in Collin County. The state historical marker tells the story of the church. Oral traditions of the community establish the founding of the frontier congregation as 1846 when the Reverend John Culwell began holding religious gatherings in the home of his brother Andrew near Honey Creek.

By 1848, the Dallas Methodist Circuit recorded the congregation as the Honey Creek Campground Church. A Cottage Hill Methodist Church history describes these campground meetings on the frontier as occasions for "spiritual ignition" and "social contact." The first documented reference to the present name of the Cottage Hill Methodist Church occurs in the minutes of the Trinity Conference of the Methodist Church in Plano in 1874.

Today, the church continues to hold Sunday services, and the congregation celebrated a sesquicentennial in 1996. Relatives of Lila Spannagel Magee, a long-time church member, say the church gets along well except for an occasional problem such as the motorist who ran over the historical marker. Lila's daughter, Linda Magee Nelson, insisted the marker be put back up more securely.

Finding Anything

The Roads of Texas (1999) by Shearer Publishing identifies precise locations of more than 25,000 U.S., state, and county roads. In addition to the roads and maps, the atlas includes fifteen pages of almanac information on state parks, ghost towns, place names, forts, missions, roadside attractions, and weather.

To locate information about any of the specific local landmark symbols appearing on any of the roads of Texas, go to the atlas of the web site of the Texas Historical Commission at atlas.thc.state.tx.us/. To find the complete text of the historical marker, search for the name of the community or town nearest the landmark symbol. The atlas contains data on more than 200,000 historic sites and properties on the National Register of Historic Places.

"BAPTIST BISCUIT EATERS" AND "CALLOUS-RUMPED SONS OF THE RANGE"

Geography and environment distinctively shaped Texas into seven natural regions, but cultural geographers and other writers used geography and environment to try to explain differences in the culture of the state. Here are just a few of the theories of Texas culture that have been advanced to explain regional differences in character and style.

Southern writer Robert Penn Warren in *All the King's Men* favored an east to west explanation of the state with the "Baptist biscuit eaters" in East Texas and the "callous-rumped sons of the range" in the West. He overlooks the Hispanic culture in South Texas. Historian of the Great Plains, Walter Prescott Webb, favored an east to west division of Texas for a different reason. He drew a line down the center of the state from Sherman in the north to Indianola on the Gulf of Mexico. East of his line the land of the Pineywoods had forests and plenty of water. The average annual rainfall exceeded 30 inches. West of Webb's line rainfall declined and the land became arid, flat, and treeless. Webb believed that the plains shaped the economy, the society, and culture of everything and everyone who entered it.

Other observers of Texas attempted to explain Texas's cultural divisions in a north to south direction. They bisected the state with lines showing the northern extent of "the Hispanic Borderland." Some have used the climate as a determining factor in the culture by dividing the state with a line separating north and south by a mean annual temperature of 66 degrees Fahrenheit. They have even drawn a line across the state that represents the "wet-dry legal border" for selling alcoholic beverages. Everything north of the line is normally dry and everything south is wet. This line happens to correspond with heavy concentrations of Baptists and Methodists in the north and Catholics and Lutherans in the south.

All of these creative attempts to offer simple explanations of Texas character and identity based on environment and cultural geography ultimately underscore the immense size and complexity of Texas. Simple explanations won't work. Texas exhibits Anglo and Latin American influences. It shows southern, western, and midwestern patterns. The Bible Belt fundamentalists and Roman Catholics intermingle with Asian immigrants. Texas has plains, mountains, forests, prairies, deserts, and even subtropical areas. When farmers and ranchers, scientists and technologists, and a few cowboys and oil tycoons intermingle with all these influences, it produces what Texas geographer Terry Jordan calls a "border province."

Finding Anything

Texas: A Geography (1984) by Terry Jordan renders a geographical picture of the origin and spread of the many cultural patterns in the Texas experience. The author charts the spread of religion, ethnic and settlement patterns, diffusion of languages and dialects, and rural and urban development. The book provides detailed information on courthouse square plans, *plaza mayors,* cemetery plots, and settlement patterns of Texas immigrants. Maps and photographs illustrate the text.

For up-to-date geographical information about Texas compiled from collaborative efforts of state and federal agencies, check the regional geography section of the web site of United States Geological Survey at www.tx.usgs.gov/. The Texas Natural Resources Information System called StratMap aids the USGS in producing much of the data on Texas. Check out the National Atlas of the United States for a great variety of statistical and spatial data on Texas.

"IT'LL CHANGE IN A MINUTE"

The High Plains area of Texas is one of the windiest regions on the North American continent during spring. Sustained wind speeds of 30 to 45 miles per hour may last several hours and make walking difficult. Wind gusts over 70 miles per hour in late winter can last over a minute. During winter, the famous Texas "blue northers" force temperature levels rapidly below freezing, and the combination of wind and temperature produce "bone-chilling conditions." Blasts of cold wind remove body-warmed air next to the skin

A bona fide Texas "blue norther" around 1950 with temperatures changing substantially over short distances. From the collections of The Dallas/Texas History and Archives Division, Dallas Public Library.

faster than the body can replenish it. Discovery of an approximate relationship between temperature, wind speed, and exposed skin led to the creation of the "windchill index." A person's ears turn white when the temperature is 35 degrees F with a wind blowing 10 mph just as quickly as they turn white with no wind at 21 degrees F. At a temperature near zero in the Panhandle with a wind gusting at 40 mph, it will "feel" like it is –53 degrees F. The windchill factor, at best, is only an approximation.

Southwest Texas experiences its own unique weather conditions derived from a scorching desert. The town of Marfa in the semi-arid Trans-Pecos region of Texas is most famous for its atmospheric phenomenon of the "Marfa Lights," which have been identified as everything from UFOs to meteors. In meteorological terms, the town of Marfa is known for another reason, the "Marfa front." Southwest Texas has a reverse form of the Panhandle "blue norther" in the form of a searing, desert-like wind. The intense heat of the Mexican desert creates a dry, torrid wind that sweeps eastward across parts of the Trans-Pecos. Marfa resides in the path of the desert air mass and is the site of the remote weather site that hourly tracks the front by sending data to weather observers who monitor its progress.

Texas's diverse geography sometimes combines with these powerful wind conditions in menacing and destructive ways. With the Rocky Mountains terminating in West Texas, cold fronts frequently move into the state from the higher elevations in the northwest. At the same time, the Gulf of Mexico and southeastern parts of the state blow warm, moist air near the land surface toward the north. When a third major source of high, dry air comes steaming out of the Mexican desert, the mixture of fronts spawns thunderstorms, funnel clouds, and tornados.

The Goliad tornado of May 18, 1902, killed 114 people. Fifty-one years later, a tornado devastated Waco on May 11, 1953, killing another 114 citizens and injuring 1,100. These tornados have been Texas's worst. Most deaths in Texas tornados occur from collapsed structures or flying debris which become lethal projectiles propelled at 300 to 400 miles per hour.

Finding Anything

Texas Weather (1995) by George Bomar analyzes the major meteorological conditions that generate Texas weather patterns. In language easy to understand for the nonscientist, the author explains the dynamics of hurricanes, thunderstorms, floods, tornados, fronts, winds, and heat waves that characterize the state's unpredictable and sometimes destructive weather. Keeping statistics to a minimum, he illustrates the text with photographs and drawings.

For a regional look at current Texas weather, including watches, warnings, statements, and advisories, go to the National Weather Service web site at www.nws.noaa.gov/. Find your Texas region on the menu and select appropriate regional areas for weather conditions, satellite images, and weather warnings.

DROUGHTS TO FLOODS TO DROUGHTS

One thing Texans usually agree on is the weather: it will change. For most of the state, the weather changes from droughts to floods. Because Texas is so large, flooding can occur in one part of Texas at the same time another part experiences severe drought. A norther can blow through the Panhandle while it is bright and sunny on the Gulf. The average annual rainfall ranges in north-south zones across the state from nearly 60 inches in Jefferson and Orange Counties in the east dropping to under 10 inches in El Paso. The midpoint and central parts of the state average approximately 30 inches annually.

In 1917, the state recorded an average rainfall of only 14.3 inches, making that year the driest year on record, and in 1956, after six years of drought, the state recorded 16 inches of average rainfall. The two wettest average years of annual rainfall occurred in 1919 and 1941 with 42 inches each year. Like disputed baseball and sports records, several Texas towns compete for the title of the city with the most recorded rainfall in a 24-hour period. Alvin claimed 43 inches for July 24–25 in 1979 and Thrall in Williamson County reported 38 inches in 1921. Albany in Shackelford County claimed the official record at 29 inches for August 4, 1978, because its site was an "official" recording station.

These variations represent extremes in temperature and precipitation, but they serve to illustrate the varied conditions that exist along the 800 miles of landscape from the northwest corner of the Texas Panhandle to the mouth of the Rio Grande in Southeast Texas. In a similar manner, the terrain from the Louisiana border near the Sabine River west to El Paso encompasses another 800-mile expanse that includes coastal plains, prairies, deserts, and rugged mountains. The Lone Star State runs the geographical gamut.

Finding Anything

The *Historical Atlas of Texas* (1988) by Ray Stephens and William M. Holmes provides informative maps of the geological, geographical, natural areas, precipitation, and native plant-life regions of Texas. The atlas contains sixty-four maps of historical and current significance to the state. A one-page interpretive essay accompanies each map. The maps include the locations of Texas historic Indians, Spanish missions, six flags and twelve state capitals of Texas, cattle trails, oil and gas discoveries, railroads, seaports, and airports.

To obtain online access to the complete text of this atlas, go to the TexShare database at www.texshare.edu/. Select the database netLibrary from the menu and retrieve the book. The netLibrary database contains an electronic library of 19,000 books. Obtain a password from a Texas public library to check out a book.

TEXAS CAVES: A "MARRIAGE OF ROCK AND WATER"

Some people admire the spectacular landscape of natural rock formations on the Texas surface. Others prefer the "marriage of rock and water" that takes place below the surface in caves. With an abundance of limestone rock from the state's ancient sedimentary past, the ebb and flow of shallow seas laid the foundation to form more than 3,000 caves. All but seven of these caves are called "wild caves," caves left in their natural state with no man-made improvements. Seven Texas caves achieved the status of "show caves" or commercial caves whose unusual formations can be viewed through scheduled tours.

The Caverns of Sonora, ten miles from Boerne, ranks among the great caves of the world. It achieved the designation of a National Natural Landmark from its stunning natural formations. Through the patient processes of nature, downward-building stalactites and upward-growing stalagmites formed hundreds of subsurface showplaces. Naturalists gave them names like Ice Cream Sundae, Crystal Palace, and Moon Milk Falls.

Each commercial cave exhibits unique features. Cascade Cavern, three miles east of Boerne, provides habitat for a species of colorless, blind salamander. One cave went nameless until a student who entered a contest wrote that the "cave is too pretty to have a name." He won the contest, and judges christened the cavern Cave Without A Name.

The Texas Department of Transportation discovered Inner Space Cavern near Georgetown by accident. Drilling core samples in construction of Interstate 35, the highway department drilled into the cave. Eventually, the cave extended 7,000 feet and archaeologists discovered the cave contained remains of Pleistocene animals. Natural Bridge Caverns contains an underground stream called Purgatory Creek. The Civilian Conservation Corps developed Longhorn Cavern in the 1930s. The oldest commercial cave in Texas, Wonder Cave, opened near San Marcos in 1903.

For Texans who prefer exploring the surface rock of the state, the Enchanted Rock, a huge pinkish granite dome, located twenty miles north of Fredericksburg, provides a dramatic counterpart to Texas caves. The giant dome, second in size to Stone Mountain in Georgia, originated from rock a billion years old.

Enchanted Rock's dominating presence 400 feet above the surrounding landscape long ago inspired a body of legend and folklore. The spirit of an Indian princess who threw herself off the rock reportedly inhabits the place. The indentations in the rock are the footprints of a chief doomed to walk the rock for his transgressions. A white woman kidnapped by Indians escaped and is believed to live on the rock. At night, visitors hear her screams from the rock.

Some of the beliefs and legends of a haunted rock have natural origins. Trapped water in the indentations may glitter in moonlight or reflect off feldspar in the dome. Alternate heating and cooling of the rock may make noises as the rock fractures. In any case, the State of Texas set aside the Enchanted Rock in 1978 as a state natural area to preserve the sights and sounds of an awe-inspiring rock.

Finding Anything

Texas Caves (1999) by Blair Pittman gives an account of the geologic origins of Texas caves, cave biology, and Texas's seven show caves. The book contains color photographs of the seven Texas show caves, spectacular shots of delicate formations, and commentary on how to explore a cave. The author describes his first exploration of the Devil's Sinkhole, and for beginners he includes a glossary of caving terms.

To find out more recent information about Texas caving, go to the web site of the Texas Speleological Association at www.cavetexas.org/. The association provides a photographic tour of Texas's seven show caves, a list of wild caves in state parks where caving is permitted, and bibliography of writings about the major caves of Texas.

THE LARGEST "BIRD" WHO EVER FLEW

Suspended from the ceiling of the Great Hall of the Texas Memorial Museum in Austin, the Texas Pterosaur looks like an antique airplane hanging in the Smithsonian Air and Space Museum. The creature had a wing span of 40 feet and was the largest flying creature ever discovered. The scientific name of the Texas Pterosaur, a flying reptile, is *Quetzalcoatlus northropi*. He flew 65 million years ago in the Big Bend Country. Doug Lawson, a University of Texas graduate student, discovered bone fragments of the creature in 1971. The find created a worldwide sensation in the field of paleontology. A Cal Tech professor even modeled an airplane after the Texas Pterosaurs.

Professional paleontologists and amateur collectors find endless opportunities for collecting significant fossils in Texas. Both groups have made important discoveries of a wide variety of prehistoric animals: mastodons, mammoths, saber-tooth tigers, and dinosaurs of many species.

The ebb and flow of the shallow sea that covered much of Texas left rich deposits of microorganisms in sediments. The buildup of sediments allowed molds to form after the organisms had decayed. More layers of sediments allowed casts to form on top of the new layers. The final retreat of the Gulf of Mexico left much rock near the surface, and fossil collectors continue to dig into it. Formation of petrified Palmwood, the official Texas State Stone, occurred as the Gulf of Mexico retreated. Mineral laden groundwater seeped into porous wood, and natural processes retained and preserved the structure of the wood.

Texas fossils reflect the great variety of the physical environment. Sediments washed down from the Rocky Mountain system make the western edge of the Panhandle Plains the youngest part of the state in geological age. Some of the more exotic fossil finds have occurred here: horses, camels, prehistoric elephants. South of the High Plains area in the Edwards Plateau region, the limestone caverns preserved fossils of mammoths and saber-tooth cats. In East Texas, the sea and marsh environment left well-preserved fossil shells and huge sea reptiles.

Just like the variations in Texas geography, the fossils of the state cover an extensive range. They include ancient antlers, dire wolf heads, vertebrate bones, turtle shells, crocodile scute, aquatic insects, conifers, and seed ferns. The record contains a great variety of fossils of living things that inhabited the seas and marsh areas of Texas like heart urchins, starfish, clams, jellyfish imprints, and dinosaur bones. Discovery, collection, and classification continue at a brisk pace.

Finding Anything

A *Field Guide to Fossils of Texas* (1996) by Charles Finsley supplies detailed information for the identification of Texas fossils. Designed for beginning and intermediate fossil collectors, the book contains more than 300 photographs and illustrations of fossils found in Texas. Descriptions of their distinguishing characteristics make this a practical guide for identifying and classifying finds.

To take a virtual tour of the fossils of Texas, see the web site of Texas Memorial Museum at www.tmm.utexas.edu/. The site includes a photograph of the Texas Pterosaur. The museum contains fossils collected from Texas geological surveys, collections donated by oil companies in drilling cores, and collections of professors and graduate students.

Check the section called "Natural Wonders: Treasures of the TMM" for a look at some of its finest specimens.

BOOKS AND WEB SITES

Nature's Divisions of Texas

Parent, Laurence. *Official Guide to Texas State Parks*. Austin: University of Texas Press, 1997.
Texas Parks and Wildlife Department. Natural Regions of Texas. www.tpwd.state.tx.us/nature/tx-eco95.htm.

Biggest Live Oak on Record

TexasEscapes.com. Historic Trees of Texas. www.texasescapes.com/TexasHistory/TexasHistoricTrees.htm.
Thollander, Earl. *Back Roads of Texas*. Flagstaff, Arizona: Northland Press, 1980.

Texas Chain Saw Massacre and *Honeysuckle Rose*

Texas Film Commission. Filmography. www.governor.state.tx.us/film.
Texas Film Commission, Office of the Governor. *Texas Production Manual*. 1988.

Ding Dong and Dime Box, Texas

Tarpley, Fred, *1001 Texas Place Names*. With sketches by Sally Blakemore. Austin:University of Texas Press, 1980.
Texas Historical Commission. www.thc.state.tx.us/.

The Longest Highway in Texas

Texas Historic Sites Atlas. Texas Historical Commission. http://atlas.thc.state.tx.us/.
The Roads of Texas. Fredericksburg, Texas: Shearer Publishing, 1999.

"Baptist Biscuit Eaters" and "Callous-rumped Sons of the Range"

Jordan, Terry with Bean, John L. and Holmes William. *Texas: A Geography.* Boulder & London: Westview Press, 1984.
United States Geological Survey. Activities in Texas. www.tx.usgs.gov/.

"It'll Change in a Minute"

Bomar, George W. *Texas Weather*. Austin: University of Texas Press, 1995.
U.S. National Weather Service. www.nws.noaa.gov/.

Droughts to Floods to Droughts

Stephens, Ray and Holmes, William M. *Historical Atlas of Texas*. Norman: University of Oklahoma Press, 1988.
Texas State Library and Archives Commission. TexShare. netLibrary. www.texshare.edu/.

Texas Caves: A "Marriage of Rock and Water"

Pittman, Blair. *Texas Caves*. College Station: Texas A&M University Press, 1999.
Texas Speleological Association. www.cavetexas.org/.

The Largest "Bird" Who Ever Flew

Finsley, Charles. *A Field Guide to Fossils of Texas*. Houston: Gulf Publishing Co., 1996.
Texas Memorial Museum. University of Texas at Austin. www.tmm.utexas.edu/.

5

CHARACTER, CULTURE, AND CURIOUS CUSTOMS

- What does it mean to refer to someone as "last year's bird nest with the bottom punched out?"
- What famous Texan said, "I always ride on the western side of a train?"
- What instrument of frontier "self-defense" was called the Arkansas Toothpick?
- Which cowboy ballad did Admiral Richard Byrd play and sing over and over on his trip to the South Pole until his "little phonograph froze?"
- How did a recording of the Reverend Sin-Killer Griffin's "Calvary Sermon" end up in the Library of Congress?
- In a masculine state like Texas, how did wildflowers like bluebonnets acquire so much political clout?
- What caused the judges of the 2003 Terlingua International Chili Cook-off to disqualify the winner for cheating?
- What is West Texas "wasp nest" bread?
- What are some good East Texas folk remedies for a nose bleed?
- Whose nineteenth-century Indian captivity autobiography turned out to be a hoax?

"DON'T DIG UP MORE SNAKES THAN YOU CAN KILL"

With millions of acres of cheap public lands to offer settlers, Texas attracted vast numbers of Americans and immigrants with the lure of making a livelihood from the land. New arrivals worked on plantations and small farms, drove cattle, hunted buffalo, fought Indians, and raised cotton. A life close to the soil and a personal homestead pervade much of the wisdom they bequeathed in proverbs and sayings.

The Texas Folklore Society, founded in 1910, advocated collecting, preserving, and presenting folk heritage like folksongs, proverbs, and sayings before older generations of settlers passed from the scene. John Avery Lomax served as the first president of the society. Through the efforts of the association, the second oldest folklore society in the U.S., a large collection of sayings, proverbs, and folk wisdom of early Texans exists.

Sayings remembered of a pioneer grandmother from Collin County who came to Texas in the 1840s reveal her strategy for surviving widowhood and raising a large family on the frontier. She urged perseverance and good judgment: "Lick by lick the cow ate the grindstone"; "Don't dig up more snakes than you can kill"; and "What can't be cured must be endured." She also had a practical morality to her words: "The polecat can't tell the buzzard that he stinks" and "Talk is cheap but it takes money to buy whiskey."

Animals, garden vegetables, cattle, and crops appear frequently in Texas expressions. A person surprised by a distinctive sound might say: "It made a noise like pourin' peas on a dried cowhide." In describing a person with bulging eyes, a cowboy might exclaim, "His eyes bugged out till you could rope them with a grapevine."

Collections of Texas wisdom in proverbs and sayings describe every kind of person, place, thing, situation, or predicament imaginable. A person not known for deep brain power might be described with terms from a bird habitat: "He hasn't got as much sense as last year's bird nest with the bottom punched out." For the overly courteous person, he's so polite "sugar wouldn't melt in his mouth." For a person who drinks like a fish, "He's a regular Strap Buckler."

For people early Texans found exasperating, a wide array of choice expressions helped make the point: "That galoot's not worth the powder and lead it would take to blow him up." Or, he'd "steal the nickels off a dead man's eyes" and "He's mighty small potatoes and few in the hill." Finally, they could say, "He amounts to about as much as a notch on a stick and the stick thrown away." For someone's unsuccessful attempts to assist an incorrigible child, they offered this prediction: "He might as well be singing psalms over a dead horse as trying to make a doctor out of that boy of his."

Finding Anything

The Best of Texas Folk and Folklore, 1916–1954 (1998) edited by Mody C. Boatright, Wilson Hudson, and Alan Maxwell is a broad collection of Texas folklore reprinted from the first four decades of publications of The Texas Folklore Society. This collection contains many fine examples of folklore collected by early Texas folklorists. In addition to proverbs and sayings of Texas pioneers, the selection includes Indian, Mexican, and Negro tales, legends, ghost stories, ballads, sermons, games, folk cures, and oil lore. The editors published the material as it originally appeared without attempting to edit for political correctness.

For additional collections of Texas folklore, go to the web site of Texas Folklore Society at www.texasfolkloresociety.org/. The site provides a history of the association and biographies of its major leaders and founders, J. Frank Dobie, John Avery Lomax, and Leonidas Warren Payne, who spearheaded the development of the society into national prominence. The web site menu lists all the major publications of the society since its founding in 1909.

"I ALWAYS RIDE ON THE WESTERN SIDE OF A TRAIN"

One of the grand literary figures in Texas letters established his reputation through the Texas Folklore Society by collecting, researching, and publishing hundreds of stories of the history, legends, and myths of the great Southwest. J. Frank Dobie grew up in a large ranching family in the 1890s on a ranch in Live Oak County. He witnessed the state's rapid transition from its frontier foundations.

As he learned ranching and Bible stories from his fundamentalist father and English literature from his mother, Ella, he acquired a passion for a way of life beginning to fade away. Ranch life in the Brush Country of Texas ranged from vital and beautiful to harsh and brutal. His mother remembers the "bawling of calves dying of thirst." His people didn't believe in voting for a Confederate veteran "solely because he was one-armed, one-eyed, half-witted, or possessed of some other defect calculated to influence the majority of voters."

When he returned from World War I, Dobie resumed a career teaching literature at The University of Texas. He took the position of Secretary of the Texas Folklore Society. Through the folklore society, Dobie defined himself and channeled his passion for the richness of Southwest culture and traditions. Through a career of encouraging authentic studies of the region, he acquired the nickname "Mr. Southwest."

Dobie's curiosity, energy, and restlessness led him to take frequent leaves of absence from The University of Texas. For a year, he left the university to manage a ranch. He said of that experience, "In the university, I am a wild man; in the wilds, I am a scholar and poet." On another occasion, he left the university when officials refused to promote him without a Ph.D. He returned and continued collecting and publishing the stories and legends of Texas.

Dobie's combative spirit and caustic wit kept him in conflict with college administrators, state legislators, and various professional groups throughout his career. He said he could explain "homemade fascism" in America by taking examples from the Texas Legislature. He called members of the professional education establishment "unctuous elaborators of the obvious." He disliked Texas braggarts. To him, the 25-story tower on the UT-Austin campus looked like a "toothpick in a pie."

His reputation as a spokesman and interpreter of the Southwest won him an appointment to teach American History at Cambridge University in 1943. He won popular acclaim for his lectures and stories of Texas. *A Texan in England*, published in 1945, capsuled his experiences. The University of Texas fired Dobie in 1947 over his unyielding demand for an extended leave of absence to write and lecture.

For the next sixteen years, the Lone Star State's "ambassador to the world" wrote and lectured, winning the Presidential Medal of Freedom in 1964, the year that he died. Two years after his death, his widow, Bertha, discovered an inscription he had penned for his tombstone. "Realizing that all gods and bibles are man-made, he had contempt for all creeds, and admiration for nobilities and sensible skepticisms."

Finding Anything

An American Original: The Life of J. Frank Dobie (1978) by Lon Tinkle is a biography of J. Frank Dobie from a writer and teacher who knew him. The author draws from letters, manuscripts, interviews, and his own recollections of Dobie for the book.

See the web site of the *Dictionary of Literary Biography* for a shorter biographical essay and literary analysis of Dobie at www.texshare .edu/. Obtain access through a Texas public library for a password and find the database in the literature section of TexShare databases. Search by the author's name. This account highlights Dobie's important books, beginning with the *Legends of Texas* (1924), which he published for the Texas Folklore Society, up through *Coronado's Children* (1931) and *The Mustangs* (1952).

JIM BOWIE AND THE ARKANSAS TOOTHPICK

In 1928, J. Frank Dobie wrote *Tales of Old Time Texas*, a collection of legends, stories, and myths of the Lone Star State. He highlights the legend of "Jim Bowie's Knife." Bowie's prowess with his famous knife and his death at the Alamo spawned a whirlwind of Bowie myth. So many legends, stories, and claims exist about him as to cloud the picture of exactly who he was, who made the "Bowie knife," or even how he died. The mystery leaves ample room for the legend to keep expanding.

When James Bowie of Logan County, Kentucky, first appeared on the southwestern frontier, knives dominated personal weaponry. Dobie called the era the "Knife Age in the Land of Violence." The knife had certain advantages over other weapons. Using a knife proved economical because it saved powder and lead. Used as a tool, it could mend saddles, cut through brush, and dig a grave. The bone or horn handle could crack coffee beans and nuts. Knives adapted well to frontier conditions, and Jim Bowie unwittingly became publicly associated with the knife.

On September 19, 1827, on a sandbar in the Mississippi River near Natchez, Jim Bowie and a group of men watched two men duel. The duel erupted in a melee killing two men and wounding two others. Shot through the lung and stabbed, Bowie survived by stabbing his adversary through the heart with "a big butcher knife." His brother, Rezin P. Bowie, claimed later he gave Jim this knife for self-defense. Eyewitnesses and combatants both circulated the story of Bowie's prowess with the knife, and the legend began.

No one knows to this day who made the first "Bowie knife," but two years after Bowie died in the Alamo, his brother Rezin claimed that a blacksmith in Avoyelles Parish, Louisiana, named Jesse Clifft made it. Rezin said he furnished Clifft the design. He described the knife as 9½ inches long and 1½ inches wide. It was simple and had no silver mounts. The original Bowie knife failed to survive all of Jim Bowie's adventures. Bowie had other knives made for his own use.

Arkansas makes its claim to the original Bowie knife through the word of an Arkansas judge named William Pope. He claims Rezin Bowie once came to Washington, Arkansas, and commissioned another blacksmith named James Black to design a knife from a pattern whittled from the "top of a cigar box." The expansive Judge Pope insists that no genuine Bowie knives have ever been made "outside the state of Arkansas." By 1840, the fame of Bowie knives had spread so far that a British Foreign Office employee in Texas reported seeing one that had been manufactured in Sheffield, England, with the engraving "The Genuine Arkansas Tooth Pick." Whether made in Arkansas, Louisiana, Texas, or Sheffield, England, the knife made famous on a Mississippi River sandbar endures to this day in fact and fiction, like Bowie himself.

Finding Anything

Tales of Old Time Texas (1955) by J. Frank Dobie furnishes many of the stories, legends, and accounts of Jim Bowie and his famous knife. He collected, verified, and unverified stories about Bowie and Bowie knives up until the "six-shooter" of Samuel Colt displaced the knife as a weapon of choice on the frontier.

For the Washington, Arkansas, connection to James Bowie, check the web site http://users.aristotle.net/~russjohn/bowie.html. It provides information on Arkansas blacksmith James Black who is also credited with forging one of the first "Bowie knives." The Arkansas Toothpick described here may be a different version, more like a large dagger. Many of these knives were made in England and not considered original. James Black's shop has been restored in the Arkansas Old Washington State Park.

ADMIRAL BYRD AND "HOME ON THE RANGE"

Admiral Richard Byrd, exploring the South Pole in the 1930s, carried along a phonograph player. To weather some of the lonely stretches of the long freezes, he played and sang to a recording of "Home on the Range." He said later no one would believe his story, especially if they knew of his singing ability. But it was true.

Without a little cowboy luck, "Home on the Range" might never have been collected and recorded. A college professor initially discouraged the collector of the song, Texan John Avery Lomax, because

John Avery Lomax (1867–1948) cofounded the Texas Folklore Society in 1909. After an English professor pronounced his childhood collection of cowboy songs as "cheap and unworthy," Lomax went on to establish a reputation as the premier collector of western ballads in America. From the collections of The Dallas/Texas History and Archives Division, Dallas Public Library.

the teacher thought cowboy songs had no value in literature. Later, on his first attempt to collect the song from a former trail cook, Lomax found the barkeep in no condition to sing. He had to come back the next morning.

John Avery Lomax enrolled as a freshman at The University of Texas in 1887. In a trunk he packed for college, he took his clothes, a pistol, "implements of personal warfare," and a little manuscript roll of cowboy songs. Lomax grew up on a small ranch near the Chisholm Trail. He began collecting songs he heard cowboys sing in camps and from friends who went "up the trail" to Kansas. When an English professor suggested they had no value, he put them away for years until he obtained a scholarship to Harvard. There, folklorist George L. Kittredge encouraged him to start a national campaign to collect western ballads.

Lomax launched this campaign by traveling the West and making personal appeals for songs in western newspapers. The campaign reaped some of the major folk treasures in American history. Texas proved to be a collector's gold mine. In the White Elephant Saloon in Fort Worth, he found the "Old Chisholm Trail" from cowhands. He found "Git Along, Little Dogies" from a Gypsy woman living in a truck in Fort Worth, and an old buffalo hunter in Abilene gave him the words and tune to "Buffalo Skinners."

In 1908, he discovered a black saloon keeper in San Antonio who had once been a cook on trail drives. On his first attempt to collect the cowboy songs, Lomax failed. The singer told him he was "too drunk to sing today. Come back tomorrow." The next morning the bar owner sang "Home on the Range," and Lomax published it in a collection of cowboy songs in 1910. It attracted little interest. Twenty years later, with the aid of the popular radio medium, the song resurfaced, becoming a top popular recording. "Home on the Range" remained a hot song as Admiral Byrd explored Antarctica for the second time.

Finding Anything

Cowboy Songs and Frontier Ballads (1910) by John Avery Lomax was a pioneering effort at collecting cowboy songs and frontier ballads. The book contained more than two hundred transcribed Texas and western ballads. It included some of the most internationally recognized frontier ballads like the "Dying Cowboy," "Sam Bass," and "Jesse James." The collection also contained additional cowboy lore like epitaphs, prayers, toasts, and wake-up calls used on roundups. Cowboys might be rousted out with "Wake up, snakes, and bite a biscuit." A concise grace before a meal was "Eat your meat and save the skin; turn up your plates and let's begin."

To hear how "real" cowboys sang songs and rounded up herds with cattle calls, go to the Archive of American Folksong at the Library of Congress. Many of the songs recorded by John A. Lomax on early portable equipment have been released on compact disc. *Cowboy Songs, Ballads, and Cattle Calls from Texas* contains thirteen tracks of songs from Lomax's original collection. See the Library of Congress sales shop web site for details of this and other compact discs of cowboy songs and ballads at http://store.yahoo.com/locshop/cowsonbalanc.html.

PRESERVING TEXAS FOLKLORE

In the 1930s, the Texas Penitentiary System employed the Reverend Sin-Killer Griffin, a holiness evangelist, as a state chaplain to black convicts. Sin-Killer had earned a reputation as a stirring revival preacher. He entered a town with a big gospel tent, a large choir, and many church workers poised to "take up the battle against sin." He wore a long coat, spoke in a deep voice, and projected a ministerial bearing.

John Avery Lomax, now the foremost collector of American folklore and folksong, obtained permission from Sin-Killer and the captain of the Darrington Prison Farm near Houston to record one of Sin-Killer's favorite sermons for the Library of Congress. For this special occasion, Sin-Killer chose his "Calvary Sermon."

On the day selected to record Sin-Killer's sermon, Lomax and his son Alan set up a recording machine in a large hall between two long dormitory wings of cells. They ran cable through the bars to Sin-Killer's pulpit and altar. A few deacons and preachers accompanied Sin-Killer to the prison farm, and they sat in a circle up front as encouragement.

After opening the service with a spiritual, Sin-Killer requested "sinner friends" to come forward and move up to the front seats. No "sinners" moved up. The Reverend Sin-Killer began to preach. Beginning with a reference to the Sermon on the Mount that they who mourn shall be comforted, Sin-Killer was simple and direct: "Let us mourn brethren." Then, after a powerful song, "Wasn't That a Mighty Storm That Blew the People Away," he prayed a prayer of gratitude that last night he didn't lie down on the "cooling board." For the communion, he distributed white bread crumbs and substituted grapefruit juice from the prison commissary for the wine.

With one more invitation to brothers, sisters, and "sinner friends all," Sin-Killer delivered his two-hour Easter sermon, interrupted only by an occasional song. He sternly warned that if you keep "foolin'" with the Master he will "shake the earth again." Dramatically, he described the moon "took with a judgment hemorrhage" and bleeds away. "Pay no 'tention to death," Sin-killer reported as Jesus's words to the dying thief. As for the Resurrection itself, he depicted Jesus's getting up out of the grave and "pulling off his grave clothes."

When the Calvary sermon ended, Sin-Killer issued a fervent plea for sinners to come forward. He could not move this tough audience, and no one came forward. Alan Lomax could record only segments of the sermon because the primitive recording equipment required him to rotate the disc every seven minutes. After Sin-Killer said goodbye to all the "sinners," Lomax played the recording for Sin-Killer. Sin-Killer and the prisoners responded enthusiastically to the recording. Sin-Killer said he always heard he was a good preacher, but now he knew it.

Finding Anything

From Hell to Breakfast (1944) edited by Mody Coggin Boatright and Donald Day contains a transcription of the Reverend Sin-Killer Griffin's sermon and a description of John and Alan Lomax's recording session. The Texas Folklore Society published it as the 19th volume in a long-running series of publications of the customs, songs, sermons, proverbs, sayings, stories, and legends of Texas. Because of the society's long association with major interpreters of Texas culture, like J. Frank Dobie, John A. Lomax, and Walter Prescott Webb, the publications constitute primary sources.

To view the entire contents of *From Hell to Breakfast* online, check the book out as an electronic book at www.texshare.edu/ as part of the TexShare service coordinated by the Texas State Library and Archives Commission. To view the book, consult your public library, obtain a password, and register. The Reverend Sin-Killer's sermon is in John A. Lomax's article "Adventures of a Ballad Hunter."

POLITICAL CLOUT OF WILDFLOWERS

Wildflowers occupy a venerated position in Texas culture, and bluebonnets command the summit. When Theodore Roosevelt visited Austin in

1905, the bluebonnet had already reigned as the Official Texas State Flower for five years. Thousands of schoolchildren lined the road to greet him, threw bluebonnets in his path, and sang *America*.

The bluebonnet, however, did not ascend to official symbol status without a fight. Bluebonnet supporters had to overcome stiff competition from two powerful economic interests in the Texas Legislature. The "open cotton boll" lobby pushed hard for cotton, the "white flower" of commerce. A future vice president of the United States, John Nance "Cactus Jack" Garner, preferred the prickly pear cactus.

When the chips were down, the Colonial Dames of America in Texas marshaled the bluebonnet forces and carried the day. To make their case, they displayed a painting of bluebonnets by Austin artist Miss Mode Walker in the chamber. This tactic illustrated with graphic force why little flowerets that resembled bonnets worn by pioneer Texas women ought to become the one and only official state flower. They won.

The Legislature designated the species *Lupinus subcarnosus,* the bluebonnet, as the official state flower. Bluebonnets were also called "buffalo clover" because early settlers and native peoples mistakenly thought buffalo ate them. Mexicans called them *conejo* because the flower's white top resembled the white tail of the cottontail rabbit.

Over the years, the bluebonnet held its own in the halls of the Legislature. Inevitably the Legislature relented to pressure and designated other official state symbols that threatened to dilute the bluebonnet's exclusive position. The pecan tree became the official state tree in 1919, but the bluebonnet lobby roared back strongly, flexed its political muscle, and secured the lyric "Bluebonnets" as the official "state flower song" in 1933.

In 1969, the Legislature began a new push of designating official state symbols. They designated "sideoats gramma" as the official state grass and petrified palmwood as the official state rock. The bluebonnet people mobilized again. In 1971, the Colonial Dames of America in Texas succeeded in obtaining legislative sanction of *Lupinus Texensis* as the species of Texas bluebonnet with official legal status. This time they broadened their influence over bluebonnets by permitting "any other variety of bluebonnet" to be recognized as the official state flower. They now had control over all the species of bluebonnets in Texas, plus any future species that might be identified. This was wildflower power.

In the 1990s, the bluebonnet people struck again. The Legislature created seventeen new official state symbols in four years. Cotton finally won recognition as the official state "fiber and fabric." The sweet onion and the crape myrtle received recognition as the state vegetable and state shrub. To counter these incursions into their domain, the bluebonnet people secured political allies in the cities and tourism industry.

They countered by designating Ennis, Texas, as the official Bluebonnet City, naming several miles of the city parks and streets as the Official Bluebonnet Trail of Texas. As a final triumph, they secured for Chappell Hill the title of the official Bluebonnet Festival of Texas. By now, the process of official state designating had gotten completely out of hand. The 2002 Legislature placed restrictions on what could become an official state symbol, but the bluebonnet had nothing to worry about. With an official city, an official trail, an official festival, an official song, and control of all species of bluebonnets in the state, it reigned supreme among symbols.

Finding Anything

Legends & Lore of Texas Wildflowers (1996) by Elizabeth Silverthorne gives an account of the history, folklore, legends, and stories that surround forty-four Texas wildflowers. The author examines buttercups, dogwood, honeysuckle, morning glories, orchids, and yuccas in addition to bluebonnets. She provides a literary and historical background to the legends, stories, and names of Texas wildflowers.

For extensive current information on Texas wildflowers, check out the web site of the Lady Bird Johnson Wildflower Center at www.wildflower. org/. The site features more than twenty years of color issues of newsletters, photographs of wildflowers, and natural history of the state's major wildflower species.

THE TERLINGUA "CHILI IMPOSTER"

People outside the perimeter of the five American and three Mexican states that border Texas find comprehending the Texas passion for chili difficult. Politicians campaign with it, restaurants give it hundreds of names, and pundits pay homage to it. Chili ranks alongside religion and football in the trinity of Texas values.

Will Rogers called Texas chili "the bowl of blessedness," and President Lyndon Johnson proclaimed that any chili made outside of Texas is a "weak, apologetic imitation of the real thing." The Legislature designated chili the "State Dish of Texas" in 1977. In elevating chili to this high standard, they cited Albert Agnor, the 1976 World Champion Chili Cooker of

Marshall and a winner of the Terlingua International Chili Cookoff as an example of the Texas standard of excellence in chili cooks.

With chili occupying the same vaulted status of the bluebonnet, little wonder that a "chili imposter" at the 2003 Original Terlingua International Chili Cook-off "rocked the chili cookoff world." Judges of the 2003 competition disqualified the winner for cheating at chili cooking, made him give back all the prizes, and banned him for life from cooking chili at Terlingua. In the chili world, some compare this penalty to Pete Rose's ban from baseball.

"Chiliheads" reported the essential facts of the case as happening like this. An established chili cook, Larry Eastep, qualified for the championship, but could not attend. His brother from Springfield, Illinois, Don Eastep, who doesn't cook chili, came to Terlingua as a spectator. Claiming his deception was only "a gag," Don moved around and among the eight-seven cooking pots long enough to scoop up a batch of chili of his own from the legitimate competitor's pots. He entered his "mongrel" concoction under his brother's name. To his amazement and discomfort, Don won the cookoff.

Caught off guard, he collected the prizes, including a necklace and a portable stove with "Terlingua Champion" painted on it, and exited. After checking up on the winner, the real cooks did not recall his cooking any chili. Soon, word of the charade circulated through the camp. Organizers quickly re-awarded the championship and the prizes to the runner-up, Dallas dentist Ted Hume.

The culprit made a quick getaway from Terlingua. He said he had no idea that mixing up all that chili could produce a championship chili recipe. Claiming it was all just a joke that went bad, he apologized to the chili world in the *Goat Gap Gazette*, an influential chili magazine. Not everyone was convinced. With something as sacred as Texas chili, organizers called for tightening security.

An examination of the consumption of spirits at the cookoff during the judging may also be in order. The instruction sheet provided for the Margarita Mix-Off says, "If you fall out of your chair at any time during the event, we will have to disqualify your judging sheet." Over the years, the Terlingua International Chili Cookoff has earned its reputation as "Mardi Gras in the Desert." Now it has the legend of "the chili imposter."

Finding Anything

"Hallie Stillwell Will Live on in Memories" by Kent Biffle is an article that appears in *Features and Fillers: Texas Journalists on Texas Folklore*

(1999) edited by Jim Harris and Carolyn Satterwhite. The article contains an account of the judging of the first Terlingua International Chili Championship Cookoff. The author pays tribute to the life of the long-time justice of the peace and first judge of the Terlingua chili cookoff who died in 1997. He describes the cookoff's three principal founders: Frank X. Tolbert, Homer Thomas Wilson (Wick) Fowler, and H. Allen Smith, who wrote extensively about chili.

For an online account of the 2003 Terlingua Chili Cookoff, see the article from *The Austin-American Statesman* (November 4, 2003) by John Kelso entitled "A 5-alarm Scandal at Chili Contest." It can be found at the web site of TexShare at www.texshare.edu/ in the InfoTrac database of newspapers. Obtain a password through a local participating Texas public library.

BURNING A HOLE IN THE TABLECLOTH

Besides chili and barbeque, chips and salsa, Texas food customs derive from the practices of many traditions. A cumulative folklore enhances many of the foods that Texans consume. One of the ways to determine if a salsa recipe meets high standards is to try a proven salsa test. Drop some salsa on a tablecloth. If it doesn't burn a hole in the cloth, it is not a good sauce.

Waco, Texas, a city with a fundamentalist reputation as the "Buckle of the Bible Belt," for decades produced churches that filled the spirit with blessings and the body with foods and food rituals. These churches broke a lot of bread together. Hardy food and socializing went hand-in-hand in all aspects of denominational life on the frontier. The breaking of heavy breads, like "corn bread," was an essential ingredient in the religious quest. One West Texas pioneer woman shunned all "light bread." She called it "wasp nest bread" because it had lots of holes in it.

In "old time" Texas religion, few events happened in a congregation that did not require food, elaborate food preparation, or food supplies. Congregations welcomed a new preacher to the church with the custom of a "pounding" or a donation party. A pound of sugar, a pound of coffee, and a pound of flour appropriately inaugurated the minister's tenure with the congregation. Congregations supply a box of staples even today.

The congregations celebrated holidays, anniversaries, and "revivals" with "dinner on the grounds" of a church or camp meeting. Food spread out on long tables under trees highlighted the festivities of all day "camp meetings." They became commonplace by the mid-1880s. In some East Texas communities, congregations set aside certain days to clean the cemetery and broke for a big meal at noon. One East Texan, Esther Huckaby, vividly remembers her cemetery cleaning experiences in Rusk County.

The family assembled on cemetery cleaning day to pull weeds, rake the area, and bring flowers and plants. They observed strict cemetery etiquette: don't be rowdy; don't walk on the graves; and don't be melodramatic, sentimental, or superstitious. At noon, they blessed the food set out on sawhorses and weathered boards covered with cotton tablecloths. Then they feasted on fried chicken, barbecue, dressing, mashed potatoes, and garden vegetables of all kinds. Lavishly cooking for a grieving family who has lost a loved one remains a fundamental Texas custom. Old timers may still remember another piece of Texas bread lore: "If the loaf is upside down on the table, it means the devil is around."

Finding Anything

Eats: A Folk History of Texas Foods (1989) by Ernestine Sewell Linck and Joyce Gibson Roach provides an extensive look at customs and folklore surrounding Texas foods. In addition to giving recipes of many Texas mainstays like red beans and rice and jambalaya, the authors provide stories and lore of such foods as eggs, bread, tomatoes, watermelons, and potatoes.

There are many good web sites on Texas food and cooking, but take a look at www.texascooking.com/ for a site that covers traditional Texas fare, cookbooks, historic restaurants, and recipes. They track many food-related Texas fairs and festivals, and they review cookbooks.

"RUB ONIONS AND SKUNK OIL ON MY CHEST"

The little science of folk remedies for ailments and diseases accumulated several centuries of local practice from the major cultures who lived in the Lone Star State. Native American, Anglo-Texan, Texas-Mexican, and Black cultures all had well-developed, coherent traditions of folk medicine before established medicine began to predominate. Shamans and medicine men believed much illness originated from malevolent spirits of the dead. The Tonkawas wore little bags of roots and herbs to ward off these spirits. Other rituals like drumming, sweat baths, and incantations provided protection from disease. Complications from battle wounds constituted a large percentage of medical problems. The Comanches knew about tourniquets and used peyote and other herbal remedies in treatments. They applied a wide assortment of herbs to reduce fever, dress wounds, and relieve pain. They used alder bark, snakeroot, and peyote to treat snakebites and attached a slice of the offending snake to the wound.

Anglo-Texans improvised cures from whatever supplies they had on hand. Common household items like soda, coal oil, kerosene, sugar, whiskey, vinegar, turpentine, and soot from wood stoves served as staples in the medicine "cabinet." They creatively supplemented these supplies with medicinal plants. They used magic and Bible verses to treat various conditions. They could rub a wart with a slice of potato or a stolen dishrag and bury the object. The wart disappeared as the object rotted. A good Anglo-Texas cure for a rattlesnake bite was to kill a chicken, and while the body of the fowl was still warm, wrap it around the bite "to draw the poison out."

Folk medicine and home remedies of East Texas have been classified like medical dictionaries. *Rub Onions and Skunk Oil on My Chest and Call Me Well* covers many ailments from chest congestion and consumption to hangovers and nose bleeds. Under "Nose Bleed," sufferers can select from a list of choices on how to stop the hemorrhage. They can put cobwebs up the nose. If this doesn't work, they can take two strips of bacon, roll them up, and form them into two cylinders. Forcing them well up the nostrils provides "almost immediate relief."

Other nose bleed remedies include inserting grated beef into the nostrils, placing a nickel under the tongue, or wearing "a piece of nutmeg on a string around your neck." If the nose continues to bleed, it is time to seek spiritual assistance. Call a friend and ask them to speak the words of Ezekiel 16:6 three times, and then say your name. This is certain to do the trick, but don't try any of these without consulting a physician.

Texas-Mexican folk medicine showed a strong influence of its religious heritage. The Virgin Mary was summoned frequently to expunge illnesses caused by the devil and Satanic powers. Black folk medical practices reflect both European and African roots. Some practices required faith in a process like hanging a key down the back of the neck to stop nose bleeds. Other rituals aimed at eradicating illnesses of supernatural origin like witches.

Finding Anything

Rub Onions and Skunk Oil On My Chest, And Call Me Well: A Collection of East Texas Home Remedies and Folk Medicines (1996) by Bob Bowman renders a humorous picture of East Texas home remedies for a host of diseases, ailments, conditions, and preventions. The author compiled the treatments from East Texans who submitted hundreds of home remedies, folk medicines, medical superstitions, and medicinal recipes.

For a broader look at Texas folk medicine and home remedies from the Native American, Afro-American, Spanish, Mexican, and Hispanic traditions, see both the bibliography and article on "Folk Medicine" by Joe S. Graham in the *Handbook of Texas Online* at www.tsha.utexas.edu/handbook/online/.

INDIAN CAPTIVITY HOAX

By the middle of the nineteenth century, Texas found itself at the center of national attention from the adventures of its earliest pioneers and mythic heroes of the revolution, the Mexican War, and famous frontier engagements. Characters coming to the Lone Star State occasionally attempted to profit from the insatiable curiosity of the reading public in the east. Some even manufactured their life experiences on the frontier. In 1859, Nelson Lee published a dramatic account of his capture and escape from Comanches. Most of his book turned out to be a hoax, but not before he had fooled some well-known historians.

Claiming he had been a Texas Ranger, a soldier, and a Comanche captive, Nelson Lee showed up in New York in November 1858 and quickly dictated an account of his life to the editors of the Baker and Taylor Company. By this time, Indian captivity stories had become bestsellers. His editors admitted that his story was not "precisely in his own words."

Before his capture by Comanches, Lee's life, in excitement, adventure, and brushes with death, rivaled the lives of mountain men, frontier Indian fighters, and veterans of the Texas Revolution. He rafted the St. Lawrence and Mississippi Rivers, participated in the Black Hawk War, and pursued pirates between Africa and Brazil on the *Delaware* and *Ontario* vessels.

He joined the Texas Navy under Commodore Moore and became a Texas Ranger. Lee assessed the four essential qualifications of a Texas Ranger were a fast horse, a sharp eye for the trail, great power of endurance, and the ability of "looking through the double sights of his rifle with a steady arm." He said he fought in the Indian engagements at Enchanted Rock and the Battle of Plum Creek. His claims placed him at the center of major historical events. At the Mier Expedition debacle, he escaped to bring the news of the defeat back to Texas.

After the war, Lee got into the cattle business. On a drive from Brownsville to California with a herd of horses, Comanches captured him and three others on April 2, 1855. They strung up, tortured, and killed his three comrades, but the Comanches spared Lee's life because they became fascinated by an "alarm watch" that he carried with him. At first, he was a slave to Big Wolf. Later, Spotted Leopard purchased both Lee and his watch. Spotted Leopard sold Lee and the watch to Rolling Thunder, who arranged for Lee to enter "into the holy estate of matrimony for the space of one moon" with Sleek Otter.

Lee's descriptions of the customs and culture of the Comanches began to raise doubt about the validity of his story. He described the Comanches as an agricultural people who planted corn, beans, and tobacco, which contradicted knowledge of their non-sedentary, hunting lifestyle. Lee's name also failed to appear in any of the muster rolls, documents, or contemporary newspapers to support the engagements he described.

Anthropologists disproved most of his claims about the Comanches, and his own story proved too good to be true. His near-death experiences that included survival from shipwrecks, rattlesnake bites, and outswimming an alligator proved difficult to swallow even in Texas.

Finding Anything

Three Years Among the Comanches (1859) by Nelson Lee depicts the fictional life of a nineteenth-century adventurer. The University of Oklahoma Press reprinted the book in 1959 with an introduction by the historian Walter Prescott Webb, who declared Nelson's account authentic. The forward to the new edition calls the work a "primary source where the author is not honest with the reader."

To access the full text of the book online, see the netLibrary database of electronic books at the TexShare web site at www.texshare.edu/. The book can be "checked out" for twenty-four hours. By obtaining a password from a local public library, Texas residents are eligible to check out this book and approximately 19,000 additional books over the Internet. The service brings the holdings of a medium-sized public or academic library to a work station.

BOOKS AND WEB SITES

"Don't Dig Up More Snakes Than You Can Kill"

Atkinson, Mary Jourdan. "Familiar Sayings of Old-Time Texans," 213–219. In Boatright, Mody C., Hudson, Wilson M., and Maxwell, Allen. *The Best of Texas Folk and Folklore, 1916–1954*. Denton, Texas: University of North Texas, 1998. Texas Folklore Society. www.texasfolkloresociety.org/.

"I Always Ride on the Western Side of a Train"

Crimm, A. Caroline Costille. "J. Frank Dobie." *Dictionary of Literary Biography*. Detroit: Gale, 2002. TexShare. www.texshare.edu/.

Tinkle, Lon. *An American Original: The Life of J. Frank Dobie*. Boston: Little, Brown & Co., 1978.

Jim Bowie and the Arkansas Toothpick

Dobie, J. Frank. *Tales of Old Time Texas*. Boston: Little, Brown & Co., 1955.

The Bowie Knife and the Arkansas Toothpick. http://users.aristotle .net/~russjohn/bowie.html.

Admiral Byrd and "Home on the Range"

Lomax, John Avery, et al. *Cowboy Songs, Ballads, and Cattle Calls from Texas*. http://store.yahoo.com/locshop/cowsonbalanc.html.

Lomax, John Avery and Lomax, Alan. *Cowboy Songs and Frontier Ballads. Revised and Enlarged*. New York: MacMillan Co., 1959.

Preserving Texas Folklore

Lomax, John A. "Adventures of a Ballad Hunter," 9–16. In Boatright, Mody Coggins and Day, Donald, eds. *From Hell to Breakfast*. Dallas: Southern Methodist University Press, 1944. Publications of the Texas Folklore Society No. XIX.

———. *From Hell to Breakfast*. Denton: University of North Texas Press, 1998. TexShare. netLibrary. www.texshare.edu/.

Political Clout of Wildflowers

Lady Bird Johnson Wildflower Center. www.wildflower.org/.

Silverthorne, Elizabeth. *Legends & Lore of Texas Wildflowers*. College Station: Texas A&M University Press, 1996.

The Terlingua "Chili Imposter"

Harris, Jim and Satterwhite, Carolyn. *Features and Fillers: Texas Journalists on Texas Folklore*. Denton, Texas: University of North Texas Press, 1999.

Kelso, John. "A 5-alarm Scandal at Chili Contest." *The Austin-American Statesman* (November 4, 2003). TexShare. InfoTrac Newspapers. www.texshare .edu/.

Burning a Hole in the Tablecloth

Linck, Ernestine Sewell and Roach, Joyce Gibson. *Eats: A Folk History of Texas Foods*. Fort Worth: Texas Christian University Press, 1989.
Texas Cooking Online. www.texascooking.com/.

"Rub Onions and Skunk Oil on My Chest"

Bowman, Bob. *Rub Onions and Skunk Oil On My Chest, And Call Me Well: A Collection of East Texas Home Remedies and Folk Medicines*. Lufkin, Texas: Best of East Texas Publishers, 1996.
Graham, Joe S. "Folk Medicine." *Handbook of Texas Online*. Texas State Historical Association. www.tsha.utexas.edu/handbook/online/ (accessed June 15, 2004).

Indian Captivity Hoax

Lee, Nelson. *Three Years Among the Comanches: the Narrative of Nelson Lee, the Texas Ranger*. Norman: University of Oklahoma Press, 1991.
———. *Three Years Among the Comanches: the Narrative of Nelson Lee, the Texas Ranger*. Norman: University of Oklahoma Press, 1991. TexShare. netLibrary. www.texshare.edu/.

6

ART AND MUSIC

Paint, Rock, Steel, and Sound

- What renowned American artist painted Big Foot Wallace's description of the death sentences of seventeen Texians who drew black beans out of a clay pot?
- What Parisian painter immigrated to Texas and created a graphic record of early San Antonio de Bexar that included an Arab trainer exercising his U.S. Army camels?
- How did modern Texas artists overcome the dominance of the "Impressionist Bluebonnet School" of Art?
- What contemporary Texas artist explored the theme of "duality" in Big Bend landscapes because of his own experience of being a twin?
- What kind of trouble did the abstract public sculpture *Night Wind* encounter in Longview?
- How much did the painted fiberglass Enron cow sculpture, *Moost-Imoovative*, sell for at Sotheby's auction in 2001?
- Which Texas county courthouse contains a statue of the Goddess of Justice without a blindfold so she can closely examine issues with both eyes?
- How did Waylon Jennings and Willie Nelson come to write the song "Good Hearted Woman" in 1969?
- What Texas blues singer obtained a pardon for a murder conviction by composing a song for a Texas governor?
- How can aspiring Texas songwriters and bands learn how to launch their performance and recording careers in the Lone Star State?

FREDERICK REMINGTON: HOW THE
WEST WASN'T WON

New York artist Frederick Remington fashioned a lucrative career in the East by painting and sculpting heroic, enduring images of the West. He created dynamic scenes of bronco busting cowboys, raiding Indians, magnificent galloping horses, stampeding cattle, and detailed trappings of western frontier life set in vigorous glory. Collections of his paintings, drawings, and sculptures deck the galleries of Texas's major museums of Houston, Dallas, Fort Worth, and the Panhandle Plains.

The romantic, sleek, and noble picture of the West in Remington's illustrations sometimes contrasted with conditions he endured in his travels. He found Texas heat and mosquitoes oppressive. On assignment for *Century* magazine in 1888, he described his visit to Henrietta in less than romantic terms. He called it a "miserable little frontier town with a little hen coop of a hotel."

Remington found Texas veterans and heroes more to his liking. Texas frontier men like William Alexander "Big Foot" Wallace, John Ford, and other Texas Rangers he called "men with the bark on." On another trip through Texas in February 1896, he extracted enough information from these ranger veterans for an article on Texas called "How the Law Got into the Chaparral."

To illustrate the article, Remington produced an oil painting called *The Mier Expedition: Drawing of the Black Bean.* One hundred and seventy-six Texans, recaptured by Mexicans after an abortive escape attempt in 1842, drew seventeen black beans from a clay pot mixed with white beans to see who would face a firing squad. Big Foot Wallace, a survivor of the expedition, left a vivid description of the scene.

A squad of Mexican officers came into the corral. Then a soldier entered with an "earthen vessel" and began to count out white beans. Next, he counted out seventeen black beans, put all the beans in the pot and covered it with a cloth. As the Texians drew the "fatal color," some made casual remarks like "the jig is up," or they have "taken my sign in at last." After all the beans were drawn, Mexican soldiers separated the two groups of prisoners, and a firing squad executed seventeen prisoners who drew black beans. To deter further escape attempts, the Mexican soldiers forced Big Foot and the other prisoners to view the bodies of their comrades before marching to Perote Prison in Mexico City.

In his painting, Remington aligned darkness and light, black and white, sun and shade in every space. The sun cast dark shadows over the Mexican guards with their rifles. The table with the vessel full of black and white beans sat on the shady side of the corral. A prisoner dressed in a white shirt and black pants held his right hand in the jar selecting a bean. Several prisoners in white shirts and black pants talked casually in the background as guards in white uniforms and black hats monitored the proceedings. Remington painted heroic men caught between opposing forces with their lives at stake. They handled their fate almost casually, and Remington loved and sold this view of the West.

Finding Anything

Painting Texas History to 1900 by Sam DeShong Ratcliffe provides analyses of important paintings of major Texas historical events. The author illustrates his study with fifty color plates and seventy-six black and white photographs. Remington's painting *The Mier Expedition: The Drawing of the Black Bean* and several other artists' works about the expedition are compared and contrasted. Artists like Remington, Robert Onderdonk, William Henry Huddle, and Julius Stockfleth painted a wide range of events in Texas history from the fall of the Alamo to the surrender of Santa Anna, the Mier Expedition, and the Galveston Hurricane.

To obtain an online view of many paintings, drawings, photographs, and memorials of the Mier Expedition, go to www.google.com/. Select the "Images" menu and search for "Mier Expedition." Remington's painting *The Mier Expedition: The Drawing of the Black Bean* appears in several web sites along with other artists' paintings of different scenes of the expedition. The original Remington oil painting belongs to the Hogg Collection in the Houston Museum of Fine Arts.

THEODORE GENTILZ AND *THE CAMEL RIDE*

Artist Jean Louis Theodore Gentilz studied drafting, painting, and engineering at the Imperial School of Mathematics and Drawing in Paris. Henri Castro hired him as a surveyor to assist in the establishment of a Texas colony on the Medina River. In 1843, Gentiltz reached Texas on the ship the *Heinrich* well ahead of Castro. In the interim, he met another young Parisian in San Antonio, Auguste Fretelliere. The two became friends.

When delays plagued the launch of Castro's colony, the two friends resorted to bartering for food when they ran short of money. Fretelliere wrote of exchanging two pistols for a mare, a milk cow and a calf, a sow with eight piglets, and some corn and a bushel of frijoles. With Castro's preparation at last complete, Gentilz and the immigrant procession departed San Antonio for their colony on the Medina River at Castroville.

For two years, Gentilz assisted Castro in surveying the towns of Castroville, Quihi, and D'Hanis. He documented some of this work with an oil painting in 1845 entitled *Surveying in Texas before Annexation to U.S.* The artist's taste for his new life inspired him to return to France in 1846 and dispose of his property. He married Marie Fargeix and brought his bride back to Texas. They settled in San Antonio and established a studio on Flores Street.

From this studio, Gentilz proceeded to sketch and paint the people and scenes of San Antonio. The Alamo lay in ruin from the destructive siege, but the city moved vibrantly on. The market was a "medley of carts, chickens, pigs running about, and women making tortillas." Side streets provided the stages for cock fights. Gentilz painted oxcarts, tamale sellers, candle sellers, drunkards, bread makers, water sellers, and a rooster race. On the plains, Comanches and other Native Americans fascinated him, and he painted chiefs, warriors on the march, Indian camps, Indian portraits, and Indians fishing with bows and arrows.

In paintings like the *Fall of the Alamo* and the *Death of Dickerson*, Gentilz revealed an interest in history and public affairs. The commotion caused by the arrival of two contingents of U.S. Army camels in San Antonio in 1857 inevitably caught his attention. The *San Antonio Herald* issued frequent reports on the camels' health, diet, and maneuvers around the city. While the camels waited to march to their home base of Camp Verde, Gentliz sketched the camels in their training exercises.

From one of these sketches, Gentilz created an oil painting, *The Camel Ride.* This painting shows Elias, the Turkish camel trainer in full Middle Eastern costume, taking one of the two-humped Bactrian camels on a training run at full gallop. Elias carries a stick and races over sandy, rocky terrain. The camel appears to be smiling, enjoying himself. After the U.S. Army camel experiment failed, the army sold the camels. Elias, the trainer, settled in Sonora, Mexico, and married a Yaqui Indian woman. He raised a large family, and his son Plutarco Elias Calles, nicknamed "El Turco," became president of Mexico in 1924.

Finding Anything

Painting in Texas: The Nineteenth Century (1967) by Pauline A. Pinckney surveys the work of more than fifty major painters who worked in Texas in the nineteenth century. The author illustrates the book with black

and white and color illustrations of the artists' works. The book highlights
primary themes, subjects, and styles in nineteenth-century Texas art.

To keep current with art exhibitions, musical events, and Texas cultural
heritage festivals on a region-by-region basis, check out the web site of the
Texas Commission on the Arts at www.artonart.com/. In addition to an-
nouncing arts and cultural events in any of the seven major Texas regions,
the site posts many event listings in major cities in each region.

LONE STAR REGIONALISM AND "THE DALLAS NINE"

In 1932, nine young Dallas artists, all less than thirty years old, exhibited
their paintings at the Dallas Public Art Gallery at Fair Park. A leading art
magazine reviewed their work favorably and referred to these artists as
"the nine." The group formed around artists Jerry Bywaters and Alexandre Hogue and included John Douglass, Otis Dozier, Lloyd Goff, William
Lester, Perry Nichols, Everett Spruce, and Thomas Still.

*Jerry Bywaters, a leading member of the group of artists called the Dallas Nine, became Director
of the Dallas Museum of Fine Arts. Above, he hosts Adelyn Breeskin, Director of the Baltimore
Museum of Fine Arts, on a visit in March 1951. From the collections of The Dallas/Texas History
and Archives Division, Dallas Public Library.*

These artists shared a number of common interests. Cliché landscapes of bluebonnets and wildflowers bored them. Some even expressed strong resentment at the rising "flood of mediocre paintings" of wildflowers and "misty paintings of cactus" that dominated Texas art. To them, impressionist renderings of fields of bluebonnets belied the realities of 1930s Texas. They viewed the landscape from a clean, sharp-edged perspective of the reality around them: soil erosion, greed for oil, rape of the land, and the Dust Bowl. Critics called their work and style Lone Star Regionalism. The Dallas Nine painted the real Southwest in oil on masonite.

Regionalists sharply depicted the dark side of nature, sometimes with giant, oversized grasshoppers and sometimes the stark scenes of parched earth. Alexandre Hogue's painting called *Drouth Stricken Area* typifies the subject and style of the Dallas Nine. In a blue West Texas sky with one cloud in it, four buzzards fly above a tall windmill standing over a circular trough that has gone dry. An emaciated cow whose ribs protrude in exquisite detail lowers her head into the dry trough for a drink. A big buzzard waits close by, perched on a board above the cow, in anticipation of his feast.

The Dallas Nine also captured man's role in the depletion of the environment. Hogue's painting *Erosion No. 2: Mother Earth Laid Bare* portrays land worn out from decades of destruction of the soil. He exhibits this view bare again with a gigantic, sandy female nude as Mother Earth laid out in front of an abandoned farm with a plow in the foreground.

In a 1940 painting called *Oil Field Girls*, Jerry Bywaters depicted the impact of the Texas oil booms on land and people. Two seductive prostitutes hitchhike by the side of a Texas road running through flat, dusty land full of oil derricks. Old tires and shabby billboards litter the roadway. A Coca Cola sign, "Hattie's Hut, Dine & Dance, Trucker's Welcome," announces a honky-tonk in the distance. An oil fire burns in the background and darkens half the sky. Because the artist exaggerated the size of the prostitutes, some critics suggested the artist compared unrestrained oil exploration to prostitution.

In 1934, the New York Museum of Modern Art selected the work of four young Dallas artists for inclusion in a major exhibition of American art to tour sixteen cities. The recognition signaled the emancipation of Texas art from the bluebonnet and wildflower school. "The clear feeling was that these Dallas artists were producing work on a level comparable to the best in the country."

Finding Anything

Lone Star Regionalism: The Dallas Nine and Their Circle, 1928–1945 written by Rick Stewart in 1985 describes "the nine" and their movement. The author published the catalog to accompany the regionalist exhibition of The Dallas Museum of Art to mark the Texas State Sesquicentennial in 1986. The book contains 147 color and black and white photographs of the paintings and sculptures assembled for the exhibit.

For a survey of the wider circle of artists who associated with the Dallas Nine, see Kendall Curlee's article "Dallas Nine" at the web site of the *Handbook of Texas Online* at www.tsha.utexas.edu/handbook/. This article lists artists and sculptors who contributed to Lone Star Regionalism. The sculptor Mark Owen, who carved a 1943 sculpture of blues singer "Leadbelly" in black serpentine stone, belongs in the group.

BIG BEND LANDSCAPES: "WHERE MOUNTAINS FLOAT IN THE AIR"

The Big Bend Country affected every population who visited it. Native Americans painted its rocks, caves, and shelters. The Spanish described it as almost unlivable in reports and journals. With increasing encroachment on their lands, Comanches and the Apaches sought refuge in it. The U.S. military explored, mapped, and surveyed Big Bend. Camels marched through it. Adventurers wandered into it and disappeared. Survivors buried their dead there in graves with wooden crosses soon obliterated by wind-blown sand.

An old cowboy once gave simple directions on how to find the Big Bend Country. He said to go south from Fort Davis until you come to the place "where the big river is kept in a stone box and the water runs uphill." At this point, you have arrived at the place where "the mountains float in the air except at night when they go away to play with other mountains." For more than a century, visual artists have attempted to capture on canvas the many faces of a region whose mountains float in air, great shadows move across the desert floor, and rivers cut hundreds of feet through solid rock. They share an affinity with the special place described by the cowboy.

After the border tensions between the U.S. and Mexico eased in the 1920s, Dallas artist Frank Reaugh took students on trips to the Big Bend and West Texas in a modified Model A to sketch landscapes. Several young artists from the Dallas Nine joined these sketching excursions. Jerry Bywaters, Otis Dozier, William Lester, and Everett Spruce deepened their understanding of the Texas landscapes in West Texas and the Big Bend.

On January 20, 1935, Franklin Roosevelt officially created the Big Bend National Park. The National Park Service hired University of Texas historian Walter Prescott Webb to write two articles on the opening of the park in 1944. With photographers and a film crew, he rafted in the Big Bend to launch the event. Part of the park's attraction arose from its uncontaminated remoteness. A Rio Grande border patrolman described it as a "tough country." To him, the Big Bend was "so tough, so big and so lonesome no one lived in it long enough to change it much." The park's undisturbed, rugged remoteness appealed to luminaries in the visual arts. Ansel Adams, Laura Gilpin, Jim Bones, Peter Koch, and many other artists painted and photographed Big Bend's multiple surfaces and facades.

Fort Worth landscape artist Dennis Blagg follows this long tradition of artists with a special connection to the Big Bend. For more than twenty years, he traveled and photographed Big Bend. Returning to his studio, he painted and sketched the landscapes on very large canvases. The unusually large canvases capture the grand scale of many Big Bend landscapes. The large scale allows multiple combinations of colors to form and reform in clouds and terrain that stretch out in changing light conditions. To Blagg, the Big Bend landscape contains great symbolism. "The desert represents a landscape of broken promise, yet it is a place of vast spiritual content—an emptiness waiting to be fulfilled."

In a painting called *Running River*, Blagg frames the Rio Grande like a "yellow ribbon" at dusk between a glowing red sky, darkened terrain, and deep green vegetation. An eight-foot wide canvas called *Edifice* presents the dramatic, bold face of a rock formation. He paints strata so delicately balanced they appear ready to crumble and fall. Blagg's landscapes contain many scenes of clouds, rain, and menacing storms in Big Bend. He considers *Passover*, a portrait of Pummel Peak caught in a storm, his best work. In a painting called *Two Peaks*, Blagg explores "the mystery of being a twin" from his own personal experience as a twin, the fifth child in a family of ten children growing up on a cotton farm in West Texas.

Finding Anything

Big Bend Landscapes (2002) by Dennis Blagg contains fifty recent oil paintings and twenty pencil drawings of scenes of the Big Bend Park and environs. The oversized book, ten inches high by twelve inches wide, effectively captures the panoramic landscapes of Blagg's canvases which often extend two full pages. The author provides short comments on each painting.

For a photographic tour of Big Bend, see the web site of the Big Bend National Park at www.nps.gov/bibe/home.htm. The "Visitor's Photo Gallery" provides a virtual tour of Big Bend through more than 100 photographs of scenes of major canyons, peaks, rivers, and wildlife from the park. The site contains additional information on archaeology, historic areas, early settlers, and natural history and backcountry information.

TEN BURIED CADILLACS AND OTHER OUTDOOR SCULPTURE IN TEXAS

As the state's "most accessible form of art and history," monuments and outdoor sculptures symbolize Texas values and cultural heritage for more people than any other visual art form. Images in stone, bronze, steel, urethane, and miscellaneous media populate parks, battlefields, public buildings, streets, highways, and trails.

Canyon, Texas, exhibits a life-size bust of Comanche Chief Quanah Parker and a 47-foot high concrete and stucco *Cowboy Tex Randall*. Carthage, Texas, commemorates country music legend "Gentleman Jim" Reeves with a 6-foot granite statue of the singer in a suit and bow tie standing behind a six-string guitar. Alvin, Texas, boasts a life-size bronze statue of Nolan Ryan on a pitcher's mound celebrating his record of no-hit games and strikeouts from a professional baseball career. The Texas State Cemetery in Austin contains hundreds of sculptures of state heritage like the life-size bronze statue of Johanna Troutman cast in 1915. In 1835, Troutman gave the Georgia Battalion a white silk flag appliquéd with a single blue star inscribed with the words "Liberty or Death."

Texas patriotism dominated public sculpture for the first 100 years of state history. One hundred and seventy-five large war memorials commemorate the service of veterans of the Texas Revolution, the Civil War, Spanish-American War, World Wars I and II, the Korean Conflict, and the War in Vietnam. Forty-five of these monuments memorialize the Texas Revolution. Seventeen monuments surround the Texas State Capitol on twenty-two acres of land. The four oldest monuments lie along the "Great Walk" created by civil engineer William Munro Johnson in 1891. They include the *Heroes of the Alamo*, *Volunteer Fireman*, *Confederate Soldiers*, and *Terry's Texas Rangers*.

The first large-scale monument created in Texas memorialized the Alamo martyrs. A simple pyramid fashioned from stone salvaged from the original Mission San Antonio de Valero (the Alamo) occupied the vestibule of the Capitol building until a fire in 1881. A new bronze *Battle of the Alamo* statue replaced it in 1891. Patriotic memorials dominated so much public sculpture that one city planner expressed the hope that his city could expand its imagination beyond the notion that "public art is an equestrian statue with a hero on his back."

Close behind patriotic themes in public sculpture, Texas honored the characters and influences of the western frontier in public spaces. Statues of lawmen, cowboys, Indians, pioneers, trail drivers, buffalo, longhorns, and mustangs predominate. After World War II, native Texan Electra Waggoner Biggs created a bronze sculpture of *Will Rogers—Riding into the Sunset* for the Will Rogers Coliseum in Fort Worth. He rides off on his favorite horse, Soapsuds.

Prosperity and the influx of new artists opened the way for experimentation with modern themes and styles in public sculpture. Sculptors began to take a tongue-in-cheek look at Texas myth and legend. In environmental art, the *Cadillac Ranch*, consisting of ten partially buried Cadillacs near Amarillo, blazed the trail. The creators buried ten vintage models from years 1949 through 1964. The public interacted with the *Cadillac Ranch* by scribbling graffiti on the doors, tops, and trunks of the vehicles.

Other artists created giant armadillos, roadside snake farms, frogs, truck stops, cowboy boots, and roadrunners. Bob Wade's eight-foot urethane and steel *Frogs*, commissioned for the Dallas Tango Club, violated a city sign ordinance and was relocated to Carl's Corner in Hillsboro. After a state-wide goodwill tour, some of the *Frogs* ended up in Houston. Not all of the public greeted the new Texas public art enthusiastically. In Kilgore, one resident protested that a 20-foot tall abstract sculpture called *Night Winds* was a waste of public funds and a "communist policy to erect ugly and meaningless objects." Kilgore College cut it down and hauled it away.

As bold, whimsical, and innovative as neo-Western art dared, it could not eclipse the Texas public's love of traditional forms of sculpture. Two years after its installation, *The Mustangs of Las Colinas*, by wildlife sculptor Robert Glen, attained recognition as the most popular public sculpture in the Dallas area. Glen sculpted a dynamic grouping of larger-than-life wild horses in full gallop across a man-made stream in Williams Square. It is one of the largest equine sculptures in the world.

Finding Anything

A *Comprehensive Guide to Outdoor Sculpture in Texas* (1996) by Carol Morris Little identifies, describes, and locates the major pieces of Texas public sculpture. The author provides the title of each work, name of the artist, medium, history of its creation, and location. A photograph of each piece of art illustrates the text. For a virtual tour of public outdoor sculpture at the Texas State Capitol, check the Monuments Guide of the web site at the Texas State Preservation Board. The site is www.tspb .state.tx.us/. This site provides a photograph and a history of the seventeen major monuments that occupy the Great Walk on the 22-acre site of the Capitol grounds.

THE HOUSTON COWPARADE

Combining public art, Texas heritage, and Houston civic pride, the city staged a fund-raising "bovine bonanza" in 2001 for the Texas Children's Hospital and Texas Children's Cancer Center. Forty-five public and private school art classes participated in a "Cows in the Schools Project." Students submitted 115 designs to judges from the school districts, and artists painted the winning designs on life-size fiberglass bovines. They generated a colorful herd of more than 300 cow sculptures, displayed in streets and plazas for two months and auctioned for charity.

Houston patterned the idea from similar successful campaigns in Chicago and New York in 1999 and 2000 based on three cow sculptures of Swiss-born artist Pascal Knapp. He designed the cows for a Zurich public art event in 1998 in which artists painted designs on three life-sized, fiberglass cow models. With more than two tons of clay, he finally achieved success with three models: a standing cow, a reclining cow, and a grazing cow. Several thousand artists in Europe and America painted Knapp's fiberglass bovines and raised millions for charities.

With the Texas longhorn cattle tradition, the CowParade Houston presented a unique opportunity for the expression of Texas history and culture. It lived up to the opportunity—perhaps more than it intended at the beginning of the campaign. Every conceivable Texas symbol ended up on a bovine in a frivolous and whimsical manner. They were fun.

There were wildflowers and bluebonnets running up cow's legs and meeting a blue sky; bovines wore lone stars, Stetsons, saddles, derricks, dinosaur scales, a space shuttle, quilts, guitars, sombreros, dollar bills, and covered wagons; and cow designs had flies, jalapeno peppers, rhine-stones, beads, piñatas, blankets, yellow roses, and even the Waco Sus-pension Bridge. One cow representing Texas Catholic heritage carried a large model of a cathedral on its back. They named this sculpture *Holy Cowthedral*. For two months, the herd of 300 painted urethane cows grazed all over Houston until the roundup for the auction.

Campaign organizers can claim a unique piece of Texas and American business history in the CowParade. They could not escape fallout from the collapse of Enron Corporation. For a $10,000 contribution, Enron sponsored a bovine in the CowParade called *Moost Immoovative* de-signed by artist Jason C. Alkire. This sculpture of a standing cow with its head up was mounted in front of Enron headquarters. The artist mounted small panes of reflective, mirror-like material on the fiberglass cow suggesting a modern, metallic effect. In November 2001, organizers removed the sculpture from the Enron site for auction by Sotheby's.

Moost Immoovative sold for $8,000 at the Sotheby's auction on De-cember 6th. The sale prompted one *Fortune* magazine columnist to sug-gest that the Enron Company was like the Enron cow. The content cannot be discerned by looking into it; it is made of mirrors. Was the company worth as much as the cow? One thing for certain, it made little difference to the kids at the Children's Medical Center of Houston. They benefited from $1.1 million in support and memories of colorful, fiberglass cows.

Finding Anything

CowParade Houston (2001) written by Thomas Craughwell and Vicki Bomke Thomson provides an exhibition catalog of cow sculptures displayed during September and October of 2001. Six artists photographed all 300 fiberglass cows in the project. These photographs show the exhibit sites in parks, plazas, buildings, shopping centers, and banks, and artists painting their designs.

To view a closeup of a photograph of each bovine in the CowParade, go to the CowParade web site at http://houston.cowparade.net/. They are arranged alphabetically by title of the piece or the artist.

JUSTICE WITH HER EYES WIDE OPEN

For more than a century, the county courthouse overshadowed all other building architecture in the Texas landscape. Many counties prominently fea-

tured their courthouses by employing the Shelbyville town plan, which posi-
tioned the courthouse at the center of a town square with traffic entering or
exiting at the corners. Other counties increased visual focus on the courthouse by designing four roads that terminated in a square directly in front of
the building. In Spanish-American influenced town plans, the courthouse
occupied a central place on a *plaza mayor* opposite a cathedral or church.
Whatever the town plan, Texas courthouses anchored the state with strong
physical structures and a visible symbol of civic pride and stable public order.

Courthouses in Comanche County contain a living record of the contributions of these structures to Texas heritage. Several counties in early Texas
history convened court under a tree, dispensed justice in residences, and
then built a simple two-room log structure as the first "court house." The
"Old Cora" log courthouse in Comanche County served this purpose until
railroad prosperity in the 1890s made possible construction of a three-story

The "Old Red Courthouse" of Dallas County is one of six court houses the county has built since
1846. It was constructed in 1892 of red granite and sandstone in Romanesque Revival style.
From the collections of The Dallas/Texas History and Archives Division, Dallas Public Library.

courthouse in Renaissance Revival style. In 1939, the county replaced it with a Moderne-Style Art Deco courthouse. After relocating five times, the "Old Cora" log courthouse shares the site in Comanche with the 1939 structure.

The new courthouse contains a restored statue of the Goddess of Justice. She dispensed justice from two courthouses for more than a century with some allowances for wear and tear. The statue lost its scales in a windstorm in 1908. Later she lost a hand, forearm, and her symbolic Sword of Justice. In Comanche, the Statue of Justice hears cases without a blindfold so that she can examine issues carefully "with both eyes."

Construction of courthouses in Texas experienced a "golden age" during the prosperous times of 1870 to 1900. These courthouses have been loosely named Victorian courthouses, but they comprise three major styles: Second French Empire, Renaissance Revival, and Romanesque. All these terms have to be applied freely. In typical Texas fashion, architects mixed and mingled, borrowed, and improvised many styles.

The period from 1900 to 1940 ushered in a new era of courthouse construction characterized by new styles sometimes called the "Texas Renaissance." Of Texas's 254 counties, almost 100 county courthouses survive from this period. With many counties passing bond issues to finance construction, counties went on a competitive building spree and built monumental structures in Beaux-Arts, Renaissance, Classical Revival, and Mission style buildings. More than twenty of these structures are listed on the National Registry of Historic Places. All these diverse styles prompted one architectural historian to write: "To study Texas is to study a large cross section of America in microcosm."

Contrasted with courthouses from earlier eras, Texas courthouses constructed since the 1950s have been described by art historians as "uninteresting," "institutional," or "lacking in cultural value." Constrained by the economy, the "most space for the most money," and practical utility, the courthouses built in the middle decades of the twentieth century suffered by comparison. Critics coined the unflattering term "early motel style" architecture to refer to flat, one-story rambling courthouses that appeared in the 1950s. The term connotes a nostalgic sense of loss of stability and authority once reflected in the majestic courthouse structures of previous eras.

Finding Anything

The Courthouses of Texas: A Guide (1993) by Mavis P. Kelsey, Sr. and Donald H. Dyal is a concise alphabetical directory of the current 254 courthouses of Texas. The authors describe the architectural style and the material composition of each courthouse and supply a color photograph. They outline the history of Texas courthouse architecture and tell how Texas counties and county seats acquired their names.

For recent online photographs of current Texas courthouses, check the web site www.texascourthouses.com/. The site provides alphabetical access to courthouses and a list of courthouses arranged by architectural styles from Texas Renaissance and Classical Revival up through Contemporary. The site describes eleven different architectural styles employed in Texas courthouses.

WAYLON AND WILLIE AND "GOOD HEARTED WOMAN"

Texas musicians and musical traditions contributed substantially to the origins and development of commercial country and western music. Texas bands, Texas songwriters, Texas history, Texas cities, Texas landscapes, and Texas musical styles exerted a prevailing influence on the industry for eighty years.

Marion Try Slaughter, II, a versatile singer of opera and popular music from Jefferson, recorded the nation's first country mega-hit in 1924. He combined the names of two West Texas towns, Vernon and Dalhart, to form his stage name and cut a double-sided Victor recording of "The Prisoner's Song" and the "Wreck of the Old 97." The recording sold more than a million copies and made Vernon Dalhart a star.

Like many conflicts in a country song, the authorship disputes often surface after a song sells a million copies. Dalhart learned "The Prisoner's Song" from his cousin Guy Massey, who owned the copyright. Novie Massey, the widow of Guy's brother Robert Massey, tells a different story. Novie says she watched her husband Robert sing it in Dallas, and Guy wrote it down. At his death, Guy willed it back to his brother Robert, but he "never did admit that he didn't write it." Is his will an admission of the true authorship of the song? Not much has changed in the music industry.

The musician known as the "Father of Country Music," Jimmie Rodgers, hailed from Meridian, Mississippi, but his signature song "T-for Texas (Blue Yodel)" and his railroad songs forged a permanent Texas connection. He built his dream home, Blue Yodeler's Paradise, at 617 West Main Street in Kerrville. Rodgers worried what people would think if they heard him on the radio singing lyrics like "I'm going to shoot poor

Thelma just to see her jump and fall." Jimmie's fans said by the time he finished the song, his sobbing, moaning, and yodeling could convince anyone "she had it coming."

In 1940, Bob Wills and the Texas Playboys put "western swing" style music on the map with "San Antonio Rose," their signature song that sold millions. A long line of country music stars emerged in the alcohol-triggered "honky-tonk" era. Many of these stars later entered Nashville's Country Music Hall of Fame: Ernest Tubb, Lefty Frizzel, George Jones, Ray Price, and Hank Thompson. Willie Nelson would lead a transition from honky-tonk country music into the new style of "progressive country" or "redneck rock."

An established Nashville songwriter with a string of credits, Nelson switched recording labels, left Nashville, and returned to Texas in 1970. He settled in Austin, forty miles from his birthplace of Abbot. From an old Austin armory turned into a club called World Armadillo Headquarters, Nelson and Texas singer-songwriter Waylon Jennings from Littlefield launched "outlaw music."

Nelson and Jennings made the nickname permanent with the recording of Willie Nelson's *Wanted: The Outlaws* album in 1975. The album contained several duets, including the smash hit "Good Hearted Woman." Jennings and Nelson wrote the song during a poker game in 1969 in a Fort Worth motel. Waylon joined Willie's card game, and they began writing the song. Waylon already had the first line: "A long time forgotten are just dreams that just fell by the way." As the poker game continued, Nelson's wife wrote down the lyrics. Waylon said they finished the song during the game and "didn't miss a hand."

Finding Anything

Sing Your Heart Out, Country Boy (1996) by Dorothy Horstman contains the lyrics and the stories behind many Texas country and western classic songs. The author includes many famous songs in the book, but two sections of the book, "Honky Tonk Songs" and "Cowboy Songs," contain the work of many star Texas songwriters.

To keep up with events that celebrate Texas music heritage and encourage rising music talent, see the web site of the Texas Heritage Music Foundation of Kerrville at www.texasheritagemusic.org/. The site offers an online newsletter reviewing performances, festivals, documentaries, and many activities of hundreds of regular performers and songwriters in Texas.

BLIND LEMON JEFFERSON AND "LEADBELLY"

In 1997, the 75th Texas Legislature designated the guitar as the Official State Musical Instrument. With characteristic humility, the legislators claimed Texas "preeminence" in pop, blues, country and western, jazz, rock, and Tejano music. In their official resolution, they conceded Spain's claim to the creation of the guitar. Because it had "transcended its national origins," Texas could claim it too. The guitar, they resolved, could not be separated from the popular culture of cowboys, sharecroppers, railroad workers, and migrant laborers who built Texas.

The Legislature did not overstate Texas's contribution to "blues" music. The state's first great blues musician, Blind Lemon Jefferson, modeled a recipe for a unique musical style called "country blues." Born in Wortham, Texas, in 1897, he moved to Dallas and began performing in the Deep Ellum district. Tradition reports that Paramount records discovered Jefferson playing on the sidewalk.

Blind Lemon Jefferson succeeded in becoming the highest selling artist in the "race records" category of the late 1920s. He influenced a rising generation of black musicians whose music proved as memorable as their names: T. Bone Walker, Lightnin' Hopkins, Clarence "Gatemouth" Brown, Robert Johnson, and Huddie "Leadbelly" Ledbetter. All these musicians owed a measure of debt to Jefferson for their successes.

"Leadbelly," known as the King of the Twelve String Guitar, grew up near Caddo Lake. He moved to Dallas and played with Blind Lemon Jefferson for five years. Then he killed a man and ended up in the Shaw State Prison Farm in Huntsville, Texas. When Texas Governor Pat Neff visited the prison in 1923, Leadbelly improvised a freedom song for the governor. He impressed the governor enough to win a pardon.

Leadbelly returned to Louisiana to play the blues. But not for long! In 1930, he assaulted a woman and received a sentence to the Angola prison farm in Louisiana. Leadbelly's musical talent and songwriting ability brought him to the attention of folksong collector John Avery Lomax. The folklorist now traveled the South collecting field hollers, spirituals, chain gang songs, and rural blues songs. In 1934, Lomax and his son Alan visited the Angola prison farm and recorded Leadbelly.

Many legends grew up around Leadbelly. Some say he acquired his name by taking a gunshot in the stomach. Others say prisoners tagged him with the nickname for his fast work pace on the chain gang. Another Leadbelly legend claimed he obtained early release from Angola by composing and singing another clemency song, but the prison warden denied

Sam Lightnin' Hopkins (1912–1982) carried on the country blues tradition of Blind Lemmon Jefferson in an album called Texas Blues *about gambling, woman troubles, slavery, and prison. From the collections of The Dallas/Texas History and Archives Division, Dallas Public Library.*

the story. When Louisiana released him, Lomax helped him record a three-volume set of songs for the Library of Congress. Leadbelly relocated to New York, and Lomax became his "manager." He performed with Woody Guthrie, Burl Ives, the Weavers, and other folk groups before he died in 1949 of Lou Gehrig's disease. Leadbelly's greatest hit turned out to be *Goodnight Irene.*

Finding Anything

Texas Music (1998) by Rick Koster tells the story of Texas popular music in the twentieth century. The author surveys the roots of many popular styles of Texas music from 1890 forward through the stories of musicians and bands. All the individual musicians and groups covered include musicians born in Texas or who spent significant portions of their careers in Texas. Besides blues, the author includes country, rock, folk, jazz, and ethnic music, soul music, and R&B. Classical musicians are selectively treated.

For a brief, straightforward account of the basic facts of Huddie Ledbetter's life, check his biography at the web site of the Rock and Roll Hall of Fame and Museum at www.rockhall.com/hof/inductee.asp?id= 140. He was inducted into the Hall of Fame in 1988.

"TEXAS, OUR TEXAS": THE TEXAS MUSIC OFFICE

Callers to the Texas Governor's Office, if placed on hold, presently hear a recording of the Texas A&M University military cadet "Fightin' Texas Aggie Band" playing the official state song, "Texas, Our Texas." Gladys Yoakum Wright wrote the lyrics and William J. Marsh composed the music to enter a 1929 state-sponsored contest to create an official state song. Legislators selected their song as the contest winner. When Alaska entered the Union in 1959 and displaced Texas as the biggest state, Marsh amended the third line of the song from "largest and grandest" to "boldest and grandest."

The Legislature's interest in Texas music increased over the last fifty years in proportion to the music industry's thriving, dynamic national and international impact. As all forms of Texas music continued to grow in popularity and commercial value, the Governor created the Texas Music Office on January 20, 1990. The music office had the specific mission of promoting the "development of the music industry" in Texas by informing the public and the music industry about "resources available in the state for music production."

By 2000, the Texas Music Office matured into a massive clearinghouse of Texas music industry information. A musician needing assistance can quickly locate 7,580 music businesses in Texas arranged in ninety-six musical categories. It functions like a large state-funded Yellow Pages devoted to a single industry. The office directory maintains listings of businesses as small as individual music teachers and guitar studios to large recording studios, music copyright law firms, music schools, high schools for the performing arts, dance halls, and music venues.

The Texas Music Office continues to add useful features to assist musicians, music groups, music associations, and the music industry. It created the Texas Talent Register that now includes 5,800 Texas recording artists. The register provides the style of music, locations, and the phone number of booking agents and management. The office maintains the most extensive calendar of annual musical events in Texas called the "Texas Music Events Calendar." It lists web sites, phone numbers, and organizers of almost 700 annual music happenings in the state such as Mardi Gras Galveston, the Rattlesnake Hunt in Walnut Springs, the North Texas Irish Festival, the Wild Hog Festival in Sabinal, and the Fiesta Amistad in Round Rock.

Musicians beginning musical careers in Texas have an excellent resource in the Music Office to use in planning a career, supporting recording endeavors, learning about songwriting competitions, and finding performance venues. It provides both a printed and online gateway to the industry.

Finding Anything

The Handbook of Texas Music (2003) edited by Roy Barkley organizes the state's musical heritage into a one-volume, comprehensive encyclopedia of Texas music. The editors specifically patterned the music encyclopedia after the *New Handbook of Texas*. They represented the Texas State Historical Association, the Texas Music Office, the UT-Austin Center for Studies in Texas History and several universities. The handbook contains contributions from musicians, teachers, musicologists, and managers of musical groups. Editors included more than 700 articles and music bibliographies illustrated with more than 100 photographs and illustrations of musicians, groups, and music memorabilia.

To expand on information provided by the handbook, see the web site of the Texas Music Office in the Governor's Office at www.governor. state.tx.us/music/. The Texas Music Office maintains an in-depth list of 231 Texas musical pioneers with online links to additional information. They provide an extensive bibliography and discography of more than 500 publications on Texas music history and heritage.

BOOKS AND WEB SITES

Frederick Remington: How the West Wasn't Won

Mier Expedition. Images. www.google.com/.
Ratcliffe, Sam DeShong. *Painting Texas History to 1900*. Austin: University of Texas Press, 1992.

Theodore Gentilz and *The Camel Ride*

Pinckney, Pauline A. *Painting in Texas: The Nineteenth Century*. Austin: University of Texas Press, 1967.
Texas Commission on the Arts Calendar. www.artonart.com/.

Lone Star Regionalism and "The Dallas Nine"

Curlee, Kendall. "Dallas Nine," *Handbook of Texas Online*. Austin: Texas State Historical Society. www.tsha.utexas.edu/handbook/online/.
Stewart, Rick. *Lone Star Regionalism: The Dallas Nine and Their Circle, 1928–1945*. Austin: Texas Monthly Press; Dallas Museum of Art, 1985.

Big Bend Landscapes: "Where Mountains Float in the Air"

Big Bend National Park. Visitor's Photo Gallery. www.nps.gov/bibe/home. htm.
Blagg, Dennis. *Big Bend Landscapes*. College Station: Texas A&M University Press, 2002.

Ten Buried Cadillacs and Other Outdoor Sculpture in Texas

Little, Carol Morris. *A Comprehensive Guide to Outdoor Sculpture in Texas*. Austin: University of Texas, 1996.
Texas State Preservation Board. Texas Capitol. Online Gallery. The Monuments Guide. www.tspb.state.tx.us/.

The Houston CowParade

CowParade Houston. The Cows. http://houston.cowparade.net/.
Craughwell, Thomas J. and Thomson, Vicki Bomke. *CowParade Houston*. New York: Workman, 2001.

Justice With Her Eyes Wide Open

Kelsey, Mavis P. Sr. and Dyal, Donald H. *The Courthouses of Texas: A Guide*. College Station: Texas A&M University Press, 1993.
Texas Courthouses.com. www.texascourthouses.com/.

Waylon and Willie and "Good Hearted Woman"

Horstman, Dorothy. *Sing Your Heart Out, Country Boy*. Nashville, Tennessee: Country Music Foundation, 1996.
Texas Heritage Music Foundation. www.texasheritagemusic.org/.

Blind Lemon Jefferson and "Leadbelly"

Koster, Rick. *Texas Music*. New York: St. Martin's Press, 1998.
Rock and Roll Hall of Fame and Museum. Leadbelly. www.rockhall.com/hof/inductee.asp?id=140.

"Texas, Our Texas:" The Texas Music Office

Barkley, Roy, et al. eds. *The Handbook of Texas Music*. Austin: Texas State Historical Association, 2003.
Texas Music Office. Texas Music History Tour. Pioneers of Texas Music. www.governor.state.tx.us/music/.

7

TEXAS-STYLE JUSTICE

"He's Innocent and He Has a Piece of Paper to Prove It"

- Why did the Texas Constitution become the nation's second longest constitution with more than 400 amendments and 80,000 words?
- Is justice "for sale" in Texas because elected judges can take campaign contributions from lawyers with cases before their courts?
- What do you need to know about Texas law when you turn eighteen?
- How does the "Value Ladder" determine penalties for crimes like burglary, theft, shoplifting, and embezzlement in Texas?
- With just China and the State of California incarcerating more prisoners than Texas, how many prisoners and prisons does Texas have?
- What crime are Texans arrested for more than any other?
- Under the Driver Responsibility Program, how much does it cost Texans for accumulating eight points of moving violations on their driving records during a 36-month period?
- What has the pro-business Texas Legislature ever done to aid consumers?
- Can a creditor seize your car and your Individual Retirement Account in Texas under a judgment for a debt?
- If you don't own anything but an old beat-up Martin guitar, why should you make a will in Texas?

THE SECOND LONGEST CONSTITUTION
IN THE UNITED STATES

In September 2003, Texas radio broadcasts, television commercials, and bumper stickers promoted the slogan "Save Your Doctor!" It sounded like physicians were in imminent danger. Sara Koehn, a *Dallas Morning News* commentator, with tongue in cheek, worried that physicians would soon be on the street corner with a cardboard sign: "Will write prescriptions for food." For Texas voters who regularly participate in elections to change the constitution, the threat to doctors constituted political hype expected from interest groups clashing over constitutional amendments. Texas legislators placed twenty-two constitutional amendments on the ballot in 2003.

Since declaring independence from Britain 228 years ago, the United States government operated under two constitutions and amended the present constitution twenty-seven times. The U.S. Constitution consists of about 7,000 words written in general terms. Since Texas won independence from Mexico 168 years ago, leaders wrote six constitutions and amended the present constitution more than 400 times.

The Texas Constitution contains more than 80,000 words and grows each legislative session. The number of words and amendments, the level of detail, and the out-of-date "deadwood" provisions make the Texas Constitution disorganized, difficult to read, and hard for courts to interpret. So far, the State of Alabama spares Texas the embarrassment of having the longest state constitution; Alabama's Constitution contains 310,296 words. Today, Texas rarely prints the full document. The ten to twenty proposed biennial amendments get printed in almanacs and newspapers, and the Legislature maintains the complete constitution at their web site.

On the surface, the Texas Constitution appears to be similar to the U.S. Constitution. It creates three branches of government: an Executive, Legislative, and Judicial branch. Like the U.S. Constitution, it also provides a Bill of Rights, a separation of powers, and a form of checks and balances.

But in authority to manage the affairs of state, the two constitutions differ substantially. The crucial difference between the U.S. Congress and the Texas Legislature lies in the broad power Congress has to make laws that are "necessary and proper" to govern the country. The framers of the 1876 Texas Constitution focused intensely on limiting governing authority, and they spelled out many specific actions the Legislature cannot take. Koehn suggests that leaders so restricted the power of state government that "whenever our Legislature wants to do something, we have to amend the darn thing."

The Texas Constitution of 1876 set aside 3 million acres of Pandhandle land to provide for construction of a new Capitol. The new structure, completed in 1888, was made from "Sunset Red" granite from the Marble Falls area. From the collections of The Dallas/Texas History and Archives Division, Dallas Public Library.

Critics of the Legislature have pointed out the flaws in the system. Unlike many states, Texas functions with a biennial legislature, low salaries, a relatively weak governor, elected judges, and unreformed county government. The disorganization, chaos, and antics of the legislators led columnist Molly Ivins to declare the Texas Legislature the "finest free entertainment in Texas. Better than the zoo. Better than the circus."

Finding Anything

Vernon's Annotated Constitution of the State of Texas (1984) published in four volumes by the West Publishing Company contains commentary on the original meaning and historical development of the Texas Constitution. This work provides annotations with comparisons to other state constitutions.

To see the complete Texas Constitution with all current amendments, go to the web site of the Texas Legislature at www.capitol.state.tx.us/txconst/toc.html. While the Legislature is in session, this web site provides useful updates on proposed amendments to the constitution and highlights of bills and pending legislation.

DO THE SCALES OF TEXAS JUSTICE WEIGH CAMPAIGN CONTRIBUTIONS?

Texas courthouses contain statues, murals, and symbols of a blindfolded figure of Justice balancing scales between competing interests and points of view. Critics of the practice of electing, rather than appointing, judges frequently allege that the size of a campaign contribution tilts the scales of Texas justice. Lawyers and judges who work under the system insist the critics are dead wrong to attack a system blessed by the Texas Constitution.

Opponents of electing judges often illustrate their view of the corrupting influence of campaign contributions by pointing to a series of lawsuits known collectively as the Texaco/Pennzoil "case." In March 1984, Pennzoil filed suit against Texaco alleging that Texaco had interfered with its takeover of Getty Oil. They charged Texaco with interfering with the "handshake deal" of J. Hugh Liedtke, the head of Pennzoil, to acquire the major interest in the Getty Oil Company.

Pennzoil hired the trial law firm of Joe Jamail of Houston to try the case in Texas district court under District Judge Anthony Farris. On March 7, 1984, Jamail contributed $10,000 to Judge Farris' election campaign after the filing of the suit. Jamail also served on the steering committee of the Judge's reelection campaign. As the trial progressed, Farris, who refused to disqualify himself, ruled several times in favor of Pennzoil. *The Wall Street Journal* reported that Pennzoil lawyers also contributed more than $300,000 to Texas Supreme Court Justices during the three years of litigation. Without ever holding a hearing, the Texas Supreme Court refused to hear Texaco's appeal of the decision. Pennzoil's trophy turned out to be the largest judgment for damages in history. The chairman of the Legislature's Jurisprudence Committee, Senator Frank Tejada, observed that the "appearance is that justice is for sale."

In 1995, responding to public concern over the integrity of its court system, the Legislature acted by passing the Judicial Campaign Fairness Act (JCFA). This act placed a limit on individual contributions in each election to $5,000. The act limited law firms from contributing more than $30,000 to individual Supreme Court candidates, and it placed a total fund limit of $300,000 a judicial candidate can accept from all political action committees. Even after passage of the act, some attorneys with cases pending before judges participated in fundraising activities for the judge.

More than a century after Judge Roy Bean became "the law west of the Pecos," the *Wall Street Journal* suggested that the "image of hang- 'em-high-justice still clings to the courts of Texas." They openly exclaimed that Pennzoil's "unbroken string of victories in the Texas State courts" was tainted by big-money politics.

Finding Anything

Texas Politics (2002) by Richard Kraemer, Charldean Newell, and David Prindle provides a candid analysis of political affairs of the state, including the selection of judges, by three political scientists. The book provides illustrations, charts, population estimates, revenue data, and political cartoons. The authors examine all six Texas constitutions and provide the chronological context.

For a look at the Texas court system, go to the web site of the Texas Judiciary Online at www.courts.state.tx.us/. This site provides a description of the two primary types of Texas courts, trial courts and appellate courts. The site provides a wide array of links to important judicial information such as foster care, indigent issues, parental notification issues, and many legal publications. Select the Overview of Texas Courts for a broad perspective on all the parts of the system.

"PAINFUL LESSONS ON THE ROAD TO MATURITY"

Turning eighteen in Texas constitutes a crucial divide in the law. For most purposes, a citizen becomes an adult under Texas law with the exception of consumption of alcoholic beverages. Texas law sometimes administers "painful lessons on the road to maturity." Becoming familiar with some of the typical lessons eighteen-year-olds have learned from firsthand experience with the Texas legal system may prevent the consequences of ignorance of the law from being exacted.

Young adults interact frequently with traffic law enforcement and the results may not be positive. Consider the case of a twenty-one-year-old college student who lent his driver's license to his nineteen-year-old brother for the weekend. When police stopped the younger brother for speeding, he showed them his brother's license, which was restricted for glasses. The officer ticketed him for speeding and not wearing glasses.

Under Texas law, both brothers then had a problem. If they kept silent about the deception, the elder brother would have two tickets on his driving record, and the Department of Public Safety would suspend his license for driving without wearing glasses. If they told the truth, the younger brother would get a ticket for speeding and a ticket for presenting someone else's license. The police then would charge the older brother for allowing his license to be used by another, and they both could lose their licenses. The consequences of the deception turned out to be both expensive and time-consuming.

Ten or more infractions often result in suspension of a driver's license in Texas. If a driver receives four moving violations in a year or seven within two years, the DPS suspends the license for one year. Drivers responsible for death or serious personal injury in an accident, driving with a suspended license, violating license restrictions, and driving while intoxicated generally receive license suspensions. Failure to carry liability insurance, ignoring out-of-state tickets, and conviction of a drug offense usually result in license suspension.

Living arrangements with the opposite sex often generate problems for young adults, and some of these situations have serious responsibilities and legal consequences. Distinguishing "living together openly" with another person from a legal "common law marriage" has consequences in Texas law. Two criteria determine a common law marriage in Texas: living together for a "reasonable period of time" and "holding yourself out to others as being married." A woman using a man's last name or a couple introducing each other as husband and wife are examples of "holding yourself out to others as being married." Using "Mr. and Mrs." on checking accounts, credit cards, and leases furnishes additional evidence. Filing a joint tax return with the Internal Revenue Service just about seals a common law marriage.

Weapons violations laws are sometimes confusing to young adults. "Certain weapons are always illegal to possess. Other weapons are legal to possess only in certain circumstances. In Texas, it is never legal to possess, manufacture, transport, or sell machine guns, sawed-off shotguns, silencers, switchblade knives, and explosive weapons like grenades or rockets. A spear, a sword, a dagger, a bowie knife, and a knife with a blade longer than 5½ inches are considered "legal weapons with restrictions." They cannot be carried "on your person."

Finding Anything

What Every 18-Year-Old Needs to Know about Texas Law (1997) by
L. Jean Wallace provides a practical, short introduction to Texas law written in understandable language. This book focuses on legal issues a young
person starting out might encounter, like how apartment leases and deposits work, how real "Miranda warning" works, alcohol related charges,
and consumer laws. The Texas Lawyers Auxiliary annually mails a booklet called *Now You Are 18* to all graduating seniors in Texas. The booklet
provides a useful updated summary of the information in this book.

To obtain online access to *What Every 18-Year-Old Needs to Know
about Texas* Law, go to the TexShare database web site through a Texas
public library at www.texshare.edu. Secure a password and find the
complete book in the netLibrary database, an electronic library of
19,000 full-text books. Most Texas public libraries provide free access to
this service.

THE TEXAS PENAL CODE AND THE "VALUE LADDER"

Establishment of a workable penal code in Texas had to overcome the
frontier legacy of lawlessness, violence, and vigilante justice. Easy access
to weapons settled disputes quickly and avenged slights to reputation and
honor. Vigilance committees operated all over Texas. In November 1875
in Bastrop County, a mob lynched a white man named Cordell for being a
"hereditary horse thief." The next year in Fort Griffin, a man caught stealing a horse was hanged from a pecan tree. The executioners left a shovel
leaning against the tree for anyone who saw fit to bury the thief. Clearly,
justice had a long way to go, but Texas jurists took up the challenge.

Texas instituted a revised Penal Code on September 1, 1994. The Texas
Punishments Standards Commission established a system of "prohibitions,
penalties, and correctional measures" to deter conduct harmful to individuals or the public. The commission envisioned the new code achieving
three objectives: to provide the criminal justice system with the power of
deterrence, the possibility of rehabilitation for offenders, and punishments
sufficient to prevent recurrence of criminal behavior.

Under the old penal code, every specific offense had a specified punishment. Each crime and its punishment were written into a statute. With
ninety or more major types of crimes and many more minor ones, this
arrangement became confusing.

The new code simplified Texas crimes and punishments by creating a system with two major categories: felonies and misdemeanors. The commission classified felonies as the most serious criminal conduct. They first subdivided felonies by the nature and seriousness of the crime into capital felonies requiring life or death sentences. Then, for less serious felonies, they created first-, second-, or third-degree felonies requiring fines and sentence to a penitentiary. For nonviolent criminal offenses, they created a system of state jail felonies requiring 180 days to two years in a state jail. The code placed lesser crimes into a class called misdemeanors: Class A, Class B, and Class C misdemeanors requiring short jail terms and fines ranging from $500 to $4,000.

Citizens of Texas reported a total of 1,005,673 burglaries, thefts, and motor vehicle thefts in 2002, with a property loss of $1.8 billion. Criminals convicted for these offenses receive a sentence according to a "Value Ladder," based on the fair market value of the property at the time it was taken. Property worth less than $20 is normally a Class C misdemeanor; property valued at $20 to $500 is a Class B misdemeanor; and property $500 to $1,500 in value is a Class A misdemeanor.

All property thefts above $1,500 are felonies. From $1,500 to $20,000, the penalty is a state jail felony. Property valued from $20,000 to $100,000 is a third-degree felony; and property valued from $100,000 to $200,000 is a second-degree felony. At the top of the punishment ladder are all first-degree property crimes where the value of the property taken exceeds $200,000.

Finding Anything

Texas Law in Layman's Language (1999) by Charles Turner and Ralph Walton surveys several fundamental issues in Texas criminal justice. Along with discussions of family law, wills and estates, and law in the workplace, the authors describe the Texas Penal Code. They provide more than ninety practical definitions of the most commonly recurring crimes in Texas.

For the full-text official copy of the Texas Penal Code, go to the Table of Contents page of the code which is found at the Legislature's web site at www.capitol.state.tx.us/statutes/petoc.html. From the Table of Contents page, it is easy to navigate through the various chapters, articles, and sections of the code even though the code is filled with many pages of legal and technical definitions.

"A BIBLE IN ONE HAND AND A BASEBALL BAT IN THE OTHER"

One of the founding fathers of the modern Texas Prison System, George J. Beto, earned the reputation of "a preacher with a baseball bat in one hand and a Bible in the other." As an ordained Lutheran minister and college president, he brought a spirit of reform to Texas prisons. As a legacy, he created the Institute of Contemporary Corrections and Behavioral Sciences at Sam Houston State University, which bears his name. When he died on December 4, 1991, the Texas prison system contained 48,000 inmates.

In just ten years, the prison population exploded 212 percent. Texas entered the twenty-first century managing approximately 110 public and private prison facilities distributed across the state, incarcerating almost 150,000 convicted felons. Eighty-four of these facilities met the criteria as prisons. Twenty-six institutions ranked as state jails for the incarceration of non-violent offenders who "commit low-level, nonviolent property crimes or drug offenses." The Texas prison system operated its own hospital in Galveston and employed 200 physicians, 1,300 nurses, 100 dentists, and 20 pharmacists.

In 1999, researchers found Texas's 150,000 inmates represented approximately 12 percent of the entire prison population of the United States. The incarceration rate in Texas exceeded the rate of all other recorded rates in the United States since the federal government began keeping records. The rate of 659 convicts for every 100,000 population constitutes another Texas "first." The average incarceration rate of all U.S. states is 388 per 100,000 of population, making the Texas rate of incarceration almost twice the national average. Not surprisingly, the Texas Department of Criminal Justice employs a staff of more than 42,000 and operates on an annual budget of more than $2 billion, making it the single largest Texas State Agency.

In 2002, the Texas Criminal Justice System incarcerated 150,000 prisoners for a wide variety of crimes. In Texas, the Department of Public Safety collects, organizes, and reports crime data.

In the class of most serious crimes, citizens reported a total of 1,137,806 serious crimes to police. Violent crimes against individuals of murder, rape, robbery, and assault constituted 122,108, while reports of property crime reached 1,015,697. Nineteen percent of these crimes resulted in an arrest. Law enforcement arrested 111,836 individuals for narcotics charges and 91,429 for driving under the influence (DUI).

Statewide, the Texas Department of Public Safety tabulated 1,417 murders, 7,986 rapes, 75,706 aggravated assaults, and 183,440 incidents of family violence. In property crime, there were 697,790 incidents of theft, 219,733 burglaries, and 98,174 automobile thefts. There were approximately 37,000 robberies. The value of stolen property totaled nearly $2 billion. Undoubtedly, crime and crime detection constitute two of the largest enterprises in Texas.

Finding Anything

Lone Star Justice: A Comprehensive Overview of the Texas Criminal Justice System (1999) by David M. Horton and Ryan Kellus Turner analyzes the origins and present operations of the Texas criminal justice system. The authors describe the Texas court system and the growth and development of the Texas prison system.

For up-to-date information on the Texas Department of Criminal Justice, go directly to the home page of their web site at www.tdcj.state.tx .us/. The web site provides access to all their publications, including their official newsletter. All of the 111 component prison facilities are linked to this site.

TEXAS SCHEDULES OF "CONTROLLED SUBSTANCES"

Texas's reputation as a hard-drinking state where saloons sprang up on the frontier like cacti and mesquite trees remains alive and well. One current web site for a distiller of a "mesquite-mellowed whiskey" claims that one Texas town in the late 1800s had eight saloons serving a population of 892 residents. True or not, more Texans today are arrested for the offense of public intoxication than for any other crime. In 2003 alone, authorities arrested 130,984 individuals for public intoxication, the crime which perennially tops the list. But Texans also are arrested for offenses arising from the use of "controlled substances," and the total number of these arrests increased 9.1 percent from 2001 to 2002.

Texas law follows U.S. law in classifying all legal and illegal drugs called "controlled substances" into five "schedules." Thousands of drugs are assigned a classification according to their potential for addiction or abuse and their "acceptable medical use."

Author and criminologist James Inciardi describes drug scheduling provisions in the *War on Drugs II*. Schedule I contains drugs the government judges to have high potential for abuse, no currently acceptable medical use in the United States, and no acceptable safe level of medical use under medical supervision. Possession, distribution, or trafficking in Schedule I drugs incur the most severe penalties. Drugs like heroin, LSD, certain amphetamines and methamphetamines like "Ecstasy," and marijuana currently receive Schedule I designation.

All remaining drugs fall into Schedules II to V, depending upon their potential for addiction or possible medical application. Cocaine, morphine, and codeine have seriously addicting properties, but these drugs have limited, acceptable medical uses so they are included in Schedule II. Schedules III and IV include various anti-depressant medications, tranquilizers, and anti-anxiety drugs like valium, xanax, and librium that normally can be authorized by a physician with one prescription and up to four refills.

In the year 2003, Texas law enforcement officers made 111,836 arrests for all types of drug abuse violations covered under Texas laws. Drug possession charges accounted for 99,721 arrests. Selling and manufacturing drugs accounted for the remaining 12,115 arrests. Marijuana possession charges accounted for 57 percent of all possession cases followed by 27 percent for cocaine or opium possession. Six percent of the arrests occurred for synthetic narcotics, and the remaining 10 percent of arrests covered a variety of substances from inhalants, steroids, methamphetamines, and prescription medications.

The Texas Health and Safety Code requires all Texas law enforcement agencies to make monthly reports on all arrests for drug offenses and on quantities of controlled substances seized during the preceding month. In 2003, state officers seized 521,422 pounds of marijuana, 929,233 dosage units of designer drugs, and 13,943 pounds of cocaine.

Agents seized a wide variety of additional drugs including heroin, morphine, codeine, PCP, mushrooms, peyote, and barbiturates, and they shut down 717 clandestine drug laboratories in Texas, with 710 producing methamphetamines. Considering the fact that none of these data includes drug seizures by federal agencies, there is a Lone Star State controlled substances problem.

Finding Anything

Vernon's Texas Statutes and Codes Annotated published by West Publishing provides authoritative updates to Texas laws and creates annotations to relevant court cases. The Texas Legislature attempted to revise all its statutes beginning in 1963. It directed the Texas Legislative Council to carry out a "formal revision" of Texas statutes to make them generally "more accessible, understandable, and usable." To date they have completed and published seventeen revised codes.

For the most recent annual data and analysis of Texas crime, see the online version of *Crime in Texas*. The Department of Public Safety makes the full report available at www.txdps.state.tx.us/crimereports/03/2003 index.htm.

DRIVING A VEHICLE BY THE POINT SYSTEM

Texans interact with the Department of Public Safety more than any other state agency. The Department enforces Texas law, provides assistance with motor vehicle problems, and issues licenses. As part of a massive transportation bill in 2002, the Legislature established the Texas Driver Responsibility program in Texas House Bill 3588. The law affects all Texans who operate a motor vehicle. The program went into effect September 1, 2003. The program grew out the state's need to finance the Trans-Texas Corridor project and emergency trauma centers.

For every conviction an individual receives for certain moving violations during a 36-month period, the Department of Public Safety assigns points to the driving record. The Department levies points for moving violations in the Class C misdemeanor category like speeding and other specified driving offenses.

A person convicted for speeding in Texas or another state, for example, accumulates two points for each final conviction. If the moving violation or speeding results in a vehicle crash, then the Department of Public Safety adds three points to the driving record. Seat belt convictions do not accumulate points, nor do speeding convictions if the person travels less than 10 percent over the posted limit. At the end of each year, the Department of Public Safety reviews the points accumulated during the previous thirty-six months of driving. When individuals accumulate a total of six points, they are required to pay a $100 surcharge to the Department of Public Safety. If they exceed six points, they pay a surcharge of $25 for each additional point. An individual who accumulates eight points pays a $150 surcharge.

For certain types of convictions, drivers will pay annual surcharges for a period of three years. DWI or DWI related offenses, failing to maintain financial responsibility, or driving with an invalid license fall into this category. For a first-time DWI conviction, the department assesses a surcharge of $1,000 annually for three years. If a driver acquires a second DWI conviction, the surcharge escalates to $1,500 per year. The surcharge is cumulative, and so a person could pay $2,500 annually for a second DWI. The Department of Public Safety sign, "DWI, You Can't Afford It," is more than a public relations campaign. The surcharges stack on top of any fines, court cost, probation fees, or restitution that a local jurisdiction levies for the offense.

The surcharge for driving with an invalid license and without financial responsibility is $250 annually for three years. Driving with an invalid license by itself is $100 per year for three years. The Department of Public Safety notifies offenders of assessments by first-class mail. Failure to pay the assessments results in revocation of the driving privilege.

Finding Anything

The *Texas Criminal and Traffic Law Manual, 2003–2004 Revised Edition* published biennially by LexisNexis includes all new or amended criminal and traffic laws passed by the Texas Legislature in the latest session. It contains the exact legislative language of the Driver Responsibility Program.

To keep track of changes in traffic laws, crime rates, and the major legal issues related to crime in Texas, see the web site of the Department of Public Safety. The agency maintains an archive of all press releases containing simple explanations of new laws. At the close of the legislative session, the Department issues a summary of new criminal laws passed by the legislature. The agency web site is www.txdps.state.tx.us/.

"I DEMAND A REFUND": THE TEXAS *DECEPTIVE TRADE PRACTICES ACT*

The Lone Star State has a long history of pro-business, laissez-faire support of the oil, agriculture, banking, and insurance industries, but Texans may not know the steps the state has taken to protect consumers from unfair trade practices. Texas has one of the strongest consumer protection laws in the nation called the *Deceptive Trade Practices-Consumer Protection Act*. Consumers understanding the provisions of this act can enhance their effectiveness in negotiating successful purchases.

The law covers a wide range of practices considered false, misleading, deceptive, or unlawful that sellers of consumer goods might do to harm a consumer. The act lists twenty-five specific misleading practices and transactions illegal in buyer-seller relationships and provides remedies consumers may take when they occur. The list covers everything from selling a house, to selling a bicycle in a garage sale, or taking advantage of someone caught in a state-declared emergency. People, who are buying or selling merchandise, need to know the wide authority of this law.

In sales transactions, whether in a flea market, a business establishment, or a garage sale, this law supports a consumer's right to have a complete and accurate statement of the condition of the merchandise. If you buy a used car and a week later you are facing a $1,200 transmission repair bill, the seller normally cannot claim exemption from responsibility because you failed to ask about it. The law makes it unlawful to fail to disclose defects in merchandise, especially if disclosure would have prevented the consumer from entering the transaction.

The Deceptive Trade Practices Act prohibits fraudulent activities from promoting a "pyramid scheme" to falsely advertising a "going out of business" sale. The act provides remedies for the consumer by making the perpetrator liable through "no-fault." This feature of the law usually means the instigator does not have to violate the law intentionally or know he is doing it to be held responsible. A person who violates the law may be responsible for up to three times the actual damages plus all court costs and attorney fees.

Finding Anything

Know Your Rights! Answers to Texans' Everyday Legal Questions (2000) by Richard M. Alderman explains the Texas *Deceptive Trade Practices Act.* Using case studies and a question and answer format, the author explains how the law works in Texas, how to file a claim, sample letters to use, and other information tips. The author covers many other areas of Texas law including debt collection, divorce and custody, credit cards, banking, bankruptcy, and other practical subjects.

The complete copy of the Texas Deceptive Trade Practices Act is available at the Texas Legislature's web site at www.capitol.state.tx.us/. Deceptive trade practices are covered under Chapter 17 in the Business and Commerce Code. For information on how to file a claim in a small claims court, how to work with a lawyer, and how to locate publications prepared by attorneys on consumer issues, also check the web site of the State Bar of Texas at www.texasbar.com/.

TWO HORSES, TWO MULES, TWO DONKEYS, AND 120 FOWL

Texas law affords consumers another important protection in the form of a limited protection of personal property for payment of a debt owed. The law sets limits on how much personal property a creditor may take in discharging a debt owed. Section 42.001 of the Texas Property Code describes this protection under the "personal property exemption." It declares that certain personal property is "exempt from garnishment, attachment, execution or seizure" if the property meets certain conditions.

The law places a financial ceiling of $30,000 on the fair market value of the exempt property that can be shielded. If "the property is provided for a family" and has a value of not more than $60,000 exclusive of any liens, it is considered exempt. If owned by a single adult, who is not a member of a family, personal property with an aggregate fair market value of $30,000, and no liens upon it, is legally exempt.

The law exempts several types of personal property from seizure over and above the financial limitations. It excludes current wages for personal services except for the enforcement of court-ordered child support; professionally prescribed health aids of a debtor or dependent; and it excludes alimony, child support, or maintenance for the support of the debtor or debtor's dependents.

Section 42.002 of the Texas Property Code lists specific items of personal property that are exempt from seizure under the $60,000 or $30,000 limits. The statute allows exemptions for home furnishings, heirlooms, "provisions for consumption," equipment used in farming and ranching vehicles, tools, books, motor vehicles, and boats used in a trade or profession. It excludes wearing apparel and jewelry up to 25 percent of the limitation, two firearms, athletic and sporting equipment such as bicycles. The law allows an exemption for a two-wheeled, three-wheeled, or four-wheeled motor vehicle for each member of a family.

The law reflects the agricultural and ranching heritage of Texas. It exempts animals and any "forage on hand" for the animal's consumption. It includes two horses, two mules, or two donkeys, and a saddle, blanket, and bridle for each. The code exempts 12 head of cattle, 60 head or other types of livestock, 120 fowl, and all household pets. The present value of any life insurance policy is protected as long as a dependent remains the beneficiary of the policy. Since 1987, Individual Retirement Accounts (IRAs) have been exempted along with the traditional Texas homestead exemption provided by the Texas Constitution.

Finding Anything

The *Texas Consumer Law Handbook* (2003) by Stephen G. Cochran contains an extensive list of the consumer-related statutes and regulations applicable to all Texans from both state and federal regulatory bodies. It covers a wide range of consumer transactions from joining a health spa, contest giveaways, mobile home standards, and "lemon" laws up through debt collection, credit reporting, credit cards, and bankruptcy.

To find out about specific Texas consumer protection credit issues, go to the web site of the Office of Consumer Credit Commissioner at www.occc.state.tx.us/. The site provides assistance with consumer brochures, publications, legal statutes, and administrative rules governing credit protections. A complete copy of the Texas Finance Code is available at this site. Title Five of this code is "Protection of Consumers of Financial Services."

WHO WILL GET WHAT AND WHEN?

The contested will of Lon Gresham of Terrell, Texas, constitutes a good example of why a well-written, well-executed will may avoid much legal time, money, and confusion in the Lone Star State. Documents filed on appeal to the Texas Supreme Court tell the story of Gresham's "homemade will," the story of a man who tried to save money by leaving instructions on how to distribute his assets in a letter.

Fearing that something "might happen" to him and that he might be "wiped out," Lon Gresham on January 12, 1950, sat down and wrote a letter on what to do in the event of his death. Lon probably did not have a lot of respect for lawyers. He believed that "crooked lawyers" would want to add a lot of "whereas and wherefores" to it. Lon desired his "affairs wound up in a reasonable way" in case of his sudden death. Lon put his letter away for a bit, read it again, and decided that it "seemed about right."

In the letter, Lon named U.C. Boyles Refrigeration Supply Co. and Charlie Hill Superior Ice Co. recipients of all his "affairs, cash, all assets." He asked that everything he had be turned over to Boyles and Hill without "any bond or court action that can be avoided." He wrote that these two gentlemen would receive $500 each "to wind up my affairs in any way they see fit."

Lon communicated in his letter some of his wishes on how his property should be distributed. He was "not much in favor" of organized charities because he felt they were too cold blooded. He also did not care much for any person "over 21" benefiting from what he termed his "Kick off." He did reveal a positive regard for children. He concluded the letter by saying he was "inclined to play the children; they are not responsible for being here and can't help themselves." Finally, he believed he had communicated his "wishes plain."

In a legal sense, it took two trips to the Texas Supreme Court to make Lon's wishes plain. To determine if his letter constituted a legal will compelled the first trip. Lon's son, Arch V. Gresham, contested the letter as soon as U.C. Boyles tried to probate it. The Texas Supreme Court finally determined the letter a legal will, but the court found Lon's sentiments in the letter too vague to constitute a legal disposition of property. The court determined Boyles and Hill to be "independent executors," and the court finally ruled Gresham's letter a legal "will which disposed of no property but appointed executors to administer the estate."

There are some good reasons for making out a will in Texas even if the property left is only a beat-up Martin guitar. Since execution of a well-thought-out will provides for an orderly exit from life, everyone involved, including the maker of the will, avoids time, money, worry, and anxiety over what to do in the absence of one. A will may be the most important legal document many people ever execute, and it deserves some thought and care. A will containing unambiguous provisions for the transmitting of property from the maker to surviving family and instructions for disposition of debt can be a valuable legacy.

Dying without a will prohibits choice as to who administers the estate, who receives property, in what amounts, and how and when this is to take place. These conditions leave open the opportunity to bequeath a lot of pain and suffering on loved ones left behind. Lon Gresham's heirs can testify to it.

Finding Anything

How to Live—and Die—With Texas Probate. 7th Edition (1995) edited by Charles A. Saunders provides an easy-to-use guide to wills and probate in Texas. The book supplies practical advice about what a will should contain, selection of executor, tax issues, and the costs of probating a will. More than twenty contributors to this volume are members of the State Bar of Texas.

For a practical guide to preparing your own Texas will, whether using an attorney or not, see the electronic book *How to Make a Texas Will: With Forms* (1998) by Karen Ann Rolcik and Mark Warda. See the netLibrary database of electronic books at the TexShare web site at www.texshare.

edu/. Authorization to use electronic books is provided through the TexShare Library consortium by means of a password furnished by Texas public libraries.

BOOKS AND WEB SITES

The Second Longest Constitution in the United States

The Constitution of the State of Texas. www.capitol.state.tx.us/txconst/toc. html.

Vernon's Annotated Constitution of the State of Texas. Four Volumes. St. Paul Minnesota: West Publishing Company, 1984.

Do the Scales of Texas Justice Weigh Campaign Contributions?

Kraemer, Richard, Newell, Charldean, and Prindle, David. *Texas Politics*. Eighth Edition. Belmont, CA: Wadworth, 2002.

Texas Judiciary Online. Overview of Texas Courts. www.courts.state.tx.us/.

"Painful Lessons on the Road to Maturity"

Wallace, L. Jean. *What Every 18-Year-Old Needs to Know about Texas Law*. University of Texas Press, 1997.

What Every 18-Year-Old Needs to Know about Texas Law. netLibrary. www.texshare.edu/.

The Texas Penal Code and the "Value Ladder"

Turner, Charles and Walton, Ralph. *Texas Law in Layman's Language*. Sixth Edition. Houston, Texas: Lone Star Books, 1999.

The Texas Penal Code. www.capitol.state.tx.us/statutes/petoc.html.

"A Bible in One Hand and a Baseball Bat in the Other"

Horton, David M. and Turner, Ryan Kellus. *Lone Star Justice: A Comprehensive Overview of the Texas Criminal Justice System*. Austin, Texas: Eakin Press, 1999.

Texas Department of Criminal Justice. www.tdcj.state.tx.us/.

Texas Schedules of "Controlled Substances"

Crime in Texas 2003. Austin, Texas: Texas Department of Public Safety. 2004.
Crime in Texas. 2003. www.txdps.state.tx.us/crimereports/03/2003index
.htm.

Driving a Vehicle by the Point System

Texas Criminal and Traffic Law Manual. Albany, New York: LexisNexis, 2003.
Texas Department of Public Safety. www.txdps.state.tx.us/.

"I Demand a Refund": The Texas *Deceptive Trade Practices Act*

Alderman, Richard M. *Know Your Rights! Answers to Texans' Everyday Legal
Questions*. Houston, Texas: Gulf Publishing, 2000.
State Bar of Texas. www.texasbar.com/.

Two Horses, Two Mules, Two Donkeys, and 120 Fowl

Cochran, Stephen G. *Texas Consumer Law Handbook*. St. Paul, Minnesota: West
Group, 2001.
Office of Consumer Credit Commissioner. www.occc.state.tx.us/.

Who Will Get What and When?

Rolcik, Karen Ann and Warda, Mark. *How to Make a Texas Will. With Forms.*
netLibrary. www.texshare.edu/.
Saunders, Charles A. ed. *How to Live—and Die—With Texas Probate*. 7th
Edition. Houston, Texas: Gulf Publishing, 1995.

8

"I'M FROM THE GOVERNMENT AND I'M HERE TO HELP YOU"

- Which Texas agency employed short story writer O. Henry as a draftsman providing him the setting for two short stories?
- How can you find state requirements to become a barber and set up a barbershop in Texas?
- What Texas physician invented the word "aerobics" and designed a fitness program that earned him the title of the "Father of Aerobics?"
- Where can you get business assistance in Texas for a genetically-engineered cotton fabric for your new line of bullet-proof fashions?
- Who drilled the first successful oil well in Texas?
- What was significant about the discovery of oil on widow Daisy Bradford's East Texas farm?
- How did a Texas agency formed to regulate railroads end up controlling oil, gas, liquefied petroleum, coal, and uranium?
- What is meant by the "Southwest effect" in the U.S. aviation industry?
- Is the typical job in the Texas economy of the future destined to be a McJob?
- How many people will you have to share Texas with in 2020?

MURDER IN THE GENERAL LAND OFFICE

Obtaining assistance from Texas state agencies requires knowledge of where to go to find aid and patience to persevere in the paperwork. Consider the plight of John H. Lockhart, a Republic of Texas veteran from Dover Hill, Indiana, who applied for his entitlement to 640 acres of land on January 4, 1861. His frustration with Texas bureaucracy began when he served in the revolution without pay and "never got one solitary cent from the Republic of Texas in the way of monthly pay."

The Commissioner of Claims of the Texas General Land Office required an "audited certificate" of pay records before he could process Lockhart's claim. Lockhart expressed his opinion that "an honest man, with all the evidence in the world, cannot get his right" while a "Rascal and Bloodsucker, can step in without the least shadow of truth and justice on his side, and sweep the platter." He volunteered that he simply could not "understand the manner in which business has been transacted" in Texas. Unfortunately, Lockhart failed to obtain his claim.

One of the first acts of the Congress of the Republic of Texas created the General Land Office. After independence from Mexico, the necessity to distinguish privately owned land with Spanish and Mexican titles from public domain land dominated the work of the agency. Texas entered the Union in 1845 with 200 million acres of public land, and the state charged the General Land Office with the responsibility of managing these lands.

American short story writer O. Henry worked as a young man in the General Land Office. At the age of twenty, William Sydney Porter left his home in Greensboro, North Carolina, to visit some family friends on a ranch in LaSalle County. He herded sheep, learned some of the ranch life, and absorbed some of the culture and characters who would show up in his later stories about Texas. When his friend Dick Hall became Land Commissioner in 1887, Porter went to work as a draftsman in the General Land Office in Austin. He worked at this position until Hall's term ended in 1891.

Porter found employment in a dynamic, active bureaucracy at a time when Texas experienced explosive growth. The Land Office distributed 70 million acres of land to settlers and 10 million acres in military bounties and donations to veterans. It granted another 30 million acres to railroads and made sizable grants to improve roads, irrigation, navigation, ships, and manufacturing. The state set the rest aside for educational endowments and dedicated projects. O. Henry worked at a small drafting desk in the Old Land Office among millions of maps and documents.

O. Henry's short story "Bexar Scrip No. 2692" about a murder in a land office suggests that he knew which closets contained skeletons. It would require many books to describe "the various schemes and plots that for the sake of the almighty dollar have left their stains upon the records of the General Land Office." Still, O. Henry craved the atmosphere of the land office. He wrote that "when you enter the building, you lower your voice, and time turns backward for you."

Finding Anything

Land: A History of the Texas General Land Office (1992) by Andrea Gurasich Morgan sketches the general history of the General Land Office. The author provides many charts, maps, and data on the impresario grants, reproductions of early documents such as an 1832 Mexican passport, a land scrip signed by Sam Houston, and land district maps. O. Henry's employment experience is illustrated with photographs of the land office buildings and a group photograph of O. Henry and other draftsmen in 1889.

For a comprehensive look at the activities, collections, and services of the Texas General Land Office, check the web site at www.glo.state.tx.us/. The map collection of the land office consists of 50,000 maps, sketches, and documents dating to the 1820s. The site also contains an online history of Texas public lands along with information on agency publications, genealogy research, and land records. They report more than 45,000 records scanned and available online as of 2004. These records constitute one of the state's most valuable sources of genealogy and family history.

BECOMING A CLASS A BARBER IN TEXAS

Texas statutes and the Texas Constitution create so many boards, commissions, and examiners who set the qualifications and standards for entering a vocation or profession that the process can become bewildering, daunting, and confusing. The *Guide to Texas State Agencies* provides a gateway to all information on the licensing requirements for Texas vocations and professions. The barbering profession provides a good example of how to locate the current standards, qualifications, and requirements to enter a profession or vocation in Texas.

The responsibility of keeping track of 23,800 barbers in Texas belongs to a barber board appointed by the governor. The State Board of Barber

Examiners consists of six members. Two members are Class A barbers who have been actively engaged in barbering for at least five years but do not own a barbershop. One member of the board holds a permit, owns a barbershop, and has engaged in barbering for five years. Another member of the board must hold a permit to operate a barber school or college, and two members represent the general public who go to barbershops and get haircuts. The State Board of Barber Examiners administers the Texas Barber Law.

The Barber Board serves as a "hands-on board," and licensed board members observe monthly license examinations, inspect new barber colleges, and barbershops. They issue health certificates for instructors and regularly inspect establishments for compliance with health and sanitation regulations. In setting the standards and qualifications, the board prescribes the detailed requirements for instruction at barber schools, licenses, shop permits, barber college permits, teacher certificates, and student certificates.

What is required to become a Class A barber in Texas? The Barber Board articulates standards and qualifications down to the smallest detail, even to the items a candidate must bring to the examination. When a candidate appears for the examination for a Class A registered barber certificate, he must bring "instruments necessary to give a practical demonstration of barbering services." If the applicant specializes in wigs, he must bring a "male wig not less than five inches in hair length." He must "clean, cut, and complete the style." At the examination, each wears a "clean and fastened barber smock" without a logo and furnishes a model eighteen years or older "on whom to demonstrate the practical work." If the applicant completes this examination successfully, he becomes a Texas Class A barber.

The *Texas Administrative Code* maintained by the Office of the Secretary of State contains all the qualifications and standards for entering all professions and vocations licensed by the State of Texas. Title 22 under Examining Boards lists the detailed requirements for a entering any licensed profession or vocation in Texas. It contains official Texas standards for barbers, dietitians, nurses, midwives, polygraph examiners, appraisers, physical therapists, and social workers, plus many more.

Finding Anything

The *Guide to Texas State Agencies* (2001), published by the Lyndon Baines Johnson School of Public Affairs, provides an explanation of the scope and authority of all major Texas government agencies. It supplies directory information such as address, telephone numbers, toll-free numbers, and fax numbers for each agency. The publication cites references to enabling legislation creating the agency and the chapter titles from the *Texas Administrative Code* of all current regulations in force.

See the web site of the Office of the Texas Secretary of State at www.sos.state.tx.us/tac/ to locate Texas standards for all licensed vocations and professions. The Secretary of State keeps all state administrative regulations current in the *Texas Administrative Code.* The Secretary of State also maintains the *Texas Register* at this web site. Boards and commissions proposing changes to regulations ordinarily must post proposals for at least thirty days for public comment.

PERILS AND PROSPECTS OF STARTING A BUSINESS IN TEXAS

Starting a new business frequently requires challenging old ideas. In 1968, being physically fit in America conjured up images of Charles Atlas and the body-building schools of the 1950s. Working one muscle against another in "dynamic tension," Atlas' devotees aspired to transform their bodies from "scrawny to brawny." Advertisements suggested that a "ninety-seven-pound weakling" could become sufficiently brawny to prevent a bully from kicking sand in his face on a beach. At the time, surveys indicated only 25 percent of men exercised regularly and a mere 100,000 persons jogged.

Kenneth H. Cooper, an Air Force physician, published *Aerobics* in 1968. He advocated oxygen-utilizing endurance activities like jogging as a means to good health. The book permanently changed America's approach to exercise and fitness by initiating an exercise movement focused on producing beneficial changes in the respiratory and circulatory systems through increases in oxygen intake. National and international success of Cooper's book initiated one of the twentieth century's most far-reaching lifestyle changes. It earned him the title of the "Father of Aerobics."

Cooper's personal interest in fitness and preventive medicine began with a waterskiing mishap he experienced as a twenty-eight-year-old, overweight and out of shape U.S. Army physician stationed at Fort Sill, Oklahoma. At 205 pounds, he was 35 pounds heavier than his normal weight. When he tried to slalom like he had as a teenager, he experienced thirty minutes of severe weakness and nausea suggestive of a cardiac arrhythmia. The episode frightened him and changed his life.

A year after his waterskiing experience, Cooper transferred to aviation physiology in the Air Force School of Aerospace Medicine in San Antonio. He embarked on his own exercise and conditioning program, obtained a master's degree from the Harvard School of Public Health, and ran the Boston Marathon. Returning to San Antonio as director of the Aerospace Medical Laboratory, he occasionally endured skeptical comments from his "more sedentary colleagues" about his personal fitness routine. His jogging colleagues known as "Cooper's Poopers" received comments like, "I'd rather die after a good meal than on a running track," or you're "crazy" to be running in this Texas heat.

Less than fifteen years after publication of *Aerobics*, 59 percent of American males exercised regularly and 34 million people jogged. Aerobics so permeated American culture by 1991 that a male contestant on television's "Love Connection" told the host that he wanted a girl with less than 10 percent body fat, a pulse rate of sixty or below, and an exercise program that included some form of "pulmonary conditioning." Aerobics had triumphed!

Cooper left the Air Force in 1970, moved to Dallas, and established a successful preventive medicine practice and facility. He named it The Aerobics Center. He continued to write and lecture extensively on preventive medicine and physical fitness, and newspapers reported him under consideration for the position of U.S. Surgeon General in 2002. It is regrettable that he did not get the job—Americans who keep fit today might receive a tax deduction for a body mass index under 25, blood pressure less than 140 over 90, and cholesterol under 200.

Finding Anything

The Aerobics Program for Total Well-Being: Exercise, Diet, and Emotional Balance (1982) by Kenneth H. Cooper outlines the author's general philosophy of physical fitness. It contains exercise charts for earning aerobic points for walking, running, cycling, swimming, and many other sports. The author explains his ideas on preventive medicine and total fitness, and he describes how they grew out of his research experiences in the U.S. Air Force.

For one of the most extensive web sites on starting a new business in Texas, go to the web site of the Texas Department of Economic Development at www.tded.state.tx.us/. This department houses the Texas Office of Small Business Assistance, which offers packages of business startup information for citizens. On its web site appears a publication called a *Guide to Starting a Business,* a reference guide for new and expanding businesses in Texas. From this web site, the agency furnishes a single list of the name, address, fax, and toll-free telephone number of more than 150 state agencies. It also establishes links to all Chambers of Commerce, City Halls, and County Clerks offices in Texas with addresses, telephone numbers, and web sites.

FROM THE BOLL WEEVIL TO THE COUNTY AGENT

In Tyler, at the corner of Broadway and W. Erwin Street, stands a historical marker entitled "The First County Agricultural Extension Agent." It designates the site of an opera house where Judge S.A. Lindsey met Seaman A. Knapp with forty-four citizens to hire William Crider Stallings for $150 a month to be the first United States County Agent. It could be the best investment the county, or the country, ever made.

The Texas Cooperative Extension Service of Texas A&M University is the largest agricultural and cooperative extension service in the nation. The service employs more than 1,000 faculty and professional staff, and it extends service to more than 10 million Texans annually. Formerly called the Agricultural Extension Service, the service grew out of the idea of "taking the university to the people" and applying knowledge to the practical arts and sciences of living.

Texas A&M University began when the *U.S. Morrill Land-Grant Act of 1862* provided land equal to 30,000 acres for each senator and representative to establish at least one college in each state. Congress intended universities founded under this legislation to teach "branches of learning related to agriculture and the mechanic arts," including "military tactics." After many delays, Texas A&M opened on October 4, 1876, with 106 students and a faculty of six.

The boll weevil infestation of 1903 devastated Texas, and many citizens abandoned farms. The U.S. Department of Agriculture responded by setting up a "demonstration farm" on the East Texas land of Walter C. Porter near Terrell. The success of the farm led to a rise in crop yields, and soon Seaman A. Knapp, the head of the Department of Agriculture, sent out a series of "lecture trains" from Houston to reach farmers with knowledge about how to deal with the boll weevil problem.

In 1906, Knapp hired William Crider Stallings as the first full-time country agent to serve a single county in the United States. Stallings had farmed several plots in Smith County, devoured information on scientific farming, specialized in breeding Poland-China hogs, and acquired a reputation for breeding a fine variety of high-yield corn.

All of these major agricultural innovations—the demonstration farm, the county agent system, "lecture trains," and taking the university directly to the people—became a part of the official mission of Texas A&M University. On January 29, 1915, the Legislature assigned the Texas Agricultural and Extension Service to Texas's oldest public university.

Today, the electronic bookstore of the Cooperative Extension Service of Texas A&M University continues the tradition. It stocks a number of relevant items on genetic engineering of crops. *Explore the Genetic Frontier: Biotechnology & Cotton—Texas' Biggest Crop* might assist anyone with a new business involving cotton. The pamphlet defines biotechnology and explains how modifying the DNA of an organism can make the traditional breeding and selection of plants and animals more useful and beneficial to humans. It describes how *Bt* cotton, a new strain, shows promise for farmers being able to grow "disease-and-drought-resistant cotton with stronger fibers for Texas's 5 million acres of cotton."

Finding Anything

A Centennial History of Texas A&M University, 1876–1976 (1975) by Henry C. Dethloff is a history of Texas A&M University celebrating its first 100 years. The book reveals the philosophy behind the creation of the Cooperative Extension Service and the applied science and technology traditions leading to it.

For a look at how the system currently operates and to obtain information and services, check the web site of the Texas Cooperative Extension, Texas A&M University at http://texasextension.tamu.edu/. This web site provides a central gateway to most of the major services. Two important links on this web site provide access to each county office of the extension service and to the Cooperative Extension Bookstore.

TEXAS'S FIRST GUSHER

The man who drilled the first successful oil well in Texas did not get much assistance from the state of Texas. In fact, the Texas Legislature delayed his permit so long that his investors got cold feet. Lyne Talia-ferro Barret drilled the first successful producing oil well in Texas at a depth of 106 feet in Oil Springs for the Melrose Petroleum Company on September 12, 1866.

As a boy, he and his brothers hunted near Oil Springs where the oil was known to rise to the surface and run into Oil Springs Branch. When Barret decided to drill his well, Colonel Edwin Drake had al-ready discovered oil in Titusville, Pennsylvania, in the experiment known as "Drake's Folly." Another Pennsylvanian, Samuel Kier of Pittsburgh, began producing "Rock Oil," a patent medicine which was a mixture of oil and salt. Kier bottled his oil-salt potion in eight-ounce bottles and advertised it as a liniment and cure-all for cholera, liver complaints, bronchitis, and tuberculosis. The recommended dosage was three teaspoons, three times a day. Kier provided testimonials from individuals who had been healed by this powerful new remedy of "Rock Oil."

Judging from his activities in acquiring leases, Lyne Barret wanted to drill an oil well before the Civil War, but the war interfered with his plans. After the war, he was smitten with oil fever. He wrote a Confederate Army friend that "Texas will be wild upon the subject in a few months." Foreshadowing the tradition of a great oil lease salesman, or an encyclo-pedia salesman, he urged his friend to invest in his Oil Springs project. He asked his friend, what is the use of working so hard for bread when "gold so temptingly invites you to reach out and clutch it?"

Barret finally secured permission to begin the project. He erected a 20-foot wooden tripod, procured an eight-foot screw-like device attached to a pipe and powered the whole configuration by a steam engine. When-ever the drill had to be removed, the crew drove a mule away from the tripod with a rope attached to his harness. The primitive system worked and struck the first producing well in Texas at ten barrels a day.

Unfortunately, Lyne Barret, the wildcatter, suffered the misfortune of many who would follow his path. After striking oil, he rushed off to New York and Pennsylvania to secure investors to put the well in full production. Unfortunately, unsettled conditions in post-Civil War Texas and the low price of oil caused his most promising investors to give up on the Texas project. He returned home, abandoned his oil project, and went into a different line of work. The field he abandoned lay dormant until 1887 when the Petroleum Prospecting Company with $100,000 of capital hit a sizable well about sixty feet from Barret's original site.

Finding Anything

The article by C. K. Chamberlain, "Lyne Toliaferro Barret: A Pioneer Texas Wildcatter," in the *East Texas Historical Journal* (March 1968) provides a detailed look at the drilling of Texas's first producing oil well. The author draws upon letters, photographs, and drawings in university archives to reconstruct the story. The same issue carries an extensive article on Dad Joiner's 1930 discovery of the East Texas Oil field.

For a short sketch of Lyne Taliaferro Barret and his partners in the Melrose Petroleum Company, see the entry in the *Handbook of Texas Online* at the web site www.tsha.utexas.edu/handbook/online/.

WILDCATTERS, DRY HOLES, AND GUSHERS

The petroleum industry catapulted Texas onto the world stage and made the Texas Railroad Commission one of the most powerful agencies in America. The adventures and exploits of a colorful oilman figured prominently in both these developments. In the history of Texas wildcatters and giant oil field discoveries, no name stands taller than Columbus Marion "Dad" Joiner. With help from an oil shaman named "Doc" Lloyd, Joiner discovered the colossal East Texas Oil Field in 1930.

On his third attempt to drill on the widow Daisy Bradford's farm in Rusk County, he discovered the oil well that launched the cataclysmic East Texas oil boom of the 1930s. After H. L. Hunt and other oilmen developed the field, it produced the largest single oil reservoir in the world at the time. It measured 34 miles long, extended 4 to 9 miles wide and comprised 135,000 acres. By 1967, the yield amounted to 3.8 billion barrels.

Myths proliferate about why Dad Joiner selected East Texas as a place to begin his wildcatting operations. One story attributes the discovery to a dream he had in Galveston in 1926. After walking along the seawall, he became despondent and even considered ending his life. Exhausted from travel, he lay down to rest and dreamed he "would discover a big oil field in East Texas!" Upon awakening, he made a detailed sketch of the place: gently rolling hills covered with timber near a small stream. People who believe the story say he took his sketch all over East Texas until he found Daisy Bradford's farm, the place of his dream.

This story belongs more to wildcatting folklore than reality. Economics dictated Dad Joiner's choice of East Texas. Cheap land, low drilling costs, and ease of acquiring the leases made conditions favorable. So, he secured about 970 acres on the widow Daisy Bradford's farm. In deciding where to drill, he called on the services of his old friend Doc Lloyd, who was living in Fort Worth. Dad Joiner believed that geology "existed to help him persuade potential investors to buy leases." For this reason, he was not at all disturbed at Doc's credentials, which included claims to the "M.D., Pg. G., and C.E." degrees.

Lloyd had several aliases and several wives and had tried several occupations, including pharmacy, chemistry, and patent medicine. Then he entered the profession of "geology." He stood six feet tall, weighed three hundred pounds, could out-drink and out-eat anyone. He promoted oil leases with a mixture of "quasi-scientific jargon" and the zest of a patent medicine man. His scientific "reports" contained dramatic images of underground lakes and rivers of oil.

Dad Joiner played along and often introduced Lloyd as "one of the greatest living scientists." But when the leases were secure, Dad Joiner picked his own site to drill. At Daisy Bradford No. 3 on Friday night, October 3, 1930, Dad Joiner struck oil. As the huge gusher blew over the top, one spectator in the large crowd uttered the immortal words, "Put out your cigarettes! Put out your cigarettes!" For certain, there was at least one "real" scientist at the site.

Finding Anything

Oil in Texas: the Gusher Age, 1895–1945 (2002) by Diana Davids Olien and Roger M. Olien examines the petroleum industry during its formative period in Texas. The authors describe the development of the Texas petroleum industry from a fledgling industry unable to attract capital into an industry giant that transformed the state and controlled the international price of oil through the Texas Railroad Commission.

The same authors examine global cultural conditions and background of the oil industry in their electronic book *Oil and Ideology: The Cultural Creation of the American Petroleum Industry* (2000). See the netLibrary database at www.texshare.edu/.

RAILROAD COMMISSION OF TEXAS: A MINI-LEGISLATURE

Six major departments report directly to the Texas governor in the executive branch of state government. Four of these agencies set policy for

Daisy Bradford No. 3. Cars jammed the road as East Texans rushed to the site of Dad Joiner's oil well drilled eight miles east of Henderson on the widow Bradford's farm. The East Texas oilfield discovered on October 3, 1930 was the largest field in the world at the time. From the collections of The Dallas/Texas History and Archives Division, Dallas Public Library.

Oilman H. L. Hunt bought the lease to Daisy Bradford No. 3 in 1930 and added surrounding leases that paved the way for building a fortune from the East Texas field. In 1969, he posed for a picture at the site of the discovery. From the collections of The Dallas/Texas History and Archives Division, Dallas Public Library.

Texas's most valuable natural resources: land, agriculture, railroads, and oil. Most organizational charts of Texas state government place the Railroad Commission of Texas to the Governor's right, symbolizing its power and influence.

The Texas Railroad Commission, the first regulatory agency created by the state, played a powerful role in development of all the state's natural resources, and it continues to wield great influence. Like other states, Texas provided generous incentives to attract railroads to the state in the 1850s. As early as 1852, the state granted railroads eight sections of 640 acres per section for every mile of completed track. Within two years, the state doubled land grants to sixteen sections per mile of railroad. In the railroad boom after the Civil War, the Texas and Pacific railway obtained in excess of five million acres in one year to build their line west from Fort Worth on to El Paso.

By the 1890s, the railroads exercised power through an organization called the Texas Traffic Association, and their pricing was regarded as discriminatory and abusive. As one Texas politician succinctly observed, "Having the power to charge what they pleased, they were never modest in fixing their compensation." To fight abusive rates, Governor James S. Hogg pushed through a plan to create a commission to regulate the railroads. In April 1891, the Legislature created the Railroad Commission of Texas. They gave it power to regulate intrastate rates and tariffs, prevent rate discrimination, correct abuses, and enforce state laws concerning railways.

The Railroad Commission acquired authority to regulate oil and gas from interrelated problems of land, agriculture, oil, and railroads. Oil discoveries created complicated new problems for railroads. Transportation became a major concern. For oil to have maximum value, it had to reach the refineries efficiently. At first, companies transported oil to refineries in railroad oil tankers pulled by steam locomotives. Then, many regions favored pipelines as the best mode of transporting oil. When a company owned both a pipeline and oil wells, it naturally transported oil from its own wells and ignored the wells of other companies nearby.

To prevent these competitive abuses, the Legislature designated oil pipelines as "common carriers" just like railroads and trucking companies and expanded the authority of the Railroad Commission to regulate the oil pipelines. By 1919, the commission was granted jurisdiction over oil and gas production, and it created its Oil and Gas Division.

Finding Anything

Petroleum Politics and the Texas Railroad Commission (1981) by David Pringle describes the political environment and economic forces behind the development of the Texas Railroad Commission as a major regulatory agency.

See the web site homepage of the Railroad Commission of Texas at www.rrc.state.tx.us/ for information on the petroleum, mining, and trucking industries of the state. The web site contains a centennial history of the agency at www.rrc.state.tx.us/history/hist.html. The homepage site provides extensive data on oil and gas production, oil rig counts, and maps. Even with recent declines in oil production, Texas ranks in the top ten oil producing "countries" of the world, and it still leads all U.S. states.

LOVE IN THE AIR: "THE SOUTHWEST EFFECT"

The story of Southwest Airline's ascendancy to major status among U.S. airlines contains many of the elements of a great Texas myth. Rollin King, an executive and a licensed pilot, moved to San Antonio and acquired a small air-taxi service called Wild Goose Flying Service. Wild Goose flew from San Antonio to small cities like Del Rio and Laredo. King named it Southwest Air in 1964, but it produced few profits.

The legend began to take on Texas-sized dimensions when King met with attorney Herb Kelleher and sketched a business plan on a napkin. He drew a triangle connecting Dallas, Fort Worth, and Houston, and explained his idea of creating an airline to fly short hauls less than 500 miles that would compete with trains and buses. The airline would serve the three cities with low fares, convenient schedules, and a no-frills approach to flying. All these ideas contrasted sharply with established standards of the airline industry. King wanted to transport Wild Goose Flying Service to a populated market. After some investigation and support from investors, Kelleher and King incorporated Air Southwest on March 15, 1967.

The fierce competition from the large carriers in the early 1970s resembled a western gunfight or a barroom brawl, and there was plenty of liquor on board. Southwest's CEO, Lamar Muse, slashed airline fares to $10 for the last flight of the week from Houston back to Dallas. He said they had to get the plane back home anyway. Braniff Airlines retaliated by lowering all its fares from Dallas to Houston to $13.

Southwest Airlines. From its founding in a risky entrepreneurial venture in 1967, the airline established a record of more than thirty consecutive years of profitability, an industry record. From the collections of The Dallas/Texas History and Archives Division, Dallas Public Library.

Not to be outdone, Muse countered by offering customers either a $13 fare or a "full-fare ticket plus a fifth of premium liquor." Muse advertisements read, "Nobody's going to shoot Southwest Airlines out of the sky for a lousy $13." Soon, Southwest Airlines ascended to the position of the largest Texas distributor of Chivas Regal Scotch, Crown Royal Liquors, and Smirnoff Vodka. Meanwhile, Braniff Airlines and Texas International fell under indictment for antitrust violations.

Southwest Airlines weathered these battles and established a record of profitability for every year over a thirty-year period while most of its competitors struggled to achieve three or four. A prominent business journal rated Southwest the "most successful airline in history," and the company several times achieved recognition as one of 100 best companies to work for in America.

One of Southwest's finest tributes came from the Office of Aviation Analysis in the U.S. Department of Transportation. Aviation analysts noticed a distinct pattern that developed in the U.S. airline industry each time Southwest Airlines announced it would enter a new market. The Department of Transportation found other airlines serving the market immediately reduced their fares and increased their flights. They called this pattern the "Southwest Effect." Carriers reduced fares by 65 percent and increased passenger traffic by 30 percent.

Finding Anything

The Southwest Airlines Way: Using the Power of Relationships to Achieve High Performance (2003) by Jody Hoffer Gittell examines the success of Southwest Airlines from a management and operations perspective. The book is based on the author's field research at Southwest and several other leading airlines over eight years.

For a short sketch of Southwest Airline history to 1995, see the *Handbook of Texas Online* at www.tsha.utexas.edu/handbook/online/. This article traces the roles of Southwest executive Herb Kelleher, the airline's expansion, the company culture, and its advertising strategies.

McJOBS AND MAQUILADORAS: THE TEXAS ECONOMY OF THE FUTURE?

In November 2003, the editors of *Merriam-Webster's Collegiate Dictionary* upset Jim Cantalupo, the Chief Executive Officer of McDonald's, by including the word "McJob" in the 11th edition of its dictionary. They defined a "McJob" as "a low-paying job that requires little skill and provides little opportunity for advancement." Another prestigious dictionary went further and defined it as "an unstimulating, low-paid job with few prospects," especially a job "created by expansion of the service sector." The Texas economy of the future will be influenced by maquiladoras and McJobs.

The Texas border has decades of experience in "outsourcing of jobs." Foreign-owned factories in Mexico called maquiladroras assemble export products from imported parts using lower-cost workers. Maquiladoras originated as part of the Texas Border Industrialization Program of 1965. Today, there are more than 3,000 maquiladoras on the Texas-Mexican border in industrial parks near Brownsville, Del Rio, Eagle Pass, El Paso, Laredo, Presidio, and Rio Grande. They account for 49 percent of all Mexican exports.

Looking at the fortunes and misfortunes of maquiladoras over the last decade reveals a picture of the complicated global economy and some of the forces at work shaping the future Texas economy. Initially, Mexico followed the successful examples of Hong Kong, Taiwan, and other Asian countries and offered tax breaks and cheap labor to get its industry started. Mexico allowed companies to import parts duty free from the U.S. as long as companies exported finished products back to America. The Mexican strategy worked. By 1990, Mexico had acquired more than 1,500 plants employing 400,000 workers.

Success of the maquiladoras fostered some of the conditions leading to their decline. Mexican wages in U.S. dollars began to rise. They rose from about $1.50 per hour up to $3.50 per hour by 2002. Double-digit economic growth in the industry over a number of years put great pressure on the local infrastructure. Problems in housing, public transportation systems, and sewer systems contributed to employee turnover and absenteeism.

The U.S. economic recession of 2001 profoundly affected the maquiladoras. Almost $3 billion in trade of vehicle ignition wiring sets, radio broadcast receivers, and various radio and television electronic parts came from El Paso, Brownsville, and Hidalgo in 2002.

After sustaining the hard blow of the U.S. recession, the maquiladoras next took a direct hit from the September 11th terrorist attacks. Vehicle and pedestrian border crossings dropped dramatically. Border closures and subsequent inspections caused innumerable delays in shipments and distribution. Many warehouse operations responded by shipping cargo north with only 20 or 30 percent of their capacity, driving up the costs. U.S. firms dependent upon just-in-time inventory management systems sought sources elsewhere.

Managements of multinational corporations began to seek off-shore sites in low-wage countries like Honduras, El Salvador, the Dominican Republic, and China. Eventually, economic events in these new locations triggered the same kind of plant closings in Mexican maquiladoras that the maquiladoras had once caused north of the border.

The Texas economy of the future, economists suggest, will continue to be influenced by the kind of "outsourcing" of jobs represented by maquiladoras. Economist Robert Reich suggested that Class I jobs, repetitive simple tasks of manufacturing, can be done by virtually interchangeable workers in any country. These jobs will be exported. Class II jobs like food servers, taxi drivers, and retail clerks require a physical presence but will remain at low wages and few benefits. Class III jobs for scientists, accountants, bankers, and professional consultants will have highest incomes, adequate benefits, and comfortable lifestyles.

Finding Anything

See the *Texas Business Review* for well-researched information about maquiladoras and many other subjects dealing with economic conditions affecting Texas. The Bureau of Business Research in the McCombs School of Business at the University of Texas at Austin publishes the journal six times a year.

To keep up with the findings of serious research into Texas economic and business conditions, check the web site of the Bureau of Business Research at www.utexas.edu/depts/bbr/. In addition to the *Texas Business Review* available at the web site, it maintains an active publication program about such subjects as market opportunities in recycling in Texas, Japanese-style networks in Texas, innovations in manufacturing, and NAFTA and trade liberalization.

MEETING NEEDS OF TEXANS IN 2020

In 1994, the population of Texas surpassed New York's population making Texas the second largest state in both area and population with 268,000 square miles and 19.5 million people. By 2000, the state added another one million people to break the 20 million mark. Two scholars estimate that Texas will reach 31 million residents by 2020, a sobering and alarming projection for state officials required to deliver basic services to citizens.

The Health and Human Services Commission coordinates and manages all Health and Human Services in Texas under an umbrella organization created in 1991. Three mammoth agencies, the Department of Health, the Department of Human Services, and the Department of Mental Health and Mental Retardation accounted for more than $12 billion in state appropriations in 2001. Thirteen additional agencies, such as the Department on Aging, the Commission on Alcohol and Drug Abuse, the Interagency Council on Early Childhood Intervention, and the Rehabilitation Commission, make this agency one of the most complex bureaucracies in all of state government.

Of all the agencies under jurisdiction of the commission, Texas Department of Health provides some of the most useful information and services in the state. Originally created as the Texas Quarantine Department in 1879, the agency now focuses on many health care issues. The agency provides a county-by-county health profile of Texas.

Dallas County in 2001 had 268,946 citizens living below the poverty line. The county reported 720 AIDS cases and more than 16,000 other sexually transmitted diseases. Of the 14,063 deaths from all causes, 5,159 died from cardiovascular disease and 3,177 died from cancers. Dallas County also recorded 361 motor vehicle deaths, 298 homicides, and 224 suicides along with 716 accidental deaths from multiple causes.

The delivery of health and human services to the residents on the Texas-U.S. border constitutes one of Texas's most complicated social problems. The problem increases in proportion to population. In 1998, thiry-one Texas counties on the border out of forty-three border counties were designated "medically underserved areas." These areas contain fewer than one physician for every 3,500 residents. The populations of many of the border counties are anticipated to rise by 100,000 residents by 2010. In twenty-three counties along the border, the Health and Human Services Commission predicts the number of residents who fall below the federal poverty level will exceed 25 percent by 2010.

The State of Texas adopts a "bare bones" policy in the provision of social and health services for citizens, preferring instead to leave this responsibility to families, charities, churches, and the federal government. In the electronic age, Texas government concentrates many agency efforts in developing computer-based information systems that link individuals needing health and human service assistance directly to any agency within state government that may provide the service.

The Texas Health and Human Services Commission currently employs this strategy for finding assistance for a health or social problem. It recommends calling one of the Area Information Centers located in one of the eleven regional health districts of Texas. Next, search "Finding Help in Texas" and then the "Reference Guide for State Programs." Finally, it suggests calling a "State Agency Toll-Free Number." This strategy may or may not work, but the web site contains all the links.

Finding Anything

Directory of Texas and National Health Promotion Resources (2001), published by the Texas Department of Health, describes Texas and national services coordinated through local service facilities. This directory assumes that effective access to health service in Texas requires information about local, state, and national health providers, both public and private. Accordingly, it lists organizations that supply services to individuals whether local, state, federal, or private. The directory lists national toll-free numbers and describes organizational missions and services.

See the homepage of the web site of the new Department of State Health Services for a comprehensive list of health and social services provided for Texans on a county-by-county basis. The new agency officially began operations on September 1, 2004. Check the list of all its programs and services at www.dshs.state.tx.us/.

BOOKS AND WEB SITES

Murder in the General Land Office

Morgan, Andrea Gurasich. *Land: A History of the Texas General Land Office*. Austin, Texas: General Land Office, 1992.
Texas General Land Office. www.glo.state.tx.us/.

Becoming a Class A Barber in Texas

Guide to Texas State Agencies. Austin: University of Texas at Austin. Lyndon Baines Johnson School, 2001.
Texas Administrative Code. Texas Secretary of State. www.sos.state.tx.us./tac/.

Perils and Prospects of Starting a Business in Texas

Cooper, Kenneth H. The Aerobics Program for Total Well-Being: Exercise, Diet, Emotional Balance. Toronto; New York: Bantam Books, 1982.
Texas Department of Economic Development. www.tded.state.tx.us/.

From the Boll Weevil to the County Agent

Dethloff, Henry C. *A Centennial History of Texas A&M University, 1876–1976*. College Station: Texas A&M University Press, 1975.
Texas A&M University. Cooperative Extension Service. http://texasextension .tamu.edu/.

Texas's First Gusher

Chamberlain, C.K. "Lyne Toliaferro Barret: A Pioneer Texas Wildcatter." *East Texas Historical Journal* 6 (March 1968), 5–18.

Devereaux, Linda E. "Lyne Taliaferro Barret." Texas State Historical Association. *Handbook of Texas Online*. www.tsha.utexas.edu/handbook/online/.

Wildcatters, Dry Holes, and Gushers

Olien, Diana Davids and Olien Roger M. *Oil in Texas: the Gusher Age, 1895–1945*. Austin: University of Texas Press, 2002.
Olien, Roger M. and Olien, Diana Davids. *Oil and Ideology: The Cultural Creation of the American Petroleum Industry*. Chapel Hill: University of North Carolina Press, 2000. TexShare. netLibrary. www.texshare.edu/.

Railroad Commission of Texas: A Mini-Legislature

Pringle, David. *Petroleum Politics and the Texas Railroad Commission*. Austin: University of Texas Press, 1981.
Railroad Commission of Texas. www.rrc.state.tx.us/history/hist.html.

Love in the Air: "The Southwest Effect"

Flynn, Keli. "Southwest Airlines," *Handbook of Texas Online*. Texas State Historical Association. www.tsha.utexas.edu/handbook/online/ (accessed June 17, 2004).
Gittell, Jody Hoffer. *The Southwest Airlines Way: Using the Power of Relationships to Achieve High Performance*. New York: McGraw-Hill, 2003.

McJobs and Maquiladoras: the Texas Economy of the Future?

Bureau of Business Research, *Texas Business Review* Austin: McCombs School of Business, University of Texas.
Fullerton, Thomas M. and Barraza de Anda, Martha P. "Maquiladora Prospects in a Global Environment." (October 2003) *Texas Business Review*. www.utexas.edu/depts/bbr/tbr/index.html.

Meeting Needs of Texans in 2020

Texas Department of Health. *Directory of Texas and National Health Promotion Resources*. Austin, TX: Texas Department Health, 2001.
Department of State Health Services. Programs and Services. www.dshs.state.tx.us/.

⑨

BLUE CATFISH, FLYING MAMMALS, SPACE SHUTTLES, AND MISCELLANY

- True or false Texas fish story? A five-foot, eight-inch tall Texan, weighing 135 pounds, caught a four-foot long, ten-inch wide catfish weighing 121.5 pounds?
- What Texas wood is the world's largest rocking chair made from and how much does it weigh?
- How did Texas get three official state mammals: a large mammal, a small mammal, and a flying mammal?
- Why did the 74th Legislature designate the monarch butterfly as the official state insect?
- How did "Cactus Jack" Garner finally get his wish?
- What is the origin of "thin as a rail?"
- What is the difference between a Texas Easter Daisy and a Texas White Dandelion?
- How did the state of Texas prison system get into the business of running a railroad?
- Why did Sig Sjoberg and the NASA Mission Operations Team receive the Medal of Freedom?
- Who performed the world's first coronary artery bypass procedure?

CODY MULLENNIX AND THE BLUE CATFISH

"Trout Fishing in America," a Dallas popular musical group, recorded a compact disc in 1990 on the Trout Records label called "Truth is Stranger than Fishin.'" Texas's 3.3 million acres of inland water churns out scores of fish tales that stretch the imagination. The story of Cody Mullennix's catching the big blue catfish on Lake Texoma falls into the category of a true Texas fish story no one will ever believe.

It happened like this. Cody Mullennix of Howe, Texas, went out on Friday, February 20, 2004, to fish on Lake Texoma. Cody is five feet eight inches tall and weighs 135 pounds. Fishing from the bank with a 14-foot surf rod and reel using dead shad as bait, Cody hooked a 121.5 pound blue catfish, forty-eight inches long. He estimated twenty minutes and 70 to 80 yards of 20-pound test line to reel in this fish. Finally, he waded out into the water and rolled the fish onto the bank.

After he got the fish on shore, he called his friend and fishing buddy, Jason Holbrook, to bring him a set of 100-pound scales to weigh the creature. The scale proved too small. They loaded the fish into the bed of his pickup truck and drove off to the Pottsboro Tackle Box for an official Texas weigh-in. The official weigh-in recorded the catfish's weight at 121.5 pounds.

Cody managed to keep the fish alive long enough to take it to the Texas Freshwater Fisheries Center in Athens, Texas. The fish survived. The center already contained a 120-pound alligator gar. On the basis of the data accumulated from previous large catfish catches, Lake Texoma fisheries biologist Bruce Hysmith estimated the fish might be as old as Cody Mullennix himself. Cody was twenty-seven when he caught the big blue catfish.

Mullennix's blue catfish eclipsed the Texas rod and reel blue cat record of 100 pounds set by Reyes Martinez at Lake Texoma in 2000. Mullennix submitted the paperwork to the International Game Fishing Association and the National Freshwater Fishing Hall of Fame to see if it qualified as a world record. The data indicates his catfish will eclipse the old world record by a good five pounds. Cody Mullennix's blue catfish story concludes with a Texas twist guaranteed to ensure no will believe it. He caught a fifty-six pound catfish on the same day and let that one go. Then he hit "the big one."

Finding Anything

Freshwater Fishes of Texas by Earl W. Chilton, II describes the Texas environment for freshwater fishing. The author gives information on forty-six species of Texas freshwater fishes found in Texas's inland rivers and lakes. With large color illustrations, the author provides information on the fishes' life habits, distribution of the species, and identifying features.

For authoritative information on both freshwater and saltwater fishing in Texas, check out the extensive web site of the Texas Parks and Wildlife Department at www.tpwd.state.tx.us/fish/. The site provides press releases, regulations, fishing reports, and tips on major activities for anglers in Texas. The site also provides photographs and audio presentations of interest to the fishing public.

THE "STAR OF TEXAS" RED CEDAR ROCKING CHAIR

Texans still find ways to live off the land and the products of the land even after the state passed the Census Bureau's marker in 1950 of more people living in urban areas than rural areas. Larry Dennis, the owner of a successful custom-made rocking chair business in Weatherford, moved his Texas Hill Country Furniture & Mercantile business to a rural stretch of Highway 281 between Mineral Wells and Stephenville in 2002.

A visitor to his new location showed him a picture of a 12-foot tall novelty chair, and Dennis began setting aside a few large cedar logs he got from his suppliers. He set his sights on the *Guinness Book of World Records* and built a 26-foot high, 8,000-pound rocking chair made of Texas red cedar.

To secure the world record requires an official measurement every bit as rigorous as the official Texas Parks and Wildlife weigh-in of Cody Mullennix's 121.5-pound blue catfish. Witnesses included a judge from Palo Pinto County, a utility executive, and a highway patrolman skilled in weighing trailer rigs. The official measurement results contained some unexpected findings.

The official height of the Star of Texas Rocker exceeded unofficial height estimates by four feet and topped out at 29 feet 10½ inches. Judges recorded the width at 12 feet 7½ inches and the rocker's weight at 5,678 pounds, falling below the estimated weight of 8,000 pounds printed on the store's souvenir coffee mugs. Owner Larry Dennis accounted for the difference in weight to the drying out of the wood. Even a couple a thousand pounds lighter, the Star of Texas Rocker dominates the roadside in front of the Hill Country Furniture & Mercantile, and the world record is in sight.

Depending on which definition of a tree to believe, Texas provides a home to more than 250 native species of trees. According to one definition in the *New Handbook of Texas*, a tree is a "plant with a trunk three

The Star of Texas Rocker on Highway 281 near Lipan, Texas, was built by Larry Dennis, owner of Texas Hill Country Furniture & Mercantile. Signs on the rocker read "World's Largest Cedar Rocker" and "Please Don't Climb on the Rocker." The rocker may be too big for two-year-old Elizabeth Mumford of Dallas. Photograph by Tracey L. Mumford, used with permission.

inches in diameter, at least 4½ feet in height with only one stem" and attains a height of 13 feet. Advocates for shrubs and woody vines disagree, but they all say Texas has plenty of all of them. Oak trees lead Texas by far in the total number of species with thirty-nine, followed by hawthorns. Next in line come groups of trees with fewer than ten species: ash, juniper, pine, hickory, acacia, and maple. The mesquite tree constitutes a class by itself because of its imperial spread. Whether in tree or shrub form, it occupies more than 60 million acres of rangeland.

The cedars of the Texas Hill Country and the Edwards plateau, the kind that make up the Star of Texas Rocker and other custom-made furniture, are actually Ashe Juniper. True cedars do not grow naturally in Texas. Texans who have cut cedar posts long enough for a robust folklore to blossom don't believe this scientific technicality. A native Texas society of cedar cutters evolved its own social order of cedarcutters, cedarchoppers, and cedarwhackers.

The cedarcutter, the truly independent master craftsman of the trade, stood at the top of the social order. Barbed wire created a great market for his cedar posts, and he had stepped into history at the right moment to fill the position. Cedarchoppers failed to get beyond the competency required to cut a few cords of oak firewood, and they occupied a lesser status among cedar cutters. At the bottom of cedar society stood the cedarwhacker. The society looked down on the cedarwhacker as "a reckless, careless rogue" who swung any sort of ax with "wild abandon." He could turn good timber into the "sorriest looking post."

The creator of the red cedar Star of Texas Rocker hails from the ancient and honorable line of the master cedarcutters who bequeathed a worthy tradition.

Finding Anything

Trees of Texas: An Easy Guide to Leaf Identification (2003) by Carmine Stahl and Ria McElvaney provides a useful guide to Texas trees. The authors describe and illustrate approximately 230 Texas trees, giving instructions on how to identify them. They furnish a Texas Parks and Wildlife color map of ten vegetation regions of the state showing Texas trees that inhabit each region.

For the story of the Star of Texas Rocker, see the web site "Texas Twisted: How the West Was Weird" at www.texastwisted.com/. This web site specializes in unusual Texas world record events. It covers off-beat events like the Fletcher's Corny Dog Eating Contest at the Texas State

Fair and San Angelo's Running of the Sheep at the Centennial celebration.

THE MEXICAN FREE-TAILED BAT AND THE NINE-BANDED ARMADILLO

The Texas Legislature for a time designated only traditional foods, patriotic plays, folk dances, vintage air planes, sea shells, and gems and minerals as official state symbols. Occasionally, they bestowed symbolic honor on a wildflower, a bird, or a fish. But the 74th Texas Legislature went completely "natural" with its official designations. Designating an official state fish in 1989 and an official state reptile in 1993 actually initiated the natural trend with the Guadalupe bass and the Texas horned lizard winning the honors.

No Legislature in Texas history has ever approached the 74th's record of seven natural designations in a single session. It went wild for mammals. Legislators began the session innocently enough by having elementary school students vote for an Official Texas State Mammal. Two popular mammals emerged in the voting. Bevo, the University of Texas longhorn steer mascot, had already achieved stardom as a weekly Saturday afternoon television star at football games. The music of Gary P. Nunn emanating from Armadillo World Headquarters and Austin City Limits catapulted the nine-banded armadillo into the spotlight.

When the voting turned out about equal between the nine-banded armadillo and the longhorn steer, the Legislature faced a political dilemma. It could not afford to alienate all those young future voters, so they compromised. They named the longhorn steer as the official "Large State Mammal of Texas," and the armadillo as the official "Small State Mammal of Texas." The Legislature praised the longhorn steer because an estimated 10 million head had been driven to mid-western markets in the frontier days of Texas. They applauded the armadillo for possessing "attributes that distinguish a true Texan: deep respect for the land, ability to change and adapt, and a fierce and undying love of freedom."

The small-mammal, large-mammal compromise appeared to work well. But an unexpected problem arose from Texans who liked bats. Supporters of the Texas urban and cave bat colonies, like Bat Conservation International, went away empty-handed. They lobbied all out for the Mexican free-tailed bats in Bracken Cave.

Bracken Cave functions as a "summertime nursery cave" to the largest concentration of migratory Mexican free-tailed bats in the world, perhaps

20 million bats. During the summer, these bats naturally consume 250 tons of insects like mosquitoes and crop pests. The role of bats in a healthy Texas ecosystem deserved recognition by the public.

In the face of such a compelling case, the Legislature had little choice except to create another official state mammal. So on May 25, 1995, the Legislature approved its third official state mammal of the session. It named the Mexican free-tailed bat the "Official Flying Mammal" of Texas. The Lone Star State is now overloaded with official state mammals: the nine-banded armadillo, the longhorn steer, and the Mexican free-tailed bat. All occupy unique places in Texas history and culture, and obviously they have political support in the state Legislature.

Finding Anything

Texas Natural History: A Century of Change (2002) by David J. Schmidly provides a readable, scientific look at the armadillo, the Mexican free-tailed bat, and many other mammals of Texas. The author examines 100 years of the natural history of mammals in Texas from the time of biologist Vernon Bailey's first biological survey of the state from 1889–1905. The book compares and contrasts conditions between present mammal populations and the past findings of Bailey's team. Very few books similar to this one exist for Texas.

For an easy-to-use electronic guide to Texas mammals, check out the web site of the *Mammals of Texas: Online Edition* (1994) by William B. Davis and David J. Schmidley at www.nsrl.ttu.edu/tmot1/. This site provides information on 181 species of Texas mammals giving distribution, physical characteristics, life histories, and photographs. It is conveniently arranged in a searchable alphabetical format.

THE MONARCH BUTTERFLY: THE OFFICIAL STATE INSECT

The 74th Legislature did not stop its official designating with mammals. Sticking with the "natural" theme, they moved from mammals to insects. They staked a claim for the Lone Star State as the "birthplace" of the monarch butterfly, saying this insect is as "beautiful and memorable as a Texas sunset." It deserved to be the state insect because it had forged a "unique relationship with Texas." It stops here for "one last rest and feeding" before it embarks on its journey to the mountains of Mexico.

The Legislature claimed the "distinction of being the birthplace of this imperial insect," and the Monarch Butterfly now had an official homestead. It explained its reasoning in a resolution. Each spring, the "skies over Texas are filled with excitement and color as many thousands of these tiny creatures return to the site of their own nativity to give birth to a new generation." Like the shape of Texas, the distinctive "rust-colored wings, marked by black veins and two rows of white spots, make the monarch butterfly instantly recognizable to all." And like Texas also, "the monarch butterfly has inspired imitators."

Not everyone agrees with the Legislature's claim about the birthplace of the monarch butterfly, but monarch butterflies make the longest annual migration of any insect. They travel from as far north as Manitoba and Ontario in Canada to the mountains of northern Mexico. Thousands of butterflies make many rest stops in Texas on a 2,000-mile migration to southern climes searching for winter homes. The Abilene Zoological Gardens achieved recognition as one of the first official sanctuaries along the eastern migration path as part of the National Monarch Project.

In making the official insect designation, the Legislature cited several important characteristics that make this insect culturally symbolic of Texans and Texas culture. It is a stately creature, renowned for its ability to "evade predators." Although delicate, it is heartily designed by nature so that its main source of nourishment is milkweed, which contains a poison-like substance unpalatable to birds and other "angry critters."

Like the Lone Star State itself, it has inspired imitators but has "remained in a league of its own." The monarch butterfly reaches great heights, "soaring above all other insects in its nobility and determination." Legitimately, Texas has more than 400 butterfly species in the state, more than half of all the species of butterflies identified in North America north of Mexico. No one could oppose such legislative elegance to a butterfly, and the monarch, *Danaus plexippus,* became the official state insect without opposition.

Finding Anything

Critters: Common Household and Garden Pests of Texas (1987) by Bill Zak examines both beneficial and dangerous insects of Texas. The author provides a color-illustrated field guide to doodlebugs, beetles, head lice, mosquitoes, root maggots, ticks, and most of the common insects of Texas. The book contains advice and control clues.

For a look at the monarch butterfly, plus a comprehensive description of the collection of 495 butterfly species that have been identified in

Texas during the last 130 years, see the natural history collections at the web site of the Texas Memorial Museum. The web site is www.tmm .utexas.edu/tnhc/invertzoology/butterfly/index.html. In addition to scientific descriptions of its collections, the site provides information on how to make a butterfly garden for Central Texas.

THE PRICKLY PEAR CACTUS AND
THE JALAPENO PEPPER

With three official state mammals and a state insect to its credit, the 74th Legislature set an all-time record for official "natural" designations. It ended the session by designating the prickly pear cactus as the "Official State Plant of Texas" and the jalapeno as the "Official State Pepper of Texas."

The prickly pear cactus waited 100 years to be officially recognized as a traditional Texas terrestrial form. Texan John Nance "Cactus Jack" Garner, most famous for saying the vice presidency isn't "worth a bucket of warm spit," argued for the prickly pear in 1901. He lost out to the bluebonnet and the Daughters of the Republic of Texas.

The time for the prickly pear had come. Native to the American Southwest and Sonoran Desert region of Mexico, the prickly pear produces a sweet, fleshy fruit and broad, edible flat stems. This plant has everything required of an official Texas symbol: a nutritious source of food, useful in landscape décor, and forage for cattle. It is a "rugged, versatile, and uniquely beautiful" plant. And it possesses one characteristic symbolic of the "indomitable and proud" spirit of Texas: "It thrives in a harsh climate that few plants can bear."

In its haste to complete the session, the Legislature omitted one small detail. It failed to name the exact species of prickly pear cactus to serve as the official state plant. History suggests this oversight may come back to haunt the Legislature. At least twelve species of prickly pear cacti thrive in Texas. The Brown-Spined Prickly Pear, the Clock-Face Prickly Pear, the Crow-Foot Prickly Pear, the Flaming Prickly Pear, the Fragile Prickly Pear, the Porcupine Prickly Pear, and the Purple Prickly Pear are species deserving official recognition. Legislative ambiguity might open the way for one species to claim hegemony as happened in the wildflower wars.

Hopefully, the popularity of the generic jalapeno pepper precludes any future conflicts with this official designation. Using a sensible legislative strategy, the jalapeno lobby strengthened their case by relating their pepper to the traditions of natural specimens like the bluebonnet, the pecan tree, and ruby red grapefruit. They staked their claim to the 9,000-year history of capsicum peppers in the Central American and Native American diet.

They noted the jalapeno as an "essential ingredient" in chili and went on to make a strong medicinal argument. They suggest that the basic chemical in the jalapeno pepper aids the treatment of "arthritis, shingles, sore muscles, and nerve disorders." Legislators noted some researchers believed these peppers are effective in fighting cancer and heart disease. A cactus and a pepper received official recognition, and the Legislature adjourned.

Finding Anything

Cacti of Texas and Neighboring States: A Field Guide (1984) by Del Weniger takes a practical and scientific look at many of the natural species of cacti that populate Texas. It provides the common names, scientific names, the range, and information on the life history of many Texas cacti.

To view photographs and illustration of the prickly pear cactus, search the Google.com web site at www.google.com/ and select "Images." Enter "prickly pear cactus" and more than 1,000 images of this species appear in different environments.

THIN AS A TEXAS RAIL

From almost any perspective, Texas is a birder's paradise. No other state has as many varieties of remarkable birds as Texas. At the beginning of the twenty-first century, the recorded number of species, living, extinct, or introduced, in Texas stood near 600. Both the size of the state and the diversity of the climate, geography, and habitat accounts for attracting the large number of bird species to the region.

The pileated woodpecker and the pine warbler live in the humid river bottoms of the eastern piney woods section of the state. The unusual brown-headed nuthatch inhabits the drier upland forests of the state. The white plumaged American oystercatcher and the big brown pelican populate the Gulf Coast. In the Llano Estacado of north and western Texas lives a distinctive burrowing owl that makes his nest in a hole in the ground like a prairie dog. The black phoebe, the white throated swift, and paisano, the legendary roadrunner, all make their homes in dry canyon regions of central and western Texas. The climate of the deepest recesses of the lower Rio Grande Valley produces semi-tropical conditions, and the birds found there are frequently beautiful and strange, like the northern jacana.

Texas went without an official state bird until 1927 when the Texas Federation of Women's Clubs asked the Legislature to support a program to protect birds by designating an official bird for the state. It asked that the mockingbird become the official "state bird of Texas" in the interest of generating "a more intelligent and sympathetic understanding of our feathered friends."

The mockingbird met all the criteria as the most appropriate species and logical choice. It was known to ornithologists, musicians, educators, and Texans "in all walks of life." It lived in all parts of the state, in winter and summer, in the city and in the country, and on the prairies and in the woods. Like a real Texan, the mockingbird could both fight and sing. Legislators described the mockingbird as a singer of a distinctive type and "a fighter for the protection of his home, falling, if need be, in its defense, like any true Texan."

Some people think the rail would have been a good choice for the Texas official state bird. The Yellow Rail, Black Rail, Clapper Rail, King Rail, and Virginia Rail all live in Texas in coastal wetland environments. Considered calculating and secretive, they can melt into their marsh environments at a moment's notice. In 1842, John James Audubon wrote in *Birds of America* that at the first sign of danger the Clapper Rail can lower his head, stretch his neck, and take off at "incomparable speed" in silence. He observed that a rail has the "power of compressing" its body so much that it seems to slide easily between the stems of marsh grasses. From the rail's uncanny ability to slip through the stems of the thickest marsh grass by compressing its body almost horizontally came the expression "thin as a rail."

Finding Anything

Birds of Texas (2002) by Fred J. Alsop, III covers many of the popular species of Texas birds. The book provides a practical field guide in identification of Texas birds and a useful introduction to birding. Hundreds of color photographs, charts, symbols, and drawings illustrate major characteristics, habitats, and scientific and common names of Texas birds. The introduction contains excellent information for individuals beginning the activity.

For excellent current information on Texas birds, visit the web site of the Texas Parks and Wildlife Department and select the "Birds and

Birding" menus. The site is www.tpwd.state.tx.us/nature/birding/. The site provides photographs of particularly unusual Texas birds, an update on current birding activities, and habitat projects and programs around the state. It delivers considerable information on birding activities in Texas state parks.

DAISIES AND DANDELIONS ON
THE CRABGRASS FRONTIER

Several species of dandelions inhabit Texas, of which the best known may be the wildflower called the Texas Dandelion, or False Dandelion. Generations of Texas children blew bubbles from its stems, fashioned long, bent "daisy" chains, and puffed seeds into the wind across lawns and fields. Its natural arrangement stimulated fantasy for wishes, predictions, and games of natural chance. "Will I marry Billy or go hang out at the beach?" Never mind that parents regarded these wildflowers as a menace to impeccable lawn care and an unstoppable weed that had earned its nickname as the "golden tramp."

The Texas dandelion blooms from February to June across the state in dry clay or sandy loams of lawns, pastures, cultivated fields, and prairies. It occurs in all regions of the state. The plant grows from eight to twenty-four inches high producing a lemon yellow flower with two or three rows. It opens in the morning and usually closes around noon. The tips of the dandelion fruits are covered with a "spreading tuft of feathery bristles that act like a parachute in the wind, scattering the seeds far and wide."

Unlike the Texas dandelion, the flower called the Arkansas Lazy Daisy, or Doze Daisy, typically remains closed until about noon. It gets its name from the fact that it opens late, and its flower buds tend to droop. It is a soft, hairy annual that can get up to twenty inches in height. It can sometimes produce as many as 250 disk flowers, and it ranges all across the state in sandy soils.

Like the Texas dandelion, Texas daisies share a rich and intriguing folklore especially in assisting participants in statistics and probability, and computing and predicting marriage and family relationships. The word daisy originates from the two Anglo-Saxon words which mean the "eye of the day," coined to refer to the flower's habit of opening in the morning and closing in the evening. This characteristic inspired the cliché "fresh as a daisy," coined by the English author Frederick Marrat in 1834.

The oxeye daisy grows wild in the northeastern corner of the state, and a seacoast variety occupies marshes, sand dunes, and mud flats. For the romantic and superstitious, this flower predicts marriage and love arrangements. It can be used roulette-style in the traditional up or down vote of "loves-me, loves me-not." In this game, the odds strongly favor the lover seeking an affirmative response because a large percentage of the oxeye petals grow in patterns with an uneven numbers of petals. Any even-numbered phrase like "this year, next year, sometime, never" will likely yield a favorable result because "never" can only be picked from a flower with even-numbered petals. The oxeye daisy is the perfect natural tool for romantic optimists.

Finding Anything

Wildflowers of Texas (2002) by Geyata Ajilvsgi is an illustrated field guide to Texas wildflowers. With more than 5,000 species of wildflowers inhabiting Texas, all the field guides select the more common flowering plants. The author examines more than 400 of the most dramatic, colorful wildflowers found across the state. Each plant included grows over a large portion of the state, covers a long blooming period, or is conspicuous in a region.

For a virtual tour of many of the wildflowers of Texas found in state parks, check the wildflower section of the web site of the Texas Parks and Wildlife Department at www.tpwd.state.tx.us/park/wildflower/. With excellent color photography, this site guide illustrates the wildflowers found in state parks covering seven major regions of Texas, from the Panhandle Plains and Big Bend to the Pineywoods and Gulf Coast. It also provides a Department of Transportation web site to check for seasonal roadside viewing of wildflowers.

WORKING ON THE TEXAS STATE RAILROAD

A major responsibility of conserving the abundant natural, cultural, and historical heritage of Texas belongs to the Texas Department of Parks and Wildlife. The agency employs 3,000 staff to manage more than 400,000 acres of public lands visited annually by nearly 20 million people. Public lands form 129 parks, natural areas, and historic sites. The department protects a fish population in 600 public reservoirs, 16,000 miles of streams and rivers, and 370 miles of coastline.

Each piece of land set aside for public use occupies a unique place in state history. The Texas State Railroad, the official state railroad, carved its own place in history. The railroad originally began in 1896 with five miles of track built by convicts to serve the iron foundry on the grounds of the state prison near Rusk. Convicts hauled wood and iron ore to the prison smelter known as "Old Alcalde," built in 1884. The prison system added five more miles to Maydelle in 1903.

Texas Governor Thomas M. Campbell got the idea that the prison could become a profit-making enterprise if the railroad became a common carrier, and he extended the line to Palestine with more convict labor. It had depots at Rusk, Maydelle, and Palestine. Advocates of prison reform decried high mortality rates and bad working conditions and complained of convicts being "lashed cruelly by a savage prison guard" during the railroad construction. To critics, the railroad was "stained with the blood of some helpless convict man or boy." But Texas built its very own railroad.

The prison foundry, which had made pig iron and pipe for the state, closed in 1913, and the railroad fell on hard times. The state tried leasing the railroad to railway companies who carried forest products and farm products like tomatoes. In the end, a bulk seed plant and pulpwood were all that remained of the market. Finally, in 1972 the state turned the railroad property over to the parks department to make a "hike and bike" trail.

The railroad idea refused to die in a state where tourism became the fastest growing industry. A group of railroad enthusiasts revived the idea of running a tourist train from Rusk to Palestine on the old prison line. In striving for historical accuracy, the state again employed inmates of the Texas prison system to refurbish the old tracks. Volunteers rounded up steam locomotives and other vintage equipment to supply the railway line, and the Texas State Railroad rose from the grave.

The Texas State Railroad now transports tourists on a twenty-five mile excursion through the Pineywoods region of East Texas between Rusk and Palestine. Pulling open-air cars, the steam locomotives cross thirty bridges, including an 1,100-foot bridge spanning the Neches River. Passengers view pines, oaks, sweet gums, elms, dogwood, sumac, and sassafras. The Texas State Railroad is a successful tourist attraction, but no one has ever figured out how to make the Texas prison system self-supporting.

Finding Anything

The *Official Guide to Texas State Parks* (1997) by Laurence Parent contains information about the Texas State Railroad State Historical Park

The "General Sherman" locomotive was the first class of train to operate in Texas in 1852. It weighed 13 tons and could reach speeds of 35 miles per hour. From the collections of The Dallas/Texas History and Archives Division, Dallas Public Library.

and all of the 129 state parks in Texas. The book describes parks by region, providing the history, natural significance, photographs, and services of each park. The book contains more than 200 color photographs, maps, and illustrations.

To find out detailed current information about each park, see the web site of the Department of Parks and Wildlife at www.tpwd.state .tx.us/parkguide/. This guide provides a rich photographic, historical, cultural, and natural history of Texas from one of the most effective state agencies.

APOLLO XIII AND THE MEDAL OF FREEDOM

In the history of American manned space flight, no mission stands out more dramatically than the flight of Apollo XIII. Over a four-day period, under real time pressure, NASA engineers, contractors at Boeing, and mission control team members solved critical problem after critical problem. Using high-tech and low-tech solutions ranging from computer software, duct tape, cardboard, and plastic bags, they rescued three astronauts on an abortive, near-tragic mission in space. Cameras framed the rescue for the world through lenses focused on the Texas mission control room at the Johnson Space Flight Center.

President Richard Nixon presented the Medal of Freedom to the entire NASA Apollo XIII Mission Operations Team for their achievement. Sig Sjoberg, the team leader, accepted the award for the group. The text of the award captured the sentiments of nearly every American who witnessed the work of the operations team via live television: "Three brave astronauts are alive and on Earth because of their dedication, and because at critical moments, the people of that team were wise enough and self-possessed enough to make the right decisions."

From the beginning of manned space exploration, Texas made a strong mark on the U.S. space program. President John F. Kennedy on May 25, 1961, urged a joint session of Congress to set a goal of "landing a man on the Moon and returning him safely to Earth." Behind him sat two politically powerful Texans needed to accomplish the President's goal: Vice President Lyndon B. Johnson, the Chairman of the U.S. National Aeronautics and Space Council, and Sam Rayburn of Bonham, the Speaker of the House of Representatives. Together, these Texans shared seventy years of Congressional experience.

A crucial component in landing a man on the moon was the construction of a new manned space management center to train astronaut crews and function as a flight control center. NASA formed a site survey team to evaluate twenty locations from Florida to California. In making a recommendation, it used criteria like proximity to academic institutions with adequate research facilities, availability of utilities, adequate housing, transportation, and attractive cultural and recreational facilities.

On September 19, 1961, NASA Administrator James E. Webb formally announced that the new Manned Space Flight Center would be built in southeastern Harris County, Texas, at the edge of Clear Lake. Officials from competing sites quickly suggested political pressure from the Vice President's office had swayed the decision. Some asked directly about what role Vice President Johnson played in the decision, and others inquired about the activities of another Texan, Democrat Albert Thomas, who headed the Independent Offices Subcommittee of the House Appropriations Committee. NASA assured critics that no political pressure was applied and that Houston's obvious attractiveness relative to the criteria cinched the decision.

Senator Lyndon Johnson and Speaker of the House of Representatives Sam Rayburn of Bonham in 1955. Both men were instrumental in securing a Texas site for the Manned Space Flight Center. It later became the Johnson Space Flight Center. From the collections of The Dallas/Texas History and Archives Division, Dallas Public Library.

The Johnson Space Flight Center brought big science to Texas in a big way. By the 1990s, the Center employed almost 20,000 workers, including 100 astronauts, on 1,600 acres with 142 buildings. The Center received more than $50 billion in federal appropriations. With such rewards came great responsibility and intense feelings of personal loss when inevitable accidents touched the Lone Star State. As the home base and training facility of astronauts, the Lone Star State was struck particularly hard by two shuttle accidents. Much of the wreckage of Shuttle Columbia would come to rest in the Pineywoods of East Texas in 2003.

Finding Anything

Apollo Expeditions to the Moon (1975) edited by Edgar M. Cortright provides a dramatic narrative and photographic survey of the many activities of the Johnson Space Center during all the Apollo missions. It includes special chapters on Apollo 13. The book contains individual accounts of major participants in important phases in the history of the moon landing from NASA administrators, astronauts, mission control directors, and engineers.

For an informative, readable survey of the creation, development, and significance of the Johnson Space Center, check the web site of the Johnson Space Center at www.jsc.nasa.gov/history/suddenly_tomorrow/suddenly. htm. In addition to information on the extensive activities of the space center, this site provides a complete electronic history of the Johnson Space Center written by Henry C. Dethloff. The electronic book is entitled *Suddenly Tomorrow Came: A History of the Johnson Space Center* (1993).

MICHAEL DEBAKEY AND THE "CITY OF MEDICINE"

While NASA engineers, astronauts, and managers at the Johnson Space Center explored the moon, launched space shuttles and sky laboratories, Houston physicians and medical scientists at the Texas Medical Center achieved parallel successes by building the largest medical center in the world. At its 50th anniversary festivities in 1993, the medical center celebrated growth of its facilities, the quality of its medical care, and the talents of its staff.

Richard C. Wainerdi, president and chief executive officer, declared that the Texas Medical Center was "Houston's gift to the world." The idea for a conglomeration of independent medical facilities whose synergy would produce beneficial results came from the trustees of the M.D. Anderson Foundation in the early 1940s. The trustees established an aggressive policy of attracting institutions of medicine, patient care, health education, and medical research. The center assembled staff, provided facilities, and developed programs necessary to "assure the highest standards of attainment in medicine."

The Baylor University College of Medicine and the University of Texas Hospital for Cancer Research, now known worldwide as the M.D. Anderson Cancer Center, became the first two institutions to anchor the medical center on a 134-acre site. The M.D. Anderson Hospital was named for Houston philanthropist Monroe Dunaway Anderson, who made his fortune in trading Texas's largest agricultural crop, King Cotton. In 1936, Monroe Anderson turned a cotton fortune into a medical foundation that initiated a medical establishment of international renown.

In the twenty years from 1970 to 1990, the founders' vision succeeded beyond expectations. In 1970, the Texas Medical Center had 3,196 students and more than 14,000 staff. Its budget was $150 million. By 1990, the total student body from all programs numbered 76,000, and the staff totaled 54,774 employees. The combined budget of all the medical center institutions exceeded $4 billion. The number of hospital beds had more than doubled from 3,256 in 1970 to 6,694 beds in 1992. By 1990, the nineteen component institutions doing medical research had received almost $2 billion in research grants.

As the Texas Medical Center created the largest medical center in the world, the center established an academic reputation that other institutions began to emulate. Michael DeBakey, with his team of surgeons at the Baylor University College of Medicine, performed the first successful coronary artery bypass surgery on November 23, 1964. DeBakey and Denton Cooley made considerable advances in heart transplantation and artificial hearts. Many faculty members associated with the Texas Medical Center became members of the National Academy of Sciences.

The Medical Center today comprises fourteen hospitals, six university systems, the nation's first High School for the Health Professions, and more than twenty other health-related programs. President Wanerdi in 1992 told a professional society that the founders envisioned a "medical center like no other." It would consist of many different hospitals, academic institutions of all kinds, and various support organizations—an entire "city of medicine."

Finding Anything

Monroe Dunaway Anderson, His Legacy: A History of the Texas Medical Center (1994) by N. Don Macon and Thomas Dunaway Anderson surveys the major events in the founding, development, and operations of the Texas Medical Center. The book also provides a short biography of the philanthropist who, perhaps more than anyone, set in motion the forces leading to the creation of the medical center.

For a look at the current membership and programs of the Texas Medical Center, check their web site at www.tmc.edu/institutions/. The site provides a direct link to all current homepages of academic and research institutions, patient care institutions, and associated health-related members, such as the McGovern Museum of Health and Medical Science, LifeGift Organ Donation Center, and the Jachimczyk Forensic Center of the Harris County Medical Examiner's Office.

BOOKS AND WEB SITES

Cody Mullennix and the Blue Catfish

Chilton, II, Earl W. *Freshwater Fishes of Texas*. Austin, Texas: Texas Parks and Wildlife Press, 2000.
Texas Parks and Wildlife Department. www.tpwd.state.tx.us/fish/.

The "Star of Texas" Red Cedar Rocking Chair

Stahl, Carmine and McElvaney, Ria. *Trees of Texas: An Easy Guide to Leaf Identification*. College Station: Texas A&M University Press, 2003.
Texas Twisted: How the West Was Weird. www.texastwisted.com/.

The Mexican Free-tailed Bat and the Nine-banded Armadillo

Davis, William B and Schmidley, David J. *Mammals of Texas: Online Edition*. 1994. www.nsrl.ttu.edu/tmotl/.
Schmidly, David J. *Texas Natural History: A Century of Change*. Lubbock, Texas: Texas Tech University Press, 2002.

The Monarch Butterfly: The Official State Insect

Texas Memorial Museum. Invertebrate Zoology Collections. www.tmm.utexas .edu/tnhc/invertzoology/butterfly/index.html.
Zak, Bill. *Critters: Common Household and Garden Pests of Texas*. Dallas, Texas: Taylor Publishing, 1987.

The Prickly Pear Cactus and the Jalapeno Pepper

Prickly Pear Cactus. Images. www.google.com/.
Weniger, Del. *Cacti of Texas and Neighboring States*. Austin: University of Texas Press, 1984.

Thin as a Texas Rail

Alsop, Fred J., III. *Birds of Texas: Smithsonian Handbooks*. New York: DK Publishing, 2002.
Texas Parks and Wildlife Department. Nature. Birding. www.tpwd.state.tx.us/ nature/birding/.

Daisies and Dandelions on the Crabgrass Frontier

Ajilvsgi, Geyata. *Wildflowers of Texas* . Revised Edition. Fredericksburg, Texas: Shearer Publishing, 2002.
Texas Parks and Wildlife Department. Wildflowers. www.tpwd.state.tx.us/park/wildflower/.

Working on the Texas State Railroad

Parent, Laurence. *Official Guide to Texas State Parks*. Austin: Texas Parks and Wildlife Press, 1997.
Texas Parks and Wildlife Department. Guide to Parks. www.tpwd.state.tx.us/parkguide/.

Apollo XIII and the Medal of Freedom

Cortright, Edgar M. *Apollo Expeditions to the Moon.* Washington, DC: National Aeronautics and Space Administration, 1975.
Dethloff, Henry. *Suddenly Tomorrow Came: A History of the Johnson Space Center.* NASA History Series SP-4307, 1993. Johnson Space Flight Center. www.jsc.nasa.gov/history/suddenly_tomorrow/suddenly.htm.

Michael DeBakey and the "City of Medicine"

Macon, N. Don and Anderson, Thomas Dunaway. *Monroe Dunaway Anderson, His Legacy: A History of the Texas Medical Center*. Houston: Texas Medical Center, 1994.
Texas Medical Center. www.tmc.edu/institutions/.

DEEPER INTO THE
HEART OF TEXAS
ELECTRONIC INFORMATION

If all information about the Lone Star State were an iceberg floating in the North Atlantic Ocean, *Finding Anything About Everything in Texas* has revealed only a small strip of the Texas Panhandle. Getting down to the remainder requires navigating some specialized electronic information sources. If you want to go deeper into the heart of Texas information, you can become familiar with a small group of effective electronic sources. The electronic sources and specialized resources described below can expand your Texas information competence without your ever having to leave your public library or home computer.

Many of these electronic sources are among the Lone Star State's best kept secrets. Agencies, libraries, foundations, and groups who make them available either cannot advertise their services or have limited resources to do so. Exploring and mastering these electronic resources refines skills needed to go deeper into the heart of Texas information and find whatever fact, idea, or document you need. You can find out almost anything about everything in Texas.

TEXAS STATE LIBRARY AND ARCHIVES COMMISSION

Start all your investigations into Texas, if you are a newcomer to the state, at the Texas State Library and Archives Commission. The state library has mounted a substantial effort and invested heavily in electronically organizing information about Texas. Through programs of the Texas State Library, you can obtain a "virtual" history of Texas at your computer, find detailed information about companies and industries in the state, and bring a 19,000-volume library of electronic books into your home to use at your computer. You can find these services at the state library web site at www.tsl.state.tx.us/. The services provided here cost you little or nothing and are coordinated through your local participating public library.

TEXAS STATE LIBRARY AND ARCHIVES COMMISSION: ABOUT TEXAS

The Texas State Library provides a valuable array of electronic resources available from the webmaster and reference department of its web site at www.tsl.state.us/ref/abouttx/index.html. The menu "About Texas" provides an excellent introduction to seventeen broad topics of Lone Star State information resources. It covers geography, history, government, preparing reports, finding county and city population data, and company, industry, and product information. In the history section of About Texas, you can find a detailed chronology and a good selection of primary documents. The site contains the record of the verdict and sentence of A.B. Davis in a court in San Augustine for the theft of "a mule and others." For stealing this mule and some other things, Judge Augustus Hotchkiss sentenced Davis to thirty-nine lashes, branded him a thief, and exiled him from Texas.

Within each broad topic about Texas, the site provides branches to seven to ten additional links. The library identifies information according to the level and ability of the searcher, providing data for students and teachers. In these sections, you can find laws that govern the display of the Texas flag, Texas official symbols, and the state seal. You find that Anahuac is the official Alligator Capital of Texas, Odessa is the Jackrabbit-Roping Capital of Texas, and Knox City is the Seedless Watermelon Capital of Texas. The state library has not yet tracked down all of the Legislature's official capital designating activities. Consider the state library's seventeen subjects and links as a current "virtual encyclopedia" of the state of Texas.

THE TRAIL TO TEXAS STATE AGENCIES

By law, the Texas State Library and Archives Commission functions as the official agency to track all publications of Texas state agencies, boards, commissions, universities, and colleges. It collects many of the physical documents produced by the state, maintaining a state depository system in public libraries and universities and creating links to the homepages of the state agencies and their publications.

The "TRAIL" web site of the state library provides one of the easiest links to the home pages of 180 Texas state agencies. The acronym TRAIL stands for Texas Records and Information Locator. Its web site provides a direct link to the online publications of these agencies. At this web site, you can find out how to select a plumber from the Texas State Board of Plumbing Examiners and where to file a complaint if you are not satisfied with the work. To find the TRAIL web site, check out www2.tsl.state.tx.us/trail/. Select "Texas State Agencies" for an alphabetical list of 180 agencies and a link to their current electronic publications.

TEXSHARE: THE ELECTRONIC REFERENCE DESK OF TEXAS

The Texas State Library programs extend much farther than merely facilitating access to information provided from state agencies. In collaboration with colleges and universities, the state library coordinates a program called TexShare for sharing resources. TexShare makes it possible for most Texans to obtain *free* information from commercial databases from their home computers using their internet connections. Citizens need only obtain a password from their local participating public library to use this service through a customized gateway program.

Library patrons without home computers or internet service may usually access TexShare databases at internet computers in their public libraries. Depending on budget, the number of databases available in Texas varies from year to year, but TexShare has been annually providing from fifteen to twenty databases to public libraries for several years. By adding an array of electronic databases to the list of services Texans can obtain from the Texas State Library and TexShare, individuals seeking information about Texas are well equipped with a set of modern information tools.

You can find a list of the databases offered to Texans by going directly to the TexShare web site at www.texshare.edu/. TexShare groups information in its databases according to ten broad subjects similar to the About Texas section of the state library. In addition to an alphabetical list of all databases, TexShare provides coverage of business, literature, science, health, and Spanish language material. Some of the databases provide citations to the articles, and others provide the full text. Almost every database provides some information about Texas, Texas authors, Texas companies, products, and industries. Additionally, they provide local, state, regional, national, and international information found in the reference department of a typical library.

HANDBOOK OF TEXAS ONLINE

One of the TexShare databases is the *Handbook of Texas Online* from the Texas State Historical Association. As a general rule to follow, consult the *Handbook of Texas Online* as a starting place for almost all information questions about Texas subjects except statistics. It contains more than 24,000 articles on Texas subjects contributed by several thousand authors.

The range of information in the handbook extends broadly to people, ideas, economic influences, disasters, literature, companies, and geography. It includes assessments of famous people and subjects in Texas history: biographies of all defenders at the Alamo, Stephen F. Austin's Old Three Hundred Colonists, all important oilfield strikes, the most famous ranches and trails, heroes and villains, lawmen and outlaws, and dead politicians. The handbook includes biographies of deceased Texans only.

Lists of 13,000 books appended to subjects in the handbook refer readers to substantial supplementary information about Texas. The handbook includes a history of all 254 counties, the most important cities, and all major ethnic groups. The handbook continues to grow as new subjects are added and old subjects revised. Check out the *Handbook of Texas Online* at the TexShare web site www.texshare.edu/, or you can go directly to the web site of the Texas State Historical Association at www.tsha. utexas.edu/handbook/online.

TEXAS ALMANAC

To find general almanac-type information covering a wide spectrum of Texas subjects, consult the *Texas Almanac*. Published biennially by the *Dallas Morning News* for more than 125 years, it has become the standard one-volume almanac of Texas facts, statistics, and short articles. Sprinkled with tables and charts, lists, maps, names, addresses, web sites, and city and county histories, the almanac contains extensive factual data on Texas. Normally published after the Legislature adjourns its biennial session, the almanac stays current with new laws and constitutional amendments. The almanac functions as a broad encyclopedia about Texas, and it also is available as a searchable database from TexShare.

The almanac contains a smorgasbord of Texas information in short articles and statistical tables. It provides charts of the population growth and population history for over 500 Texas cities, covering every United States Census since 1850. Like traditional almanacs, it lists cities, towns, counties, officeholders, mayors, tax assessors, county clerks, commissioners, and attorneys general. Articles include information on soils, climate, vegetation, history, and geography. Check out the *Texas Almanac* at www.texshare.edu/.

WORLDCAT DATABASE

WorldCat is the world's largest library database containing the records of 42,280,435 books and 2,532,722 journals, magazines, and media. A group of libraries created it by merging the catalogs of the most important libraries in the United States, Europe, and Latin America.

Why is the WorldCat database useful to individuals seeking information about Texas? WorldCat provides two major features. Within a few minutes, a patron can produce an extensive list of books on a subject by searching subjects, authors, and titles of books. Then, using a special location feature in the database, a patron can generate a list of libraries in Texas who own the books. Patrons can order a book or go directly to the library and borrow it with a free TexShare borrower's card. Check the WorldCat database at the TexShare web site at www.texshare.edu/.

NETLIBRARY.COM

The TexShare Customized Gateway Service provides direct access to the full text of "electronic books" placed online by publishers through a company called netLibrary. The netLibrary database contains more than 19,000 books accessible through a home computer or a Texas public library. To browse this large collection of electronic books by subject, go to the TexShare web site at www.texshare.edu/ and select netLibrary. The web site will provide instructions on how to register, log in, and check out an "electronic book."

When you find an item you want to "check out," reserve it for a 24-hour period. Patrons may print from the books for personal research within the guidelines of copyright fair use. The netLibrary service contains many books about Texas. Several Texas university presses have placed some of their books in this electronic collection, creating a large core of books about Texas.

BUSINESS & COMPANY RESOURCE CENTER

For locating a large span of information on companies, products, industries, business rankings, and markets, TexShare offers databases specializing in business and commerce. Business and Company Resource Center provides information to individuals in business, undergraduates, and graduates doing case study work. It furnishes extensive information on large Texas companies such as Texas Instruments. The database entry on Texas Instruments gives a short history of the company from its roots in Geophysical Service, a petroleum-exploration company before World War II, through its attainment of its leading market share in analog chip and digital signal processor industries in 2001.

Texans can view a decade-by-decade summary of Texas Instrument's successes and failures in the semiconductor industry. It concludes with an analysis of plans for reshaping the company for the twenty-first century. It lists principal subsidiaries along with significant articles from *Business Week, Fortune, Dallas Business Journal,* and the business press. In addition to investment reports, market share data, brand and product information, the database provides useful ranked lists of company performance data. Check out the Business and Company Resource Center at the web site www.texshare.edu/.

INFOTRAC CUSTOM NEWSPAPERS

To find newspaper articles about Texas gathered from a selected list of 100 national and international newspapers, go to the TexShare web site and select "InfoTrac Custom Newspapers." This database comes from the list of databases at the web site www.texshare.edu/. The database provides full text without pictures of many articles from Texas leading newspapers such as the *Houston Chronicle,* the *Austin American Statesman,* and Knight-Ridder newspapers.

InfoTrac covers all sections of the newspapers from Arts and Entertainment to Sports, Business, and Politics. If you are interested in knowing good places to hike in the Hill Country, you can often find in-depth articles of places written by newspaper staff from the Austin press. Articles cover the trails of Enchanted Rock State Park, considered to be the "king of the mountain" of hiking spots of Central Texas and the Lake Georgetown Goodwater Trail. Coverage of state government and the governor's office is extensive, but full-length features cover all aspects of Texas. The articles vary in length from a few hundred words up to 4,000 words.

EBSCOHOST NEWSPAPERS

To find coverage of local Texas news, check out the EbscoHost newspapers database. This database provides selected full text articles for twenty-three national and international newspapers plus transcripts to radio and television programs such as *All Things Considered,* political commentators, and television news programs. Because it also attempts to provide regional coverage, it selectively covers eleven newspapers distributed over Texas's major geographical sections.

In addition to the news coverage of Dallas, Houston, and Austin provided by the InfoTrac database, EbscoHost newspapers provide eight additional newspapers across the state. They cover Amarillo, Beaumont, Brownsville, Fort Worth, Harlingen, McAllen, Odessa, San Antonio, and Waco.

For instance, if you want to know why insurance premiums surrounding the mold problem in Texas have sky-rocketed, you can read the *McAllen Monitor* about how contractor Landmark settled a claim with the Edinburg School district for $16 million for mold discovered in a four-year-old high school. Check the EbscoHost newspaper web site and its accompanying regional business news web site at www.texshare.edu/.

DICTIONARY OF LITERARY BIOGRAPHY

To find literary criticism, bibliographical data, and biographical information on major Texas authors, go to the *Dictionary of Literary Biography* in the TexShare database. The web site is at www.texshare.edu/. The database includes a lengthy bibliography of the major writings of the author, a selected list of uncollected works in periodicals, and a critical analysis of the author's work. For a Texas author such as J. Frank Dobie, the database provides a list of twenty-six of the author's books, forty-eight articles and edited works, and miscellaneous uncollected works.

EBSCOHOST DATABASES

EbscoHost provides four databases that furnish valuable information on history, social science, and science. The databases can be searched individually or collectively with a single search request. Each database is designed for a different audience. MAS Ultra—School Edition targets high school libraries and provides full text for more than 500 popular general interest publications dealing with current events and popular culture. It indexes *Billboard* magazine.

MasterFILE Premier focuses on the general public with a multidisciplinary database of almost 2,000 publications covering events back to 1975. It provides 91,600 biographies of influential people, 75,000 primary source documents for research, and 107,135 photographs, maps, flags, and illustrations. It is updated daily.

EbscoHost offers Academic Search Primer, a multidisciplinary academic database to 4,450 scholarly publications. The database provides the full text of 3,500 peer-reviewed academic journals back to 1975. A person seeking information on AIDS among African-Americans in Texas can search "AIDS" and "Texas" and retrieve several articles from a hit list such as "Optimizing Care for African-American HIV-Positive Patients," *AIDS Patient Care and STDs* (Oct. 2003). The information provided targets the advanced students and specialist researcher.

A Religion and Philosophy Collection covers the articles and journals of world religions, major denominations, biblical studies, and religious history. It emphasizes religion and philosophy, history of philosophy, moral philosophy, political philosophy, philosophy of language, and epistemology. All points of view concerning legal and religious issues of gay marriage can be found in this database. The collection includes more than 300 full-text journals. All four EbscoHost databases reside at the TexShare web site www.texshare.edu/.

A GUIDE TO THE HISTORY OF TEXAS

To make a systematic study of most subjects in Texas history requires a visit to one or more of the excellent special collections of archives and documents in libraries, museums, and historical societies. These institutions preserve and transmit knowledge of Texas history and culture. More than fifty universities in the state teach Texas history courses. Several hundred municipal, county, and state historical and genealogical societies actively study and collect Texas history. More than twenty-five academic and public libraries across the state collect archives, manuscripts, and rare books about Texas, and state agencies and museums collect Texas materials. Texas is a historically conscious state, and almost all of these institutions have active web sites describing their collections.

During the Texas sesquicentennial in 1986, two editors collaborated on a descriptive guide to the Lone Star State's vast collections of research materials and important manuscript holdings. The effort produced *A Guide to the History of Texas* (1988) edited by Light Townsend Cummins and Alvin R. Bailey, Jr. The editors consider their pioneering work "a starting point for research in Texas history."

The editors provide more than a starting point. The first half of the book consists of a series of essays describing the major historical writing during each period of Texas history. Articles by specialists cover the Spanish and Mexican Period, Texas Independence, the Civil War and Reconstruction, the Frontier Period, and the modern period. The second half of the book describes the major archival depositories in Texas with detailed descriptions of their best-known collections at the time.

As a direct result of Internet expansion, librarians and archivists placed thousands of their collection inventories on the web. Many of the collections described in this guide, along with many more that have been added, are available at the web sites of the libraries and agencies. All of the web sites of Texas community colleges, colleges, universities, and technical schools can be found at a single web site called CollegeForTexans.Com from the Coordinating Board of Higher Education. The common link is found at the web site www.collegefortexans.com/cfbin/inst.cfm.

PHOTOGRAPHIC COLLECTIONS IN TEXAS

One of the richest sources of the history of Texas captured in photographs is *Photographic Collections in Texas: A Union Guide*, a publication compiled by Richard Pearce-Moses under the sponsorship of the Texas Historical Foundation. This guide describes several million photographs found in Texas libraries, historical societies, universities, museums, government agencies, and corporations. Many of the photographic collections deal with some important aspect of the Lone Star State history. No other union list of photographic collections exists for the state.

The photographic collections described usually include the scope of the collection, including the number of photographs, the type, and time period. The guide describes the primary locations of the photographs, the major subjects and landscapes, the names of important people photographed, and photographers and photographic studios.

Geographical coverage spans collections from the petroleum industry in the Midland-Odessa region, the Sawdust Empire of the Pineywoods, the Corps of Engineers collections of the Gulf Coast, and even 7,000 photographs from the Catholic Church's collection of the early Hill Country. The Texas Historical Foundation created in 1953 also takes an active role in preserving photographs and other artifacts of Texas heritage. Check out their web site and their magazine at www.thfonline.org/. All of the institutions described in the photographic union guide have their own web sites.

TEXAS HISTORICAL COMMISSION DATABASE

In 1953, the Texas Legislature created the Texas State Historical Survey Commission to mark important historic sites across the state. Today, the commission functions in preservation activities in architecture, archaeology, history, and community heritage. It assists in economic development, heritage tourism, and urban planning. The Texas Historic Site Atlas contains information on more than 250,000 historic sites in Texas at http://atlas.thc.state.tx.us/. It contains all sites in the National Register of Historic Places in Texas, the text of all historical markers, historic cemeteries, courthouses, and state trails.

INDEX TO TEXAS MAGAZINES AND DOCUMENTS

A unique quarterly publication called the *Index to Texas Magazines and Documents* facilitates tracking obscure articles written about Texas in current magazines and journals. Since 1986, the college library of the University of Houston-Victoria has published a quarterly index to a select group of Texas magazines. These magazines and journals contain articles dealing with Texas business, education, government, and political science subjects. Presently, the list of magazines covered includes twenty-seven journals created in Texas by state agencies, university research centers, museums, and commercial publishers. Editors have expanded coverage to include history, criminal law, environment, wildlife, and health. Ten of these magazines are available in electronic form, and the index includes the web addresses.

Magazines such as *Texas Monthly, Texas Observer, Journal of Big Bend Studies,* and the *Panhandle-Plains Historical Journal* cover all geographical areas of the state. Coverage of these articles provides "Quotes of the Week" columns in *Texas Weekly* from politicians like Governor Rick Perry and former Governor Ann Richards, restaurant reviews from all over the state, and Texas commentary on major criminal law decisions of the U.S. Supreme Court. Major coverage of state environmental and wildlife issues is a priority. *The Index to Texas Magazines and Documents* provides a unique look at the last twenty years of Texas culture from the pages of twenty-seven journals and magazines.

A TEXAS ELECTRONIC REFERENCE DESK

About Texas. The Texas State Library and Archives Commission. www.tsl.state.us/ref/abouttx/index.html.
Business & Company Resource Center. TexShare. www.texshare.edu/.
Coordinating Board of Higher Education. CollegeForTexans.com. www.college fortexans.com/cfbin/inst.cfm.
Dallas Morning News, Inc. Texas Almanac. www.texshare.edu/.
EbscoHost Databases. TexShare. www.texshare.edu/.
EbscoHost Newspapers. www.texshare.edu/.
Gale Publishing. Dictionary of Literary Biography. www.texshare.edu/.
InfoTrac Custom Newspapers. TexShare. www.texshare.edu/.
netLibrary.com. TexShare. www.texshare.edu/.
Texas Historical Commission. Texas Historic Site Atlas. http://atlas.thc.state.tx .us/.
Texas Legislative Budget Board. Publications, Reports and Links. Texas Fact Book. Austin, Texas: Legislative Budget Board, 2004. www.lbb.state.tx.us/.
Texas State Historical Association. Handbook of Texas Online. www.tsha.utexas .edu/handbook/online/.
Texas Record and Information Locator. TRAIL. www2.tsl.state.tx.us/trail/.
Texas State Library and Archives Commission. www.tsl.state.tx.us/.
TexShare. Public Libraries. www.texshare.edu/.
WorldCat Database. TexShare. www.texshare.edu/.

RANDOM ACCESS INFORMATION
DEVICES CALLED BOOKS

Abernethy, Francis Edward, ed. *Some Still Do: Essays on Texas Customs*. Publications of the Texas Folklore Society Number XXXIX. Austin: The Encino Press, 1975.

Cummins, Light Townsend and Bailey, Alvin R. *A Guide to the History of Texas*. New York: Greenwood Press, 1988.

Graves, John. Photographs by Vincent J. Musi. "Texas Hill Country," *National Geographic Magazine* (April 1999) 104-121.

Kenney, T. Nathaniel. Photographs by James L. Stanfield. "Big Bend: Jewel in the Texas Desert." *National Geographic Magazine* (Jan. 1968) 104-133.

Pearce-Moses, Richard. *Photographic Collections in Texas: A Union Guide*. College Station, Texas: Published for the Texas Historical Foundation by Texas A&M University Press, 1987.

Jenkins, John Holmes, *Basic Texas Books: An Annotated Bibliography of Selected Works for a Research Library*. Revised Edition. Austin, Texas: Texas State Historical Society, 1988.

———. *Cracker Barrel Chronicles: A Bibliography of Texas Town and County Histories*. Austin, Texas: Pemberton Press, 1965.

Snapp, Elizabeth and Snapp, Harry Franklin. *Read All About Her! Texas Women's History, A Working Bibliography*. Denton: Texas Woman's University Press, 1995.

Stewart, Marjorie and Locher, Karen. *Index to Texas Magazines and Documents*. Victoria, Texas: University of Houston-Victoria College Library, 1986.

U.S. Works Progress Administration. Federal Writers' Project. *The WPA Guide to Texas: With a New Introduction*. Austin, Texas: Texas Monthly Press, 1986.

CREDITS

INDEX